£1.99
W40

A Load of Wit

A Load of Wit

Des MacHale

PRION

This edition first published in 2005 by

Prion
an imprint of the
Carlton Publishing Group
20 Mortimer Street
London W1T 3JW

The contents of this book were first published by Prion as
Wit on Target (1998) and *Ready Wit* (2004).

A catalogue record for this book is available from the British Library

ISBN 1 85375 558 3

Typeset by e-type, Liverpool
Printed in Great Britain
by Mackays

Contents

Contents

Art

Art

Painting is the art of protecting flat surfaces from the weather and exposing them to the critic.

Ambrose Bierce

He was the world's only armless sculptor. He used to put the chisel in his mouth and have his wife hit him on the back of the head with a mallet.

Fred Allen

Any fool can paint a picture, but it takes a wise man to be able to sell it.

Samuel Butler

Andy Warhol is the only genius with an IQ of 60.

Gore Vidal

What has happened to architecture since the Second World War that the only passers-by who can contemplate it without pain are those equipped with a white stick and dog?

Bernard Levin

Who among us has not gazed at a painting of Jackson Pollock's and thought 'What a piece of crap'?

Rob Long

Modern art is what happens when painters stop looking at girls and persuade themselves they have a better idea.

John Ciardi

William Orpen never got under the surface until he got under the sod.

Oliver St John Gogarty

A painter who has the feel of breasts and buttocks is saved.

Auguste Renoir

He has returned from Italy a greater bore than ever; he bores on architecture, painting, statuary and music.

Sydney Smith

There are three kinds of people in the world: those who can't stand Picasso, those who can't stand Raphael and those who have never heard of either of them.

John White

Of course William Morris was a wonderful artist and an all-round man, but the art of walking round him has always tired me.

Max Beerbohm

Donner wanted to be an artist because he heard there were opportunities to meet naked women.

Tom Stoppard

A portrait is a painting with something wrong with the mouth.

John S. Sargent

Mona Lisa has the smile of a woman who has just dined off her husband.

Lawrence Durrell

A highbrow is the kind of person who looks at a sausage and thinks of Picasso.

A.P. Herbert

Art

An amateur is an artist who supports himself with outside jobs which enable him to paint. A professional is someone whose wife works to enable him to paint.

Ben Shahn

He will lie even when it is inconvenient, the sign of the true artist.

Gore Vidal

Who is this chap Augustus John? He drinks, he's dirty and I know there are women in the background.

Bernard Montgomery

Turner's *The Slave Ship* resembles a tortoiseshell cat having a fit in a plate of tomatoes.

Mark Twain

Mona Lisa looks as if she has just been sick or is about to be.

Noel Coward

Mr Whistler has always spelled art with a capital 'I'.

Oscar Wilde

If only people knew as much about painting as I do, they would never buy my pictures.

Edwin H. Landseer

Graham Sutherland's portrait of me makes me look as if I were straining at stool.

Winston Churchill

When having my portrait painted I don't want justice, I want mercy.

Billy Hughes

Rembrandt painted 700 pictures. Of these 3000 are in existence.

Wilhelm Bode

If you have a burning restless urge to paint, simply eat something sweet and the feeling will pass.

Fran Lebowitz

An enraged cartoonist burst into the office of the editor of the *New Yorker* and shouted 'You never use my stuff but you publish the work of a fifth rate artist like Thurber.' The editor immediately sprang to my defence. 'Third rate' he said.

James Thurber

The world's worst piece of art is reputed to be *Le Remède* by Antoine Watteau. It depicts a reclining Venus about to receive an enema administered by her chambermaid.

Bruce Felton

The day is coming when a single carrot, freshly observed, will set off a revolution.

Paul Cézanne

I'm an artist and in a court of law that's next worst to an actress.

Joyce Cary

Art

The art galleries of Paris contain the finest collection of frames I ever saw.

Humphry Davy

The Acropolis is beige! My colour!

Elsie De Wolfe

Psychology is in its infancy as a science. I hope, in the interests of art, it will always remain so.

Oscar Wilde

Borrowing is for amateurs, stealing is for artists.

Steve Jobs

I always pat children on the head whenever I meet them, just in case they turn out to be mine.

Augustus John

There are moments when art almost attains the dignity of manual labour.

Oscar Wilde

I will never accept an unsigned painting from Picasso. If he doesn't sign it, I don't know which way to hang it.

Auguste Rodin

On the staircase stood several Royal Academicians, disguised as artists.

Oscar Wilde

With twenty seaside resorts planning to open up nude and topless beaches this summer, I really do not see that we have any need to keep the Elgin Marbles in Bloomsbury any longer.

Auberon Waugh

A wife could never have painted the Mona Lisa. Just as she got to the tricky bit of the smile, someone would have yelled upstairs for a clean shirt.

Ronald Ellis

I am glad all the old masters are dead and I only wish they had died sooner.

Mark Twain

One of the disadvantages of inviting Utrillo over for dinner was that he would disappear into the bedroom and drink all your wife's perfume.

Waldemar Januszczak

This row about Prince William being filmed going into lectures would never have happened in my day. Art students never went to lectures.

Eamonn Butler

I was the first person to teach Peggy Guggenheim about painting. What a tragedy that I wasn't the last.

Bernard Berenson

The cleaners thought my art was rubbish and put it in the bin.

Damien Hirst

Art

It takes courage for an adult to draw as badly as I do.

Mel Calman

When I asked her if she liked Le Corbusier, she replied,
'Love some, with a little soda water.'

Peter De Vries

A good statue can be rolled downhill without damage.

Michelangelo

If you can kill a snake with it, it ain't art.

Lyle Bonge

It does not matter how badly you paint as long as you don't
paint badly like other people.

George Moore

The difference between a bad artist and a good artist is that
the bad artist seems to copy a good deal, but the good artist
does copy a good deal.

William Blake

Modern artists always sign their names at the bottom of
their paintings so that people will know which way up to
hang them.

Frank Muir

Artists are, without exception, exhibitionists, voyeurs,
homosexuals, sadists, masochists, alcoholics or a
combination of two or more of these.

Edmund Bergler

I know so many men in London whose only talent is for washing. I suppose that is why men of genius so seldom wash; they are afraid of being mistaken for men of talent only.

Oscar Wilde

It is much easier for a Scotsman to be a genius than to be an artist.

Oscar Wilde

Dissatisfied with the Faith, I took up photography at which I became so good that in moments of depression I felt I was a born photographer. Tiring of churches, I tried cows, and I discovered with pleasure that cows are very fond of being photographed, and, unlike architecture, don't move.

Oscar Wilde

A picture is a representation in two dimensions of something wearisome in three.

Ambrose Bierce

I had to leave art school in Paris because the piles of underwear I dropped on the floor grew taller and taller.

Nancy Mitford

The politician in art is one the lowest of all living things.

Allen Tucker

A primitive artist is an amateur whose work sells.

Grandma Moses

Art

If it were not for the intellectual snobs who foot the bill, the arts would perish with their starving practitioners – let us thank heaven for hypocrisy.

Aldous Huxley

I don't mind whether my crumpled sheet of A4 paper listed for the Turner Prize is art or not. It is to me.

Martin Creed

Michelangelo was a good man, but he didn't know how to paint.

El Greco

I was named as the world's most famous artist only because Rembrandt didn't have his own TV show.

Rolf Harris

When Millais said 'Art', he meant British Art, and when he said 'British Art', he meant the painting of John Everett Millais.

Walter Sickert

To find the cloakroom in my penthouse, just turn right after the Picasso.

Jeffrey Archer

That portrait of Prince Charles by some Russian woman was brilliant, wasn't it? And that cunning stunt with the sunglasses – I can never get the eyes right either.

Giles Coren

Hitler – now there was a painter! He could paint an entire apartment in one afternoon. Two coats!

Mel Brooks

If I say it isn't art, then it isn't art.

Tracey Emin

Throwing a football is comparable to painting a canvas or playing the piano. The difference is that Beethoven didn't play the 'Moonlight' Sonata and Van Gogh didn't paint the *Potato Eaters* with Mean Joe Green charging at them from the blind side.

Jim Plunkett

So infinitesimal did I find the knowledge of art west of the Rocky Mountains, that an art patron actually sued the railroad company for damages because the plaster cast of Venus de Milo, which he had imported from Paris, had been delivered minus the arms. And what is more surprising, he gained his case and the damages.

Oscar Wilde

French nudes look as if they had just taken off their clothes; Greek nudes as if they had never put them on.

Sam Hall

If Auden's face looks like that, what must his balls look like?

David Hockney

Art

Because of a telephone mishearing the Prime Minister was incorrectly quoted in later editions of *The Times* yesterday on museum charges. His remark should have read, 'You expect to pay for going to the Louvre.'

Fritz Spiegl

Business

Business

Few great men would have got past Personnel.

Paul Goodman

The upper crust is just a bunch of crumbs held together by dough.

Joseph A. Thomas

We don't seem to be able to check crime, so why not legalise it and then tax it out of business?

Will Rogers

The secret of ensuring a man's wealth is when the little beggar is ten years old, have him castrated and his taste buds destroyed. He'll grow up never needing a woman, a steak or a cigarette. Think of the money saved.

W.C. Fields

The only reason I made a commercial for American Express was to pay for my American Express bill.

Peter Ustinov

Every morning I get up and look through the Forbes list of the richest people in America. If I'm not there, I go to work.

Robert Orben

I am proud to be paying taxes in the United States. But I could be just as proud for half the money.

Arthur Godfrey

They were a people so primitive they did not know how to get money except by working for it.

Joseph Addison

Actuaries have the reputation of being about as interesting as the footnotes on a pension plan.

George Pitcher

More and more these days I find myself pondering on how to reconcile my net income with my gross habits.

John Nelson

These are the guidelines for bureaucrats;
1 When in charge, ponder.
2 When in trouble, delegate.
3 When in doubt, mumble.

James H. Boren

Two guys were looking at some shirts in a shop window. One said 'That's the one I'd get', when the owner of the shop, a Cyclops, came out and kicked his head in.

Craig Charles

You can't put your VISA bill on your American Express card.

P.J. O'Rourke

I am very fond of fresh air and royalties.

Daisy Ashford

No real English gentleman, in his secret soul, was ever sorry for the death of a political economist.

Walter Bagehot

What if everything is an illusion and nothing exists. In that case, I definitely overpaid for my carpet.

Woody Allen

Business

To make a million, start with $900,000.

Morton Shulman

A criminal is a person with predatory instincts who has not sufficient capital to form a corporation.

Howard Scott

Money is something you have got to make in case you don't die.

Max Asnas

I came by the racetrack today but it was closed, so I just shoved all my money through the gate.

W.C. Fields

People say sailing is an expensive sport, but to own a racehorse is the equivalent of burning a yacht on the front lawn every year.

Adam Nicholson

I performed badly in the Civil Service examinations because evidently I knew more about economics than my examiners.

J.M. Keynes

Gentlemen prefer bonds.

Andrew Mellon

When you've got them by their wallets, their hearts and minds will follow.

Fern Naito

Most of my contemporaries at school entered the World of Business, the logical destiny of bores.

Barry Humphries

Today you can go to a gas station and find the cash register open and the toilets locked. They must think toilet paper is worth more than money.

Joey Bishop

It is unforgivable to deny racegoers facilities for losing their money swiftly and painlessly.

Hugh McIlvanney

Whoever said money can't buy happiness simply hadn't found out where to go shopping.

Bo Derek

Less than perfect financial circumstances are the keenest spur to further endeavour.

Joe Davis

A bargain is something you can't use at a price you can't resist.

Franklin P. Jones

All I ask is a chance to prove that money can't make me happy.

Spike Milligan

In the business world an executive knows something about everything, a technician knows everything about something – and the switchboard operator knows everything.

Harold Coffin

Business

One is always excited by descriptions of money changing hands. It's much more fundamental than sex.

Nigel Dennis

You walk into an estate agent's office and all the roulette tables become desks.

Dylan Moran

If advertisers spent the same amount of money improving their products as they do on advertising then they wouldn't have to advertise them.

Will Rogers

I handed one of my creditors an IOU and thought thank God that's settled.

Richard Brinsley Sheridan

Never underestimate the effectiveness of a straight cash bribe.

Claud Cockburn

I told the Inland Revenue I didn't owe them a penny because I live near the seaside.

Ken Dodd

It is better to give than to lend, and it costs about the same.

Philip Gibbs

If you think your boss is stupid remember; you wouldn't have a job if he was any smarter.

Albert Grant

Only one fellow in ten thousand understands the currency question, and we meet him every day.

Kin Hubbard

Boswell, lend me sixpence – not to be repaid.

Samuel Johnson

It is better to have a permanent income than to be fascinating.

Oscar Wilde

We didn't actually overspend our budget. The allocation simply fell short of our expenditure.

Keith Davis

It is the height of bad taste to have anything business-related in your briefcase. Briefcases are for taking the contents of the stationery cupboard home with you at the end of the day. Only photocopier repairmen have their work in their briefcases – 15 different screwdrivers, a copy of the *Sun* and a list of exotic, faraway locations where the vital missing part will have to be supplied from.

Guy Browning

I'm spending a year dead for tax reasons.

Douglas Adams

George Orwell would not blow his nose without moralising on the conditions in the handkerchief industry.

Cyril Connolly

Business

One way to solve the traffic problem would be to keep all the cars that are not paid for off the streets.

Will Rogers

Don't buy shares in companies whose chairmen can play consistently below their handicap. Either they are playing too much golf or they cheat.

Jeff Randall

I am not a paranoid deranged millionaire. Goddamit, I'm a billionaire.

Howard Hughes

There is only one thing for a man to do who is married to a woman who enjoys spending money, and that is to enjoy earning it.

Edgar W. Howe

Consultants are people who borrow your watch to tell you what time it is and then walk off with it.

Robert Townsend

If you owe the bank $100, that's your problem. If you owe the bank $100 million, that's the bank's problem.

John Paul Getty

I have never been in any situation where having money made it worse.

Clinton Jones

The only man who makes money following the horses is one who does it with a broom and shovel.

Elbert Hubbard

Economics is useful only as a form of employment for economists.

J.K. Galbraith

Unquestionably there is progress. The average American now pays out twice as much in taxes as he formerly got in wages.

H.L. Mencken

Anyone who lives within their means suffers from a lack of imagination.

Oscar Wilde

Recession is when your neighbour loses his job. Depression is when you lose yours. And recovery is when Jimmy Carter loses his.

Ronald Reagan

When I come home from the races my wife never asks any questions if I tell her I just ate a $380 hot dog.

Tom Conway

I don't know much about being a millionaire but I'll bet I'd be darling at it.

Dorothy Parker

Ocean racing is like standing under a cold shower tearing up £5 notes.

Edward Heath

Business

When a person with experience meets a person with money, the person with experience will get the money and the person with the money will get some experience.

Leonard Lauder

We don't just honour credit cards – we venerate them!

Dale McFeathers

They say it's better to be poor and happy than rich and miserable. But couldn't some compromise be worked out, like being moderately wealthy and just a little moody?

John Henry

I'd give a thousand dollars to be a millionaire.

Lewis Timberlake

I need enough to tide me over until I need more.

Bill Hoest

What is a thousand dollars? Mere chicken feed. A poultry matter.

Groucho Marx

Part of the $10 million I spent on gambling, part on booze and part on women. The rest I spent foolishly.

George Raft

Waiter, take away this bill – I never ordered it.

Cyril Connolly

I never refuse money. I come from a family where it was considered unlucky to refuse money.

Patrick Kavanagh

A male boutique is where you go in to buy a tie and they measure your inside leg.

George Melly

Remember, your sales resistance is lower with a salesman who calls after the kids have gone to school. When you realise he isn't one of the kids that missed the bus, you're so happy you'll buy anything.

Phyllis Diller

If you want to steal money don't rob a bank – open one.

Bertolt Brecht

Messrs Muir and Norden regret they have no machinery for the return of cheques.

Frank Muir

There is no point in borrowing if you mean to pay it back.

Marcus Clarke

If you don't want to work you have to earn enough money so that you don't have to work.

Ogden Nash

Time is money, especially overtime.

Evan Esar

Business

Capitalism without bankruptcy is like Christianity without hell.

Frank Borman

Hard work never hurt anyone who hired somebody else to do it.

Jay Kaye

Anyone who believes that exponential growth can go on forever in a finite world is either mad or an economist.

Kenneth Boulding

Business ethics means never telling a lie unless you can get away with it.

Kenneth Cook

I had a hard time at the bank today. I tried to take out a loan and they turned me down. Apparently, they won't accept the voices in my head as references.

Steve Altman

I've known Jack Buck for twenty years and he still cannot spell my name. He sent me a cheque the other day made out to 'bearer'.

Yogi Berra

Alexander Hamilton started the US Treasury with nothing and that was the closest our country has ever come to being even.

Will Rogers

God must love the rich or else he wouldn't divide so much among so few of them.

H. L. Mencken

Being a millionaire is a bit like being poor, but having a hell of a lot of money.

Griff Rhys-Jones

The FBI are looking for Osama bin Laden's financial advisor. How good can this guy be? His top client is living in a cave and driving a donkey. It doesn't sound like he is getting the best return on his investments.

Jay Leno

He's got a wonderful head for money. There's a long slit on the top.

David Frost

Why does a bank have to have all those Vice-Presidents? The United States is the biggest business institution in the world and they have only one Vice-President and nobody has ever found anything for him to do.

Will Rogers

One cannot touch a fig leaf without it turning into a price tag.

Saul Bellow

Companies run by engineers don't make any money, but companies run by accountants don't make anything at all.

Peter Kruger

Business

The buck doesn't even pause here.

Donald Regan

How can I be overdrawn when I've still got lots of cheques left in the book?

Gracie Allen

The first rule of consumerism is never to buy anything you can't make your children carry.

Bill Bryson

That money talks, I can't deny. I heard it once – it said 'goodbye'.

Richard Armour

How come banks lend billions to Third World countries but chain down their pens?

Dave Barry

There are few things in this world more reassuring than an unhappy Lottery winner.

Tony Parsons

Large increases in cost with questionable increases in performances can be tolerated only in racehorses and women.

William Thomson

My con-victims may have been respectable but they were never any good. They wanted something for nothing and I gave them nothing for something.

Joseph Weil

Success means having to worry about every damn thing in the world, except money.

Johnny Cash

A footballer has been reported for throwing a coin into the crowd. They were lucky: think what damage could have been caused if he'd hurled his wallet.

M.O. York

Some people get so rich they lose all respect for humanity. That's how rich I want to be.

Rita Rudner

People will swim through shit if you put a few bob in it.

Peter Sellers

My wife had an accident at the bank the other day. She got in the wrong line and made a deposit.

Henny Youngman

Poise is the ability to keep talking while the other fellow picks up the bill.

Michael Hodgin

Elias Mutumbe, a Kenyan forger, has been jailed for three years after issuing a series of high-value banknotes bearing his own likeness.

Trevor Danker

When a man says his word is as good as his bond, always take his bond.

Hugo Vickers

Business

I may be good for nothing, but I'm not bad for nothing.

Mae West

I cut myself so severely in forcing open the kid's moneybox that I had to spend the contents on lint and bandages.

W.C. Fields

She couldn't stand up under torture. If the Gestapo took away her Bloomingdale's charge card, she'd tell them everything.

Woody Allen

My bank manager went for a heart transplant, but they couldn't find a stone of the right size.

Dave Allen

Fifteen years ago one could have bought the Federal Steel Company for twenty million dollars. And I let it go.

Stephen Leacock

If you had your life to live over again – you'd need lots of money.

Jackie Mason

Money cannot buy you everything, but it sure puts you in a great bargaining position.

Doug Larson

The purpose of studying economics is to learn how to avoid being fooled by economists.

Joan Robinson

Banks are really aggressive with their marketing these days, aren't they? A guy robbed a bank of $5,000 last week and they tried to talk him into opening a savings account with it.

Henny Youngman

If I had a dollar for every time I've forgotten something, I don't know how much I'd have.

Steven Wright

Poets are terribly sensitive people and the thing they are most sensitive about is cash.

Robert Warren

It's not a sin to be rich – it's a bloody miracle.

W.F. Dettle

If talk is cheap, why is the phone bill always so high?

Les Dennis

They lived on money borrowed from each other.

George Moore

She had so many gold teeth she used to sleep with her head in a safe.

W.C. Fields

Fake underpants are really the bottom end of the counterfeit market.

David Westcott

Business

A little note came with my credit card bill. It said: 'Leave home without it.'

Edgar Argo

The ink on the new euro notes is poisonous, but the European Central Bank assures us that a health risk arises only if a person eats 400 or more of the notes at once.

Shelly Brady

The universal formula for the art of making good films is to be in command of the art of borrowing money.

John Ford

Angels we have heard on high,
Tell us to go out and buy.

Tom Lehrer

During World War Two, I had $20,000 invested in Nazi Germany just in case the little bastard won.

W.C. Fields

We made *Stagecoach* for $250,000. In Hollywood, that's considered the price of a good cigar.

John Ford

One hundred dollars invested at seven per cent interest for one hundred years will become $100,000, at which time it will be worth absolutely nothing.

Lazarus Long

If the subjects are living in splendour they can clearly afford to pay their taxes. If they are living frugally, they must be hiding money away and can also afford to pay their taxes.

Cardinal Morton

A fool and his money are soon partying.

Michael Powell

I've saved enough money to pay my income tax, now all I have to do is to borrow some to live on.

Lou Costello

Forty years ago people worked twelve hours a day and it was called economic slavery. Now they work fourteen hours a day and it's called moonlighting.

Robert Orben

In the *Bitter End*, my salary was in the high two figures.

Woody Allen

I myself have been in debt ever since I reached the age of discretion. To be in debt, in fact, is one of the plainest signs that the age of discretion has been reached, and those who are monotonously solvent have probably never fully grown up.

A.J.A. Symons

If Bing Crosby can't take it with him, he's not going.

Bob Hope

Never hire anybody whose CV rhymes.

Rita Rudner

Business

A tired chairman is a bad chairman. A dead one is usually worse.

Nicholas Goodison

I used to go to the office three times a week for an hour a day, but I have since struck off one of the days.

Oscar Wilde

Wouldn't it be nice if hospitals and schools had all the money they needed and the army had to hold jumble sales to buy guns?

Petra Kelly

Drink and Drugs

Drink and Drugs

I don't like people who take drugs – like customs men for example.

Mick Miller

It was what I would call a three-man wine – two men had to hold you down so that a third could pour it down your throat.

George Lang

I haven't touched a drop of alcohol since the invention of the funnel.

Malachy McCourt

There is only one thing to be said in favour of drink and that is that it has caused many a lady to be loved that otherwise might have died single.

Finley Peter Dunne

Customers in an Irish pub are asked not to throw lighted cigarette ends on the floor. People leaving have burned their hands and faces.

Tony Butler

Have you heard about the Irishman who joined Alcoholics Anonymous? He still drinks but under a different name.

Aubrey Dillon-Malone

I never drink because I was born intoxicated.

George Russell

I seldom took a drink on the set before 9 a.m.

W.C. Fields

The Bishop was talking to the local Master of Hounds about the difficulty he had in keeping his vicars off the incense.

P.G. Wodehouse

It was a French physician, naturally enough, who first described the disease known as cirrhosis of the liver.

Richard Selzer

The conclusion of your syllogism, I said lightly, is fallacious, being based upon licensed premises.

Flann O'Brien

The best way to cure a hangover is to avoid alcohol the night before.

Cathy Hopkins

I drink too much. Last time I gave a urine sample it had an olive in it.

Rodney Dangerfield

What I like to drink most is wine that belongs to others.

Diogenes

You suck on that cigarette because you didn't suck on your mom long enough when you were a kid. That's the absolute truth. If I could buy a pack of breasts, I would. I'd be smoking forty to fifty packs a day. I'd be down the news stand first thing every morning: 'Gimme a pack of 44Ds. You can leave the nipples on 'em'.

Denis Leary

Drink and Drugs

Reality is just a crutch for people who cannot cope with drugs.

Robin Williams

The best pitch I ever heard about cocaine was back in the early eighties when a street dealer followed me down the sidewalk going 'I got some great blow, man. I got the stuff that killed Belushi'.

Denis Leary

I've stopped drinking. But only while I'm asleep.

George Best

During the war I consumed German wine but I excused myself that I was not drinking it but interning it.

Winston Churchill

I've been told alcohol is a slow poison. I'm in no hurry.

Robert Benchley

W.C. Fields was fond of playing the golf course sideways with his pal Oliver Hardy. He liked being in the trees where he could drink without scandalising the natives.

Jim Murray

I never drank anything stronger than beer before I was twelve.

W.C. Fields

Prohibition is better than no liquor at all.

Will Rogers

I am so holy that when I touch wine, it turns into water.

Aga Khan III

It was a non-smoker who committed the first sin and brought death into the world and all our woe. Nero was a non-smoker. Lady Macbeth was a non-smoker. Decidedly the record of the non-smokers leaves them little to be proud of.

Robert Lynd

An old wine-bibber having been smashed in a railway collision, some wine was poured on his lips to revive him. 'Pauillac 1873', he murmured and died.

Ambrose Bierce

The Campaign for Real Ale is the last refuge of bearded Trotskyite Morris dancers.

Alun Howkins

Real ale fans are just like train-spotters, only drunk.

Christopher Howse

There are all sorts of methods of giving up smoking. My aunt used to pour a gallon of petrol over herself every morning. The idea being that she couldn't light up without turning herself into a human fireball. It didn't stop her – she'd be in the living room and you'd hear a cough and a woosh. She was up to forty wooshes a day by the end of it.

Paul Merton

Drink and Drugs

I'm not really a heavy smoker any more. I get through only two lighters a day now.

Bill Hicks

I am a drinker with a writing problem.

Brendan Behan

Spanish wine is foul. Catpiss is champagne compared to this sulphurous urination of some aged horse.

D.H. Lawrence

The worst alcoholic beverage on record was found when two women in Idaho were arrested on charges of manufacturing and selling an ersatz brandy which was distilled from water, vodka and urine.

Mark Fowler

I make it a rule never to smoke while I'm sleeping.

Mark Twain

Back in my running days, I would tremble and shake for hours upon arising. It was the only exercise I got.

W.C. Fields

The answers to life's problems aren't at the bottom of a bottle, they're on TV.

Homer Simpson

If I ever become an alcoholic, friends won't suspect I am hiding bottles. They would think it was just my housekeeping.

Phyllis Diller

I never drink at home, because I never go home.

Keith Floyd

Never trust a brilliant idea unless it survives the hangover.

Jimmy Breslin

I don't like to drink in front of the kids, but when they're around, who needs it?

Phyllis Diller

He never touches water. It goes to his head at once.

Oscar Wilde

Coffee is a pretty powerful stimulant. I had a friend who drank twenty cups a day at work. He died last month, but a week later he was still mingling in the company lounge.

Milton Berle

Why is it that drug addicts and computer nerds are both called users?

Clifford Stoll

My boss wouldn't dare to sack me – I'm too far behind in my work.

Joey Adams

I have given up smoking again. God, I feel fit. Homicidal but fit. A different man. Irritable, moody, depressed, rude, nervy, perhaps; but the lungs are fine.

A.P. Herbert

Drink and Drugs

Drinking was never a problem until I needed a new liver.

Larry Hagman

Always do sober what you said you'd do drunk. That will teach you to keep your mouth shut.

Ernest Hemingway

I was sitting in a bar nursing a drink and my nipples were getting very soggy.

Emo Philips

I've formed a new club called Alcoholics Unanimous. If you don't feel like a drink, you ring another member and he comes over to persuade you to go to the pub.

Richard Harris

Luckily I've always been able to hold my drink and I've never done anything shameful or undignified under the influence of alcohol that I can recall.

Les Patterson

I've never actually drunk the national drink of Holland, but I often sprinkle a few drops on the Y-fronts before a heavy night on the job.

Les Patterson

If I didn't have a problem with alcohol, I would drink all the time.

Havelock Ellis

'Never trust a man who doesn't drink,' was one of my father's favourite expressions and he died plenty trustworthy.

Les Patterson

I ruined my health drinking to other people's.

William Hamilton

I'm a light drinker. As soon as it gets light, I start to drink.

W.C. Fields

How would I rank sex, smoking and vodka in order of preference? All three at once.

Kate Moss

The odour of sanctity was clearly distinguishable from his breath and person.

Mervyn Wall

If God had intended us to drink beer, He would have given us stomachs.

David Daye

If you ever reach total enlightenment while drinking beer, I bet it makes the beer shoot out your nose.

Jack Handey

I've been drunk for about a week now, and I thought it might sober me to sit in a library.

F. Scott Fitzgerald

Drink and Drugs

Although man is already ninety per cent water, the Prohibitionists are not yet satisfied.

John Bangs

Princess Margaret was staggeringly good-looking.

Brian Appleyard

The only Olympic curling standards I can recall were for heavy drinking.

Magnus Linklater

Whisky was invented by the Irish as embrocation for sick mules.

David Daiches

'Credit' and 'Aaaargggh' – those two words are usually coupled together in the Old Pink Dog Bar.

Douglas Adams

Give a man a beer, waste an hour. Teach a man to brew and waste a lifetime.

Bill Owen

I drink with impunity, or anybody else who invites me.

Artemus Ward

The problem with the designated driver program is that it's not a desirable job. But if you ever get sucked into doing it, have fun with it. At the end of the night, drop everybody off at the wrong house.

Jeff Foxworthy

March is the month that God designed to show those who don't drink what a hangover is like.

Garrison Keillor

It's all right to drink like a fish – if you drink what a fish drinks.

Mary Poole

I thought I was dancing until somebody stepped on my hand.

J.B. White

Bacchus is a convenient deity invented by the ancients as an excuse for getting drunk.

Ambrose Bierce

If smoking is good enough for beagles, it's good enough for me.

Richard Littlejohn

My uncle Mike used to tell me about the Battle of Gettysburg. All he would say was, 'It was horrible. I went six whole days without a drink.'

John Ford

The Heineken Uncertainty Principle – you can never be sure how many beers you had last night.

Aaron Fuegi

Gin is intoxication reduced to its simplest essence.

Ralph Bates

Drink and Drugs

An alcoholic is a man who, when he buys his ties, has to ask if gin makes them run.

F. Scott Fitzgerald

I drink to your charm, your beauty and your brains: which gives you a rough idea of how hard up I am for a drink.

Groucho Marx

Passive smoking is really outrageous. They should buy their own.

B.J. Cunningham

It is an odd but universally held opinion that anyone who doesn't drink must be an alcoholic.

P.J. O'Rourke

Nicotine patches are great. Stick one over each eye and you can't find your cigarettes.

Bill Hicks

Recovering from a hangover, he resolved, having moved his eyeballs, never to move them again.

Kingsley Amis

Say No to drugs. That'll bring the price down.

Geechy Guys

I was left in no doubt as to the severity of the hangover when a cat stamped into the room.

P.G. Wodehouse

I was asked to do a benefit for babies born addicted to crack. I agreed, but I think we both knew what they're going to spend the money on.

Laura Kightlinger

American beer should be put back in the horse.

H. Allen Smith

Sure I lost weight during twenty years of smoking. How much does a lung weigh?

Michael Meehan

There used to be a notice in our rugby club bar which read: 'We open at 9:30 am and close at 11 pm. If you still haven't had enough to drink in that time, the management feel you can't have been trying.'

Bill Mulcahy

I'm all in favour of drug tests as long as they are multiple choice.

Kurt Rambis

Cocktails have all the disagreeability, without the utility, of a disinfectant.

Shane Leslie

I drink only to steady my nerves. Sometimes I'm so steady, I don't move for months.

W.C. Fields

I never drink water; I'm afraid it may be habit-forming.

W.C. Fields

Drink and Drugs

France is the largest country in Europe, a great boon for drunks who need room to fall.

Alan Coren

Kevin Keegan is not fit to lace George Best's drinks.

John Roberts

My New Year's Resolution is to give up drinking out of damp glasses.

Brendan Grace

I don't drink or take drugs these days. I am allergic to alcohol and narcotics. I break out in handcuffs.

Robert Downey Jr.

These nicotine patches seem to work pretty well, but it's kind of hard to keep them lit.

George Carlin

My drinking days, I think, are over. The human liver, unless it is Graham Greene's, can take so much and no more.

Anthony Burgess

Don't drink until your children are in bed. I tried this rule once – they got so sick of being tucked in at 4.30 in the afternoon.

Phyllis Diller

Education

Education

I'm a philosophy major. That means I can think deep thoughts about being unemployed.

Bruce Lee

Smartness runs in my family. When I went to school I was so smart my teacher was in my class for five years.

George Burns

Metaphysics is an attempt to prove the incredible by an appeal to the unintelligible.

H.L. Mencken

What's on your mind, if you will forgive the overstatement?

Fred Allen

Headmasters of schools tend to be men.

Clare Short

He was about to open his lecture, when one of his students rose in his seat and asked a question. It is a practice which, I need hardly say, we do not encourage; the young man, I believe, was a newcomer in the philosophy class.

Stephen Leacock

He respects Owl, because you can't help respecting anybody who can spell TWESDAY, even if he doesn't spell it right.

A.A. Milne

One of my school reports read as follows – 'This boy shows great originality, which must be crushed at all costs'.

Peter Ustinov

A plumber who has Latin is a better plumber than one who does not.

Enoch Powell

I don't think one 'comes down' from Jimmy's university. According to him, it's not even red brick, but white tile.

John Osborne

Hamlet is the tragedy of tackling a family problem too soon after college.

Tom Masson

What did I do for my college? I drank for it.

Evelyn Waugh

I am the Roman Emperor, and am above grammar.

Emperor Sigismund

Macaulay not only overflowed with learning, he stood in the slop.

Sydney Smith

He may be dead; or, he may be teaching English.

Cormac McCarthy

Teenage boys left alone for an evening with an older brother while their parents are out do not study mathematics. They study fratricide.

Mary Riddell

College athletes used to get a degree in bringing your pencil.

Ruby Wax

Education

On many American campuses the only qualification for admission is the ability to find the campus and then discover a parking space.

Malcolm Bradbury

At New York University I majored in advanced fondling. I minored in foreplay.

Woody Allen

The Romans would never have conquered the world if they had to learn Latin first.

Heinrich Heine

The great advantage of an English public school education is that no subsequent form of captivity can hold any particular terror for you. A friend who was put to work on the Burma railway once told me that he was greeted, on arrival, by a fellow prisoner-of-war who said, 'Cheer up. It's not half as bad as Marlborough'.

John Mortimer

Why don't they pass a constitutional amendment prohibiting anybody from learning anything? If it works as good as Prohibition did, in five years Americans would be the smartest race of people on earth.

Will Rogers

I would rather be governed by the first three hundred names in the Boston telephone book than by the Faculty of Harvard University.

William F. Buckley

Grammar schools are public schools without the sodomy.

Tony Parsons

There is nothing as stupid as an educated man, if you get him off the thing he was educated in.

Will Rogers

There is only one thing that consoles me about my exams. They cannot possibly ask everything I don't know.

Stanisfer Ryan

My schooldays were the happiest days of my life – which gives you some idea of the misery I've endured over the past twenty-five years.

Paul Merton

Historians are like deaf people who go on answering questions that no one has asked them.

Leo Tolstoy

Sixty minutes of thinking of any kind is bound to lead to confusion and unhappiness.

James Thurber

The intellect of the Prince of Wales is of no more use than a pistol packed in the bottom of a trunk in the robber-infested Apennines.

Prince Albert

Your head is as empty as a hermit's address book.

Rowan Atkinson

Education

I was thrown out of NYU for cheating – with the dean's wife.

Woody Allen

My wife was a Latin scholar. On our honeymoon I asked her to conjugate but she declined.

Don Foreman

If I had known I was going to be president of Bolivia, I would have learned to read and write.

Enrique Penaranda

I have been described as 'A lighthouse in the middle of a bog', brilliant but useless.

Conor Cruise O'Brien

Charlemagne either died or was born or did something with the Holy Roman Empire in 800.

Robert Benchley

Chess is the most elaborate waste of human intelligence outside an advertising agency.

Raymond Chandler

An encyclopaedia is a system for collecting dust in alphabetical order.

Mike Barfield

We schoolmasters must temper discretion with deceit.

Evelyn Waugh

Lectures at our university are optional. Graduation is also optional.

Brian Quinn

The founding fathers in their wisdom decided that children were an unnatural strain on parents. So they provided jails called schools, equipped with torture called education.

John Updike

By the time I was thirteen I realised I'd be more successful at something physical rather than mental.

Arnold Schwarzenegger

Intelligence was a deformity which must be concealed; a public school taught one to conceal it as a good tailor hides a paunch or a hump.

Cyril Connolly

He was very weak in verbs, for he has learned all his French from menus, which contain only nouns.

L.P. Hartley

You have mastered the colon, though the semi-colon you handle with less assurance, while your use of the apostrophe makes my flesh creep.

Logan Pearsall Smith

Non-philosophers often have trouble making out why philosophers remain fascinated by questions they themselves gave up as hopeless at the age of six or seven.

Frank Kermode

Education

As a young man Peter's ugliness was so remarkable that his fellow undergraduates formed themselves into a committee to consider what could be done for the improvement of Peter's personal appearance.

Hesketh Pearson

Find out what Bill Gates wants your school to do. Don't do it.

Theodore Roszak

I love kids – I used to go to school with them.

Tommy Cooper

Examinations are pure humbug from beginning to end. If a man is a gentleman, he knows quite enough, and if he is not a gentleman whatever he knows is bad for him.

Oscar Wilde

I get all my ideas from a mail order company in Indianapolis, but I'm not prepared to give you their name.

Douglas Adams

No academic ever becomes chairman until he has forgotten the meaning of the word 'irrelevant'.

Francis Cornford

Medieval studies is just a branch of the entertainment business.

Bruce McFarlane

A statesman is any politician it's considered safe to name a school after.

Bill Vaughan

Education

Oxford University is a sanctuary in which exploded systems and obsolete prejudices find shelter and protection after they have been hunted out of every corner of the world.

Adam Smith

I always begin at the left with the opening word of the sentence and read towards the right and I recommend this method.

James Thurber

Anyone who stares long enough into the distance is bound to be mistaken for a philosopher or mystic in the end.

Patrick White

Education is a wonderful thing. If you couldn't sign your name you'd have to pay cash.

Rita Mae Brown

Rarely is the question asked: what is our children learning?

George W. Bush

'Gullible' isn't in the dictionary and you can confirm that by looking it up.

Steven Wright

Pardon my long preamble. It's like a chorus girl's tights – it touches everything and covers nothing.

Gertrude Lawrence

Horace Greeley wrote so illegibly that a fired employee used his letter of discharge as a letter of recommendation for another job.

Robert Hendrickson

Education

The better class of Briton likes to send his children away to school until they are old enough and intelligent enough to come home again. Then they're too old and intelligent to want to.

Malcolm Bradbury

Having no education I had to use my brains.

Bill Shankly

The first thing to have in a library is a shelf. From time to time this can be decorated with literature, but the shelf is the main thing.

Finley Peter Dunne

There is speculation. Then there is wild speculation. Then there is cosmology.

Martyn Harris

I'd prefer a smart idiot to a stupid genius any day.

Samuel Goldwyn

I am always prepared to recognise that there may be two points of view – mine and the wrong one.

John Gorton

I have a daughter who goes to SMU. She could have gone to UCLA here in California, but that would have been one more letter for her to remember.

Shecky Green

How do you know if a teacher has a hangover? Movie day!

Jay Mohr

A short neck denotes a good mind. You see, the messages go quicker to the brain because they've got shorter to go.

Muriel Spark

Why does Sea World have a seafood restaurant? I'm halfway through my fish burger and I realise, Oh my God, I could be eating a slow learner.

Lynda Montgomery

Richard Burton has a tremendous passion for the English language, especially the spoken and the written word.

Frank Boughs

We don't believe that libraries should be places where people sit in silence, and that's the main reason for our policy of employing wild animals as librarians.

John Cleese

Latin, being a dead language, will live forever.

Samuel Johnson

The Provost of Eton does nothing and the Vice-Provost helps him.

Tim Card

Intelligence is in inverse proportion to the ability to fill in forms correctly.

David Scott-Gatty

The only function of a student at a lecture is to be present when a great mind communes with itself.

Denis Donoghue

Education

In prison, I studied German. Indeed, this seems to be the proper place for such study.

Oscar Wilde

At an examination we were allowed to take into the examination anything we could carry. I gave a piggyback to a postgraduate student.

Dirk Mollett

President Clinton returned today to the university where he didn't inhale, didn't get drafted and didn't get a degree.

Maureen Dowd

If you're going to be any good as a teacher, you've got to like the little swine.

James Darling

There is nobody more irritating that somebody with less intelligence and more sense than we have.

Don Herold

Even if you learn to speak correct English, to whom are you going to speak it?

Clarence Darrow

The word 'seminar' is derived from 'semi' and 'arse', any half-assed discussion.

Aaron Fuegi

The Glasgow College of Technology demands mathematical proficiency to the standard of undertaking long division together with proven ability to 'carry one' in hard sums.

Tom Shields

Stay in college, get the knowledge. And stay there until you're through. If they can make penicillin out of mouldy bread, they can sure make something out of you.

Muhammad Ali

Dean is to faculty as hydrant is to dog.

Alfred Kahn

It is good for David Blunkett to experience at the heated NUT conference in Blackpool what teachers have to put up with from unruly pupils.

Nigel de Gruchy

The government pays a £5 decapitation fee for every pupil in the school.

Tom Shields

Luck played no part in my winning the school prize – I deserved it.

Margaret Thatcher

The Ken Starr report is now on the Internet. I'll bet Clinton is glad he put a computer in every classroom now.

Jay Leno

Science, physics, maths were out of my range; so were modern languages. Tone-deaf, there was no future in my trying to understand them. Dead languages, of which no one was certain of the correct pronunciation, were the answer. I joined Belk's Classical Sixth.

Woodrow Wyatt

Education

Leave to repeat the examination will be granted only with the permission of the principal, which will normally be refused.

Edward Fahy

I was privately educated by goats.

Peter Cook

Ideas are like umbrellas. If left lying about, they are particularly liable to a change of ownership.

Tom Kettle

One of the disadvantages of having children is that they eventually get old enough to give you presents they make at school.

Robert Byrne

We did have a form of Afro-Asian studies which consisted of colouring bits of the map red to show the British Empire.

Michael Green

Those who do not remember history are condemned to repeat it – next semester.

Lee Barnett

I chose a single-sex Oxford college because I thought I'd rather not face the trauma of men at breakfast.

Theresa May

When I received my honorary degree from the University of Durham an onlooker remarked on seeing the formal procession of graduands: 'I think it's a Gypsy Wedding.'

P.D. James

My school report said that I was every inch a fool.
Fortunately I was not very tall.

Norman Wisdom

He teaches at a prison, a mental hospital and a local school.
He says that compared with the schoolchildren, the
murderers and psychotics are models of good behaviour.

Alan Bennett

The CSE exams are unavoidable for anyone trying to join
the civil service. Based on the results, the Treasury has first
choice of the cream, which enables that department to foul
up the British economy.

Frederick Forsyth

I'm really smart. I know a whole lot, but I just can't think
of it.

Morey Amsterdam

Tell your kids' teachers you strongly believe the best
punishment is having them stay after school.

Phyllis Diller

Food

Food

There are two things in life I like firm and one of them is jelly.

Mae West

A winkle is just a bogey with a crash helmet on.

Mick Miller

I didn't complain about the steak, dear. I merely said I didn't see that old horse that used to be tethered outside here.

W.C. Fields

I was polishing off the last mouthful of a dish in a restaurant when I heard one waiter whisper to another, 'He's actually eating it'.

Gilbert Harding

At big dinners my motto always is 'Eat it now, you can always vomit it later'.

Derek Nimmo

In Spain, attempting to obtain a chicken-salad sandwich, you wind up with a dish whose name, when you look it up in your Spanish-English dictionary, turns out to mean 'Eel with the Big Abscess'.

Dave Barry

I no longer prepared food or drink with more than one ingredient.

Cyra McFadden

The trouble with eating Italian food is that five or six days later you're hungry again.

George Miller

All these cereals they have: Cracklin' Oat Bran and Honkin Fibre Chunks. Cereal used to come with a free prize and now it comes with a roll of toilet paper in every box.

Denis Leary

God invented vegetables to let women get even with their children.

P.J. O'Rourke

For a long time I thought coq au vin meant love in a lorry.

Victoria Wood

Parsley is gharsley.

Ogden Nash

There is no such thing as a little garlic.

Aga Khan III

Whatever you tell them, people always make your tea or coffee the way they like it.

Russell Bell

Ask your child what he wants for dinner only if he's buying.

Fran Lebowitz

Food

There is nothing worse than being stuck up in the Andes Mountains in a plane crash with your anorexic friend Freddy.

Denis Leary

'Escargot' is French for 'fat crawling bag of phlegm'.

Dave Barry

Far too many cooks spoil the broth.

Wayne G. Haisley

Baseball feels better than sex and almost as good as eating watermelon.

Teddy Tannenbaum

The *Mayflower* left Plymouth for Massachusetts to check out some likely sites for McDonald's restaurants.

Russell Bell

Mexican food is delicious and perfectly safe as long as you are careful never to get any of it in your digestive system.

Dave Barry

Cottage cheese has no flavour – it's like kissing your sister.

Cathy Hopkins

Never serve oysters in a month that has no paycheck in it.

P.J. O'Rourke

Did you ever notice they never take any fat hostages? You never see a guy come out of Lebanon going 'I was held hostage for seven months and I lost 175 pounds. I feel good and I look good and I learned self-discipline. That's the important thing.'

Denis Leary

Turkish food is edible Greek food.

A.A. Gill

I've had matzo ball soup three meals in a row. Isn't there any other part of the matzo you can eat?

Marilyn Monroe

It would be nice if the Food and Drug Administration stopped issuing warnings about toxic substances and just gave me the names of one or two things still safe to eat.

Robert Fuoss

A recipe is a series of step-by-step instructions for preparing ingredients you forgot to buy in utensils you don't own to make a dish the dog won't eat the rest of.

Henry Beard

The food in that restaurant is terrible. And such small portions.

Woody Allen

There are very few shops in the country, but the ever resourceful farm folk have come up with a number of ingenious if disgusting ploys to circumvent this inconvenience. They won't just go out and buy a carton of milk like proper people, so what do they do? They squeeze it out of a cow! God only knows who first came up with that one, but it seems to work. Apparently cows are full of the stuff.

Russell Bell

Food

The chip is the great British contribution to world cuisine.

John Cleese

Organic is just another word for dirty fruit.

Ruby Wax

Easter eggs go on sale for a short period because they are
basically horrible. Something happens to chocolate in the
process of turning it eggshaped that makes it taste like
something that has spent 20 years at the back of a
cupboard. The pagan tradition is strong enough to
persuade people to pay £3.99 for this experience once a
year, but no way are they going to repeat it more often. By
the time a year has passed they have forgotten how
unpleasant Easter eggs are and they then buy them again.

Robert Crompton

After a good dinner, one can forgive anybody, even one's
own relations.

Oscar Wilde

He looked at me as if I was a side dish he hadn't ordered.

Ring Lardner

A good reducing exercise consists of placing both hands
against the edge of the table and pushing back.

Robert Quillen

Take those scales out of the bathroom; the right place for
them is in front of the refrigerator.

Richard Needham

I work for a company that makes deceptively shallow dishes for Chinese restaurants.

Woody Allen

Extra food is allowed for weddings, golden weddings, funerals and other festivities.

Edith Somerskill M.P.

Anything is good if it's made of chocolate.

Jo Brand

The Texas recipe for chili is to put a pot of chili on the stove to simmer. Let it simmer. Meanwhile, broil a good steak. Eat the steak. Let the chili simmer. Ignore it.

Allan Shivers

Inhabitants of underdeveloped nations and victims of natural disasters are the only people who have ever been happy to see soyabeans.

Fran Lebowitz

The food was so tasteless you could eat a meal of it and belch and it wouldn't remind you of anything.

Red Foxx

My doctor has advised me to give up those intimate little dinners for four, unless there are three people eating with me.

Orson Welles

English vegetables taste as though they have been boiled in a strong soap.

W.C. Fields

Food

I was eating a lot of frozen TV dinners when I realised they would probably taste better if they were warm.

Yakov Smirnoff

I feel the end approaching. Quick, bring me my dessert, coffee, and liqueur.

Pierette Brillat-Savarin

Do you know what breakfast cereal is made of? It's made of all those little curly wooden shavings you find in pencil sharpeners.

Roald Dahl

Cantonese will eat anything in the sky but airplanes, anything in the sea but submarines and anything with four legs but the table.

Amanda Bennett

Bertrand Russell looked like a vegetarian vulture.

A.A. Gill

Most vegetarians I ever see looked enough like their food to be classed as cannibals.

Finley Peter Dunne

Who bothers to cook TV dinners! I suck them frozen.

Woody Allen

One of the most popular Soviet meals is the bread sandwich. That is two slices of bread with another slice of bread in between. They have the same thing in America – it's called a Big Mac.

Yakov Smirnoff

The most dangerous food is wedding cake.

James Thurber

On ringing a restaurant to ask if they had wheelchair access I was told that they accepted all major credit cards.

Pat Fitzpatrick

The perfect lover is one who turns into a pizza at 4 a.m.

Charles Pierce

When compelled to cook, I produce a meal that would make a sword swallower gag.

Russell Baker

I believe that if I ever had to practise cannibalism, I might manage if there was enough tarragon around.

James Beard

Every morning I get up and I make instant coffee and I drink it so I'll have enough energy to make regular coffee.

Steven Wright

The dumbing-down of notices on food packets has just about reached its limit. I recently bought a packet of peanuts and it said CONTAINS: PEANUTS. INSTRUCTIONS: OPEN PACKET, EAT CONTENTS.

Robin Young

Why is a carrot more orange than an orange?

Ambrose Dukes

Food

I eat like a vulture: unfortunately, the resemblance doesn't end there.

Groucho Marx

My Uncle Joe was a philosopher, very deep, very serious. Never eat chocolate after chicken he'd tell us, wagging his finger.

Mel Brooks

The first time I fried organic wheat bread, I thought I was chewing on roofing material.

Robin Williams

Gélée of duck has the consistency of Pamela Anderson Lee's implants, and was so salty and horrid it was like licking an Abyssinian shotputter's armpit.

A.A. Gill

Age does not diminish the extreme disappointment of having a scoop of ice cream fall from the cone.

Jim Fiebig

Avoid beans as you would matricide.

Pythagoras

Dining on durian is like eating vanilla custard in a latrine.

Anthony Burgess

A nutrient is a chemical added to breakfast cereal to allow it to be sold as a food.

Mike Barfield

Vegetarians have wicked, shifty eyes and laugh in a cold, calculating manner. They pinch little children, steal stamps, drink water and grow beards.

J.B. Morton

I don't eat fish. They are my friends.

Johnny Weissmuller

Women should try to increase their size rather than decrease it, because I believe the bigger we are, the more space we'll take up, and the more we'll have to be reckoned with.

Roseanne Barr

Edible adj: good to eat, and wholesome to digest, as a worm to a toad, a toad to a snake, a snake to a pig, a pig to a man, and a man to a worm.

Ambrose Bierce

This piece of cod passes all understanding.

Edwin Lutyens

By the time they had diminished from 50 to 8, the other dwarfs began to suspect 'Hungry'.

Gary Larson

I've known what it is to be hungry, but I always went right to a restaurant.

Ring Lardner

I personally prefer a nice frozen TV dinner at home, mainly because it's so little trouble. All you have to do is have another drink while you're throwing it in the garbage.

Jack Douglas

Food

The reason there is such a food shortage in Russia is that the government stockpiles all the food for the army. Whatever the army doesn't use after a year, the government sells to the public.

Yakov Smirnoff

Processed 'cheese'. The word should always, like Soviet 'democracy' be framed in quotes, for no matter what the law may say, I refuse to call this cheese. The best I can say for it is that it is not poisonous. The worst, that it represents the triumph of technology over conscience. In the preparation of this solidified floor wax, every problem is solved: packaging, keeping, distribution, slicing, cost. One problem alone is not solved: that of making cheese.

Bob Brown

The only constant factor of American eating competitions is the basic rule of competition: 'Heave and you leave.'

Frank McNally

As part of a beauty regime it was probably fabulous. As food it was like eating soggy knicker and vinegar crisps.

A.A. Gill

Oh, the superb wretchedness of English food. How many foreigners has it daunted, and what a subtle glow of nationality one feels in ordering a dish that one knows will be bad and being able to eat it.

Cyril Connolly

In spite of their real opinions of editors as parasites and literary phonies, authors should be extra polite to them at all times, remembering that in that direction lie some of the most tasty lunches available in New York.

Paul Fussell

The vol-au-vent is the single nastiest thing ever invented as a food that doesn't involve an initiation ceremony. This one was like eating a ripe camel's conjunctive eye socket.

A.A. Gill

I'm told there are now restaurants where you can eat with the liposuction machine attached. Say, buddy, I'll have the cheesecake with two scoops of ice cream and crank me up to nine on the machine.

Jerry Seinfeld

Serve coffee early in the meal and very hot. If the guest burns his tongue he won't be able to taste anything.

Phyllis Diller

Chicken? Why do you give me these pedestrians to eat?

Oscar Wilde

From experience, I know that anything ending in '-os' on a restaurant menu is pronounced 'heartburn'.

Hugh Leonard

If I didn't cook the way I did, my husband would never have been able to buy enough food for our five kids. They've yet to ask for seconds and they never complain about the school lunch program.

Phyllis Diller

Food

I have a sign on my fence which says: 'Salesmen Always Welcome. Dog food is Expensive.'

Emo Philips

The Italians invented birth control – they call it 'garlic'.

Harlan Ellison

Boiled British cabbage is something compared with which steamed coarse newsprint bought from bankrupt Finnish salvage dealers and heated over smoky oil stoves is an exquisite delicacy. It is something lower than ex-Army blankets stolen by dispossessed Goanese dosshouse-keepers who used them to cover busted-down hen houses in the slum district of Karachi.

William Connor

A restaurant I used to frequent in Cork advertised: 'Eat here and you'll never eat anywhere else again.'

Niall Toibin

Lots of men are jealous of me because I have this extraordinarily beautiful wife who does great Indian and Italian.

Michael Caine

There is nothing on earth so savage – even a bear robbed of her cubs – as a hungry husband.

Fanny Fern

It is impossible to have a failure with chutney; there's nothing to set and no ingredient barred.

Robert Morley

I hate McDonald's. I can't think of anything I hate more than McDonald's apart from Pot Noodle.

Terence Conran

French chefs, if they cared to try, could produce an excellent and nutritious meal out of cigar stubs and empty matchboxes.

Norman Douglas

Restaurants are like ladies: the best are often not the most enjoyable, nor the grandest, the most friendly, and the pleasures of the evening are frequently spoiled by the writing of an exorbitant cheque.

John Mortimer

I did toy with the idea of doing a cookbook. I think a lot of people who hate literature but who love fried eggs would buy it if the price was right.

Groucho Marx

Get your haggis right here! Chopped heart and lungs, boiled in a wee sheep's stomach. And it tastes as good as it sounds.

Matt Groening

Maybe there is no actual place such as Hell. Maybe Hell is just having to listen to our grandparents breathe through their noses when they're eating sandwiches.

Jim Carrey

Food

The sprout was developed by Brussels agronomists, this being the largest cabbage a housewife could possibly carry through the teeming streets.

Alan Coren

I don't like to eat snails. I prefer fast food.

Jim Strange

You should try everything once except incest and steak tartare.

Philip Howard

Due to the shape of the North American elk's oesophagus, even if it could speak, it could not pronounce the word 'lasagne'.

Cliff Clavin

My diet tips are – don't eat breakfast, don't eat lunch and don't eat dinner.

Ken Follett

Don't be put off by the Formica tabletops; the chef used to cook for Onassis before he took to the bottle.

Robert Morley

Whenever I want a really good meal, I have the most wonderful meatloaf recipe. All I have to do is mention it and my husband takes me out to eat in a terrific restaurant.

Phyllis Diller

It's a funny fact that no matter what you eat it always comes up à la King.

Barry Humphries

I'm a Volvo-vegetarian. I'll eat an animal only if it was accidentally killed by a speeding car.

Ron Smith

A friend is someone you don't have to talk to anymore once the food is on the table.

Sabrina Matthews

The downfall of most diets is that they restrict your intake of food.

Fran Lebowitz

Never work before breakfast; if you have to work before breakfast, eat your breakfast first.

Josh Billings

What is the best of British cuisine? Well, a good fish finger butty is hard to beat.

Jamie Oliver

I took Calista Flockhart out to dinner and I think she ate just one pea.

Gordon House

'Twas a good dinner enough, to be sure, but it was not a dinner to ask a man to.

Samuel Johnson

I asked the waitress for another steak because the one she served me was too tough. She told me she couldn't take it back because I'd bent it.

Tommy Cooper

Food

Prefaces are an intolerable nuisance which stop you from getting to the main event, like a protracted wedding breakfast.

Frank Muir

I'm so unlucky that if a woman got cut in half, I'd get the half that eats.

Les Patterson

Liquorice is the candy equivalent of liver.

Michael O'Donoghue

I find eating chocolate as thrilling as having sex, but then I've never had sex.

Britney Spears

If man were immortal, do you realise what his meat bills would be?

Woody Allen

There is only one fruitcake in the entire world and people keep sending it to each other.

Johnny Carson

I have not gained weight. I have merely trimmed upwards.

Roseanne Barr

If you don't want your kitchen full of stinking odours, stop cooking.

Erma Bombeck

The longer the menu description, the less you will get on your plate.

Shirley Lowe

Why does sour cream have a 'use by' date on it?

John Law

I captured some people who tried to assassinate me. I ate them before they ate me.

Idi Amin

The general rule about eating mammalian carnivores is don't eat anything that might eat you or has more offensive droppings than yours.

A.A. Gill

Schizophrenia beats dining alone.

Oscar Levant

The thing women like most in bed is breakfast.

Robin Williams

I'm that hungry I could eat a baby's bottom through a cane-chair.

Les Patterson

I asked the barmaid for a quickie. I was mortified when the man next to me said, 'It's pronounced "quiche".'

Luigi Amaduzzi

Food

When I buy cookies, I just eat four and throw the rest away. But first I spray them with disinfectant so I won't dig them out of the garbage later. Disinfectant doesn't taste all that bad though.

Janette Barber

I always eat olives on a string in case I may not like them.

Max Miller

Ah, the speed with which the plates of soup are placed before the customers: not a drop splashes over, but then there is never more than a drop to start with.

Robert Morley

Coffee just isn't my cup of tea.

Samuel Goldwyn

Seize the moment. Remember all those women on the *Titanic* who waved away the dessert trolley.

Erma Bombeck

If you want to spend your money in a way that really shows, buy rich food.

Beth Gurney

Vegetarians are on a par with cannibals, since they eat not for nutrition but for moral effect.

Felipe Fernandez-Armesto

How do they always get fish the right size to fit the batter?

Tom Shields

The only ailment chicken soup can't cure is neurotic dependence on one's mother.

Arthur Naiman

In Indiana there was a law prohibiting people from travelling on buses within four hours of eating garlic.

Richard Wilson

One morning I was making tea in my pyjamas. I really must get a teapot.

Chic Murray

She used to diet on any kind of food she could lay her hands on.

Arthur Baer

I don't mind eels, except at meals.

Ogden Nash

My cooking is modern Scottish – if you complain you get head butted.

Chris Bradley

Sahara dessert tastes terrible.

Patrick Murray

'Snacktrek' is the peculiar habit, when searching for a snack, of constantly returning to the refrigerator in hopes that something new will have materialized.

Rich Hall

Food

Buy a box of liquorice and you'll always have candy in the house.

George S. Kaufman

Love is just a substitute for chocolate.

Miranda Ingram

I once ate an entire bar of chocolate.

Claudia Schiffer

A mind of the calibre of mine cannot derive its nutriment from cows.

George Bernard Shaw

The Greasy Spoon served plates of fat. You could have sausages in your fat or fried eggs in your fat. You could have the sausages and the fried eggs together, but that meant you got double the amount of fat.

Clive James

For my ordinary workaday teas I ate only flapjacks or crumpets, shortcake and gingerbread, Swiss roll and chocolate biscuits and one or two cakes which needed eating up.

Robert Morley

What is sauce for the goose is propaganda.

Ogden Nash

Everything my wife cooks, even coffee, tastes like chicken.

Woody Allen

Toast making is apparently like nose picking, in that it's best if you do it yourself.

Brendan O'Connot

The first time my wife cooked me dinner I almost choked to death on a bone in her chocolate pudding.

Woody Allen

Bert spent hours making something he called butter. This was a mix of margarine, one part per million of real butter and a secret ingredient that, after being vigorously and noisily whipped for hours, became a bowl of pallid, tasteless paste, which he claimed was good for us.

Bill Tidy

Last week I bought a frozen Mexican dinner, but now I wish I had brought him into the house and let him warm up a little.

George Carlin

My self-prepared dinners are in two courses: the first served at 6.30 pm and the second – two Alka-Seltzers – at 3.30 am.

Hugh Leonard

Vegetables are interesting, but lack a sense of purpose when unaccompanied by a good cut of meat.

Fran Lebowitz

I thought my mother was a bad cook, but at least her gravy used to move about a bit.

Tony Hancock

Food

My wife told me she'd love to eat out for a change, so I moved the dining room table into the garden.

Les Dawson

If your husband is on a special diet, like three meals a day, use all the shortcuts you can find. I even buy frozen toast.

Phyllis Diller

In our recipe for Banana Trifle last week, we inadvertently omitted the bananas. Apologies all round.

Fritz Spiegl

Lawyers and Other Professions

Lawyers and Other Professions

My friend Malcolm is a very shy and sensitive used car salesman.

Benny Hill

I remember once going into an undertakers, lying on the floor, and shouting 'shop'.

Spike Milligan

I have knowingly defended a number of guilty men, but the guilty never escape unscathed. My fees are sufficient punishment for anyone.

F. Lee Bailey

A popular Washington stop is the Supreme Court, where the justices frequently ask the spectators to help them decide a tough case by registering their opinions on the applause-o-meter.

Dave Barry

The O.J. Simpson jury they ended up choosing had to swear they'd never heard about a case that had been in the papers every day for a year and a half. And then they ask them to rule on DNA. These idiots didn't even get that far in the alphabet. They wondered why the N came before the A.

Jackie Mason

To escape jury duty in England, wear a bowler hat and carry a rolled-up copy of the *Daily Telegraph*.

John Mortimer

Lawyers and Other Professions

The Metropolitan Police Force is abbreviated to the MET to give more members a chance of spelling it.

Mike Barfield

Reading isn't an occupation we encourage among police officers. We try to keep the paperwork down to a minimum.

Joe Orton

Fear of the policeman is the beginning of wisdom.

Charles Pasqua

Even if a farmer intends to loaf, he gets up in time to get an early start.

Edgar W. Howe

If brains were a virus, policemen would be the healthiest people in the world.

John O'Dwyer

In England, justice is open to all – like the Ritz Hotel.

James Mathew

The one great principle of the English law is to make business for itself.

Charles Dickens

Detectives are just policemen with smaller feet.

Whitfield Crook

Make crime pay – become a lawyer.

Will Rogers

Lawyers and Other Professions

There are four kinds of homicide: felonious, excusable, justifiable and praiseworthy.

Ambrose Bierce

The physician can bury his mistakes but the architect can only advise his client to plant vines.

Frank Lloyd Wright

Can't wait to be arrested and go all the way to the witness stand. 'Do you swear to tell the whole truth and nothing but the truth, so help you God?' 'Yes. You're ugly. See that woman in the jury? I really fancy her. Should I keep going or are you going to ask me questions?'

Steven Wright

I thought I was an honest guy, and just doing what everyone else was doing – bending the rules.

Manny Goldstein

The Russian police have a Missing Persons Department; that's where they decide which persons are going to be missing.

Yakov Smirnoff

I was ashamed of being a lawyer, so now I manually masturbate caged animals for artificial insemination.

Virginia Smith

A man was beaten up and robbed and lay dying on the roadside. A social worker came along and said, 'Tell me the name of the man who did this. He needs help immediately.'

Murray Watts

A man may as well open an oyster without a knife, as a lawyer's mouth without a fee.

Barten Holyday

I would much prefer to be a judge rather than a coal miner because of the absence of falling coal.

Peter Cook

The only way you can beat the lawyers is to die with nothing.

Will Rogers

The finding of a gibbet in an unexplored part of Africa gave me infinite pleasure as it proved that I was in a civilised society.

Mungo Park

Injustice is relatively easy to bear; what stings is justice.

H.L. Mencken

Mr Haughey cannot be named for legal reasons.

Charlie Crow

The only difference between a dead skunk lying on the road and a dead lawyer lying on the road is that there are skid marks near the skunk.

Patrick Murray

Most journalists of my generation died early, succumbing to one or other of the two great killers in the craft – cirrhosis or terminal alimony.

John Hepworth

Lawyers and Other Professions

The function of the expert is not to be more right than other people but to be wrong for more sophisticated reasons.

David Butler

A crowded police court docket is the surest of all signs that trade is brisk and money plenty.

Mark Twain

The only difference between a female lawyer and a pit bull terrier is the lipstick.

Patrick Murray

My will is as follows: count up the lawyers in the state and divide my money among them. If there should by any miracle be any left, let my relatives all of them, God bless 'em, fight over it.

Will Rogers

A group of white South Africans recently killed a black lawyer because he was black. That was wrong. They should have killed him because he was a lawyer.

Whitney Brown

Happiness is your dentist telling you it won't hurt and then having him catch his hand on the drill.

Johnny Carson

A lawyer with his briefcase can steal more than a thousand men with guns.

Mario Puzo

Lawyers and Other Professions

A lot of people criticise supermodels and I think that's very unfair, because they can't answer back.

Jo Brand

A leading authority is anyone who has guessed right more than once.

Frank Clark

Some tortures are physical and some are mental, but the one that's both is dental.

Ogden Nash

A Scottish lawyer was so proper in his behaviour that when mugged he pursued his assailant by shouting 'Stop alleged thief, Stop alleged thief'.

Ron Neil

Every time you think you've been screwed by publishers in every possible way, you meet one who has read the *Kama Sutra*.

Cathy Crimmins

The police officer told me to walk in a straight line. And when I had finished he said, 'You call that a straight line?' I shouldn't have, but I replied, 'The closest you'll ever come to a straight line is if they ever do an electroencephalogram of your brainwave.'

Emo Philips

An architect can be described as someone who forgets to put in the staircase.

Gustave Flaubert

Lawyers and Other Professions

Marriage is really tough because you have to deal with feelings and lawyers.

Richard Pryor

I think the law is far too laxative on criminals.

Yogi Berra

In law, nothing is certain but the expense.

Samuel Butler

A peer condemned to death has a right to be hanged with a silken cord. It's a bit like insisting that the electric chair had to be a Chippendale.

Charles Mosley

I suppose publishers are untrustworthy. They always certainly look it.

Oscar Wilde

I was arrested during a demo but the police realised that the sooner they released me the less likely they were to see themselves portrayed in one of my comedies.

Carla Lane

Apologists for the legal profession contend that lawyers are as honest as other men, but that is not very encouraging.

Ferdinand Lundberg

Journalism is a profession whose business it is to explain to others what it personally does not understand.

Lord Northcliff

If crime went down one hundred per cent, it would still be fifty times higher than it should be.

John Bowman

The police have stated that the discovery of a woman's body in a suitcase is being treated as 'suspicious'. It is nice to see that the spirit of Sherlock Holmes lives on.

Sydney Wilkins

Electronic books will do for the ophthalmologists what taffy and caramels did for dentists.

Martin Arnold

She has been kissed as often as a police-court bible, and by much the same class of people.

Robertson Davies

Court TV is holding a fantasy trial of Osama bin Laden. They got the idea a couple of years ago from the Los Angeles trial of O.J. Simpson.

David Letterman

Bookie Bob is a very hard guy indeed. In fact, the softest thing about him are his front teeth.

Damon Runyon

I am not a housewife. I did not marry a house.

Wilma Scott

Where there is a will, there is a dead person.

Ronnie Shakes

Lawyers and Other Professions

A psychoanalyst is a non-swimmer who works as a lifeguard.

Thomas Szasz

I'm a lawyer, but not an ambulance chaser. I'm usually there before the ambulance.

Melvin Bell

I tried to walk a fine line between acting lawfully and testifying falsely, but now realise that I did not fully accomplish that goal.

Bill Clinton

You never know how much a man can't remember until he is called as a witness.

Will Rogers

I'd like to be a mortician because I enjoy working with people.

Emo Philips

There is nothing quite as good as burial at sea. It is simple, tidy and not very incriminating.

Alfred Hitchcock

Whatever faults they may have, lawyers could be an important source of protein.

P.J. O'Rourke

A lawyer is a person who writes a 10,000-word document and calls it a 'brief'.

Franz Kafka

Al Capone was a Neapolitan whose surname, in Italian, means a castrated male chicken.

Joe Bonanno

This court has a duty to protect an accused person against the folly of his legal advisers.

Lord Cameron

Some men would run away to the Foreign Legion to recover from a disastrous love affair, but others ran to the Prison Service to forget that they were members of the human race.

Charlie Richardson

Lawyers are said to be more honourable than politicians, but less honourable than prostitutes. This is an exaggeration.

Alexander King

They have reintroduced the death penalty for insurance company directors.

Douglas Adams

Dust! At the very least they could give a man about to die a clean electric chair!

Michael Sclafoni

A consultant is somebody who steals your watch when you ask him the time.

Laurence J. Peter

Lawyers and Other Professions

Found guilty of embezzling £5,000, Mr Thanes Nark Phong, a hotel cashier from Bangkok, had his sentence reduced from 865 years to 576 years because 'his testimony proved useful'.

Trevor Danker

I did not get a life sentence. The judge gave me ninety-nine years.

Clarence Carnes

It is indeed a burning shame that there should be one law for men and another law for women. I think there should be no law for anybody.

Oscar Wilde

I'd probably be famous now if I wasn't such a good waitress.

Jane Siberry

Someone high on crack marches into a post office with a toy gun, poses for the closed-circuit television camera, drops his social security card on the way out and the police still have to use a slot on *Crimewatch* to catch him.

Jeremy Clarkson

We must present ourselves at Holloway Gaol at four o'clock. After that it is difficult to gain admission.

Oscar Wilde

The judge sentenced me to a hundred hours of community work with the mentally disadvantaged. I asked him if I got credit for the time I spent in court.

Emo Philips

Lawyers and Other Professions

A man who has no office to go to – I don't care who he is – is a trial of which you can have no conception.

George Bernard Shaw

Never insult a police officer while he's doing a body cavity search.

Fraser McClure

During the 1980s, dairy farmers decided there was too much cheap milk at the supermarket. So the government bought and slaughtered 1.6 billion dairy cows. How come the government never does anything like this with lawyers?

P.J. O'Rourke

They would have been working class if there was any work.

Roddy Doyle

They were as scarce as lawyers in Heaven.

Mark Twain

Justice is just a legal decision in your favour.

Ambrose Bierce

My husband has a talent for inaccurate précis.

Mary Archer

Bigamy is the only crime where two rites make a wrong.

Bob Hope

The longevity of my ancestors has been entirely dependent upon the fluctuating benevolence of juries.

Sean Desmond

Lawyers and Other Professions

Why are lawyers thought of so badly? Why are we found near the bottom of nearly every public opinion ranking of occupations? The answer is simple: because we deserve it.

Alan Dershowitz

What do you throw a drowning lawyer? His partner.

David Letterman

An alibi means you can prove you were somewhere else when you committed the crime.

Jimmy Durante

The function of an advertiser is to make women unhappy with what they have.

Earl Puckett

A jury is the stupidity of one brain multiplied by twelve.

Elbert Hubbard

A lawyer is one who protects us against robbery by taking away the temptation.

H.L. Mencken

The Irish Navy was vastly superior to the British Navy. In the Irish Navy, the sailors could always go home for their tea.

Ronnie Drew

The only profession where you can consistently be wrong and still get paid is a weather forecaster.

David Feherty

Lawyers and Other Professions

I was recently stopped for driving at 39 mph in a 40 mph limit. 'Nobody does that at 2 am unless he's been drinking, sir,' said the policeman. After a negative breathalyser test, the officer asked why I had been travelling below the speed limit on a clear road. 'Because there was a police car behind me,' I said.

Alan Calverd

I murdered one of my relatives – it was a dreadful thing to do, but she had thick ankles.

Thomas Wainewright

My uncle's dying wish was to have me sitting in his lap; he was in the electric chair.

Rodney Dangerfield

Lawyers should never marry other lawyers. This is called inbreeding, from which come idiot children and more lawyers.

Ruth Gordon

The worst job I ever had was working the photo machine at the bus station. I was the only one at the Christmas party.

Steven Wright

Top civil servants are called mandarins because they are small, fruity and give you the pip.

William Kerr

Literature

Literature

Fiction writing is great. You can make up almost anything.

Ivana Trump

It's not a good idea to put your wife into a novel – not your latest wife anyway.

Norman Mailer

If you are in difficulties with a book, try the element of surprise; attack it at an hour when it isn't expecting it.

H.G. Wells

I was reading Proust for the first time. Very poor stuff. I think he was mentally defective.

Evelyn Waugh

Kingsley Amis once said that sex is a great cure for a hangover, which indeed must be the case, because if you thought Kingsley Amis was going to make love to you, you'd certainly avoid getting drunk in the first place.

Joseph O'Connor

Blurbs that appear on the back cover are written by friends of the author who haven't read the book but owe the poor guy a favour.

Art Buchwald

The principle of procrastinated rape is said to be the ruling one in all the great best-sellers.

V.S. Pritchett

Literature

One of the greatest creations of the human mind is the art of reviewing books without having to read them.

G.C. Lichtenberg

Vita Sackville-West looked like Lady Chatterley above the waist and the gamekeeper below.

Cyril Connolly

Dorothy Thompson is the only woman who had her menopause in public and got paid for it.

Alice Roosevelt

I like to take a Trollope to bed, but if one is not available, I will settle for a Wodehouse.

Harold Macmillan

Last time I was in Spain I got through six Jeffrey Archer novels. I must remember to bring enough toilet paper next time.

Bob Monkhouse

I hope you get as much pleasure reading my book as I got spending the money you paid me for it.

Dan Poynter

Anthologies are just pre-digested food for the brain.

Rebecca West

In Australia, not reading poetry is the national pastime.

Phyllis McGinley

Literature

Evelyn Waugh's style has the desperate jauntiness of an orchestra fiddling away for dear life on a sinking ship.

Edmund Wilson

I can write better than anyone who can write faster, and I can write faster than anyone who can write better.

A.J. Liebling

Victor Hugo was a madman who thought he was Victor Hugo.

Jean Cocteau

I should like to see a custom introduced of readers who are pleased with a book sending the author some small cash token: anything between half-a-crown and a hundred pounds. Not more than a hundred pounds – that would be bad for my character – not less than half-a-crown – that would do no good to yours.

Cyril Connolly

The Sitwells belong to the history of publicity rather than of poetry.

F.R. Leavis

The high-water mark, so to speak, of Socialist literature is W.H. Auden, a sort of gutless Kipling.

George Orwell

If we wish to know the force of human genius, we should read Shakespeare. If we wish to see the insignificance of human learning, we may study his commentators.

William Hazlitt

Word has somehow got around that the split infinitive is always wrong. That is of a piece with the outworn notion that it is always wrong to strike a lady.

James Thurber

Outside of a dog, a book is a man's best friend and inside a dog it's too dark to read.

Groucho Marx

How come there's no other name for thesaurus?

Wright Stevens

I always start writing with a clean piece of paper and a dirty mind.

Patrick Dennis

The only reason I visit my friends is so I can look over my own library.

Walter Scott

If even all my ex-girlfriends buy my book it will be a best-seller.

Rod Hundley

I will not meet Swinburne because I have no wish to know anyone sitting in a sewer and adding to it.

Thomas Carlyle

I make it a policy not to read reviews. Instead, I measure them with a ruler. The longer they are the better I feel.

Joseph Conrad

Literature

I read half of my autobiography, then I skipped through. I know what it's about though.

Dominique Morceau

Book reviewers are little old ladies of both sexes.

John O'Hara

Agatha Christie has given more pleasure in bed than any other woman.

Nancy Banks-Smith

Isn't it a shame that Maxwell Anderson's poetic licence has expired.

Noël Coward

The most important thing for poets to do is to write as little as possible.

T.S. Eliot

I adore adverbs; they are the only qualifications I really much respect.

Henry James

I have no sense of humour. In illustration of this fact I will say this – by way of confession – that if there is a humorous passage in the *Pickwick Papers* I have never been able to find it.

Mark Twain

Write something, even if it's just a suicide note.

Gore Vidal

One of the surest signs of Conrad's genius is that women dislike his works.

George Orwell

Gertrude Stein and me are just like brothers.

Ernest Hemingway

In cases of any impudent literary letters from married women, I write to the husband warning him that his wife is attempting to enter into correspondence with strange men.

Evelyn Waugh

One watches Stephen Spender use the English language with the same horrified fascination as watching a Sèvres vase in the hands of a chimpanzee.

Evelyn Waugh

Curll's inaccurate biographies are one of the new terrors of death.

John Arbuthnot

Beware of the man who denounces women writers – his penis is tiny and he cannot spell.

Erica Jong

H.G. Wells throws information at the reader as if emptying his mind like a perpetual chamber pot from a window.

Henry James

Literature

Mr Wordsworth never ruined anyone's morals, unless, perhaps, he has driven some susceptible persons to crime in a very fury of boredom.

Ezra Pound

The writings of Henry Brougham are long and vigorous, like the penis of a jackass.

Sydney Smith

If you imagine a Scotch commercial traveller in a Scotch commercial hotel leaning on the bar and calling the barmaid Dearie, then you will know the keynote of Burns' verse.

A.E. Housman

Joseph Heller's *God Knows* even looks exactly like a real book, with pages and print and dust jacket and everything. This disguise is extremely clever, considering the contents; the longest lounge act never performed in the history of the Catskills.

Paul Gray

The book I would most like to have with me on a desert island is *Thomas's Guide to Practical Shipbuilding*.

G.K. Chesterton

I am always glad when one of those poets dies for then I know I have all of his works on my shelf.

George Crabbe

Honest criticism is hard to take particularly from a relative, a friend, an acquaintance or a stranger.

Franklin P. Jones

What would I do if I had only had six months to live? I'd type faster.

Isaac Asimov

The difference between reality and fiction is that fiction has to make sense.

Tom Clancy

The main difference nowadays between poetry and prose is that, dreadful though it is, poetry doesn't go on for nearly so long.

Richard Ingrams

Poets are often described as dealing with the big wide world in a 'childlike' way. Presumably this means that they are always knocking things over, tearing things up and screaming blue murder if they don't get their own way.

Craig Brown

There is nothing as rare as a Woollcott first edition except perhaps a Woollcott second edition.

Franklin P. Adams

Writing a poem is a bit like being sick. It is quick and efficient and you always feel better afterwards.

Sara-Jane Lovett

The only imaginative fiction being written today is income tax returns.

Herman Wouk

Literature

I wrote a few children's books – not on purpose.

Derek Alder

I've sold too many books to get good reviews any more.

John Grisham

Harold Acton's *Humdrum* reads like a painstaking attempt to satirise modern life by a Chinaman who has been reading *Punch*.

Cyril Connolly

Novels should exclude all women with a nape to their necks.

Cyril Connolly

I always pulp my acquaintances before serving them up in a book. You would never recognise a pig in a sausage.

Frances Trollope

I was surprised to see that Amazon.com was taking orders for a novel I hadn't even begun.

Lawrence Norfolk

If I had to live my life over again there is only one thing I would change. I wouldn't read *Moby Dick*.

Woody Allen

I hear my autobiography is a terrific book. One of these days I may even read it myself.

Ronald Reagan

Listen to the editor and nod – then put it back later.

Whitney Balliett

The writing on the wall may be a forgery.

Ralph Hodgson

Of all the honours that fell on Virginia Woolf's head, none pleased her more than the *Evening Standard* award for the tallest woman writer of 1928, an award she took by a neck from Elizabeth Bowen.

Alan Bennett

Study Andy Rooney. Watch everything he does. And don't do it.

P.J. O'Rourke

What was special about Ernest Hemingway was his insistence that all his wives should learn to shoot straight.

Mary Hemingway

Once you've put one of Henry James' books down, you simply cannot pick it up again.

Mark Twain

My first idea was to print only three copies of my poem: one for myself, one for the British Museum, and one for Heaven. I had some doubt about the British Museum.

Oscar Wilde

Knight's Biography of Rossetti is just the sort of biography Guildenstern might have written of Hamlet.

Oscar Wilde

Literature

To write an autobiographical novel is to live on capital, hence permissible only if, like Proust, you know you will not live to write about anything else.

Cyril Connolly

I never read anyone else's books except my own.

Barbara Cartland

Sapper, Buchan, Fleming – Snobbery with Violence.

Alan Bennett

To become a great writer, whatever you do – avoid piles.

T.S. Eliot

There are too many people around who mistake a love of reading with a talent for writing.

Stanley Ellin

Astray by Charlotte M. Yonge and three other writers needed four people to write it and even to read it requires assistance; all the same it is a book that can be recommended to other people.

Oscar Wilde

The first joke in my book is 'it's aardvark but it pays well'.

Spike Milligan

Anyone can become a writer. Merely consider any novel by Judith Krantz and you'll know it's true.

Harlan Ellison

The word 'I'll' should not be divided so that the 'I' is one line and the 'll' is on the next. The reader's attention, after the breaking up of the 'I'll', can never be successfully recaptured.

James Thurber

I put things down on sheets of paper and stuff them in my pockets. When I have enough I have a book.

John Lennon

A classic is a book everyone is assumed to have read and which they often assume they have read themselves.

Alan Bennett

Don't write a book unless it hurts like a hot turd coming out.

Charles Bukowski

Cyril Connolly's lost masterpieces give a piquancy to his criticism, as childless women make the best babysitters and impotent men the most assiduous lovers.

Malcolm Muggeridge

I like a thin book because it will steady a table, a leather volume because it will strop a razor, and a heavy book because it can be thrown at a cat.

Mark Twain

Some men borrow books; some men steal books; and others beg presentation copies from the author.

James Roche

Literature

My writing is like fine wine; the more you read, the more you get from it. Reading it just once is like taking a dog to the theatre.

V.S. Naipaul

I called the book *Men Without Women* hoping it would have a large sale among the fairies and old Vassar Girls.

Ernest Hemingway

There are two kinds of books: those that no one reads and those that no one ought to read.

H.L. Mencken

It is a great kindness to trust people with a secret. They feel so important while telling it.

Robert Quillen

Surely Alan Wall has written this book before.

Steve Jelbert

Quarrelsome poets are like ferrets fighting for the mastery of a septic tank.

Sean O'Brien

The story goes that I first had the idea for *The Hitchhiker's Guide to the Galaxy* while lying drunk in a field in Innsbruck (or 'Spain' as the BBC TV publicity department has it, probably because it's easier to spell).

Douglas Adams

There is nothing wrong with writing, as long as you do it in private and wash your hands afterwards.

Robert Heinlein

Somerset Maugham is a bedbug on which a sensitive man refuses to stamp because of the smell and the squashiness.

Roderic O'Connor

My advice to young writers is to socialise. Don't just go up to a pine cabin all alone and brood. You reach that stage soon enough anyway.

Truman Capote

T.S. Eliot's face had deep lines. I cannot say the same for his poetry.

Melville Cane

I'd rather flunk my Wasserman test,
Than read the poems of Edgar Guest.

Dorothy Parker

Marivaux spent his life weighing nothing in scales made of spiders' webs.

Voltaire

Footnotes in a book are as banknotes in the stockings of a harlot.

Walter Benjamin

The advance for a book should be at least as much as the cost of the lunch at which it was discussed. When I proposed this formula to an editor, he told me it was unrealistic.

Calvin Trillin

Literature

Anticipator plagiarism occurs when someone steals your original idea and publishes it a hundred years before you were born.

Robert Merton

Alas! Lord and Lady Dalhousie are dead and buried at last, Which causes many people to feel a little downcast.

William McGonagall

Little Truman Capote had a voice so high it could be detected only by a bat.

Tennessee Williams

There have been a couple of books written about me by the critics, but I haven't read them because I don't want to know what my work is about.

Alan Bennett

What is my favourite book? I haven't read a book in ages. I have a big stack of them.

Albert Reynolds

Parcels have always exercised an odd fascination for me – one always expects something of a sensational nature, and one is always disappointed. In that respect they resemble the modern novel.

Peter Ackroyd

I had occasion to read the Bible the other night and believe me it is a lesson in how not to write for the movies. The worst kind of overwriting. Whole chapters that could have been said in one paragraph. And the dialogue!

Raymond Chandler

Nobody is more confident than a bad poet.

Martial

J. Gwenogfran Evans declared he knew so much about
Welsh poetry that he could tell by intuition when words
had been added or subtracted by incompetent bards, and
corrected texts at will. In one poem of just 6,300 words
he made 3,400 changes and even this is not a complete
list.

Adrian Gilbert

Never trust a writer who uses his initials.

A.A. Gill

This fellow called at my door and said, 'I'd like to read
your gas meter.' I said, 'Whatever happened to the classics?'

Emo Philips

Once Martin Amis starts chucking a few words together,
apparently he's harder to dislodge than a barnacle on heat.

Armando Iannucci

Jeffrey Archer is still slopping out his excrement in prison.
It's the authorities' fault – they shouldn't have given him a
typewriter.

Andy Parsons

The best thing I ever wrote was a cheque for £5,000 that
didn't bounce.

Patrick Kavanagh

Literature

Wordsworth announced that he could write like Shakespeare if he had a mind to. So you see it's the mind that's wanting.

Charles Lamb

There is the view that poetry should improve your life. I think people confuse it with the Salvation Army.

John Ashbery

Unlearned men of books assume the care,
As eunuchs are the guardians of the fair.

Edward Young

Listen carefully to first criticisms of your work. Note just what it is the critics don't like then cultivate it. That's the part of your work that's individual and worth keeping.

Jean Cocteau

I would advise Zola, now that the family tree of the Rougon-Macquarts is complete, to go and hang himself from the highest branch.

Alphonse Daudet

A serial is a literary work, usually a story that is not true, creeping through several issues of a newspaper or magazine. Frequently appended to each instalment is a 'synopsis of preceding chapters' for those who have not read them, but a direr need is a synopsis of succeeding chapters for those who do not intend to read them. A synopsis of the entire work would be still better.

Ambrose Bierce

Never read a book and you will become a rich man.

Timothy Shelley

I read a book once – green it were.

Brian Glover

There's nothing to beat curling up with a good book when there is a repair job to be done around the house.

Joe Ryan

I read about writers' lives with the fascination of one slowing down to get a good look at an automobile accident.

Kaye Gibbons

God and I both knew what this poem of mine meant once; now God alone knows.

Friedrich Klopstock

I'm working when I'm fighting with my wife. I constantly ask myself, 'How can I use this stuff to literary advantage?'

Art Buchwald

There is a famously wild Scottish man of letters, who, when asked to sign a pile of his novels, whipped out his penis, urinated all over the books and snarled, 'There's mae ****ing signature.'

Wendy Holden

Nominations to find Britain's favourite poem included 'The Rhubarb of O'Mark I am'.

Dennis O'Driscoll

Literature

After I read Kafka at College, I went home for Christmas
and suddenly saw my family anew, with complete clarity.

Jonathon Frazen

Let us treat children and fairies in a more summary manner.
Nowadays if in reading a book I come across a word
beginning with 'c' or 'f' I toss it aside.

J.M. Barrie

Miss Tompkins belongs to the 'rhyme at all costs' school of
poetry.

Patrick Murray

Virginia Woolf subscribed to the theory that the pen was
mightier than the sword; and I once saw the mighty Evelyn
Waugh reel under a savage blow from her Parker 51.

Alan Bennett

The difference between owning a book and borrowing a
book is that when you own a book you can get food on it.

Susan Catherine

Darius Clayhanger's lingering death will never be bettered
in literature because I took infinite pains over it. All the
time my father was dying, I was at his bedside making
copious notes.

Arnold Bennett

J.K. Rowling's imagination was so amazing that I wanted
to crawl into her head. Now, of course, I want to crawl into
her bank balance.

Richard Harris

Literature

The title for my next book is 'Are the Commentators on Hamlet Really Mad or Only Pretending to be?'

Oscar Wilde

A famous passage found in column 1,303 of the Annual Report of the Library at Alexandria for 250 b.c. indicates that the disappearance, exchange, and loss of umbrellas is a phenomenon closely associated with libraries.

Norman Stevens

It is part of prudence to thank an author for his book before reading, so as to avoid the necessity of lying about it afterwards.

George Santayana

My advice to aspiring authors is to marry money.

Max Shulman

No modern literary work of any worth has been produced in the English language by an English writer – except, of course, Bradshaw.

Oscar Wilde

When the author was on the scaffold he said goodbye to the minister and the reporters, but did not say goodbye to the publishers sitting below. He said merely, 'I'll see you later.'

J.M. Barrie

Although Rupert Brooke never succeeded in becoming the first modern poet, he may deserve to be called the first modern undergraduate, a title of comparable significance.

Michael Levenson

Literature

The reason modern poetry is difficult is so that the poet's wife cannot understand it.

Wendy Cope

As soon as war is declared, it is impossible to hold the poets back.

Jean Giraudoux

The library is the room in a country house where the murder takes place.

J.B. Morton

Writers as a rule don't make fighters, although I would hate to have to square up to Taki or Andrea Dworkin.

Jeffrey Bernard

Jules Janis once rewrote one of his own manuscripts rather than try to decipher it for the printer.

Robert Hendrickson

A man who takes a half page to say what can be said in a sentence will be damned.

Oliver Wendell Holmes

People who write fiction, if they had not taken it up, might have become very successful liars.

Ernest Hemingway

There are seventy million books in American libraries, but the one you want is always out.

Tom Masson

Literature

It is to be noted that when any part of this paper appears dull, there is a design in it.

Richard Steele

Only when he has lost all curiosity about the future has one reached the age to write an autobiography.

Evelyn Waugh

I have the ultimate rejection slip – the publishers burned my manuscript and sent me the ashes.

Mike Lanford

Genius can write on the back of old envelopes but mere talent requires the finest stationery available.

Dorothy Parker

There is a great discovery still to be made in literature – that of paying literary men by the quantity they do not write.

Mark Twain

A literary collaboration is a partnership based on the false assumption that the other fellow can spell.

Ambrose Bierce

Plagiarism is unoriginal sin.

Daniel Finkelstein

What a man Balzac would have been if he had known how to write.

Gustave Flaubert

Literature

All Shakespeare did was to string together a lot of old well-known quotations.

H.L. Mencken

To my generation, no other English poet seemed so perfectly to express the sensibility of a male adolescent as A.E. Housman.

W.H. Auden

I haven't read Karl Marx. I got stuck on that footnote on page two.

Harold Wilson

Edith, Osbert and Sacheverell Sitwell – two wiseacres and a cow.

Noël Coward

The pen is mightier than the sword, but no match for the gun.

Leiber Stoller

Although Harriet Beecher Stowe credited the Almighty with writing *Uncle Tom's Cabin*, with her own role as merely transcribing His dictation, she credited herself with the royalties.

Barry Phelps

Most recovering addicts have found God – or at least a publisher.

Calvin Trillin

Literature

I prefer Shakespeare's sonnets to his plays because they're shorter.

Spike Milligan

My novel is the funniest thing since *War and Peace*.

Cathy Loue

Alan Bennett took over the job of national teddy bear after John Betjeman's death left it vacant.

Phil Baker

Plagiarism is taking something from a person and making it worse.

George Moore

Poets are terribly sensitive people and the thing they are most sensitive about is money.

Robert Warren

Bugger the adjectives. It's the nouns and verbs that people want.

Barbara Castle

Like many classics, the New Testament is not very well written.

Norman Mailer

The English may not be the best writers in the world, but they are the best dull writers.

Raymond Chandler

Literature

My brother Brian has just written his memoirs. Memoirs me arse. You could write that fellow's memoirs on the back of a stamp and still have enough room left for the Koran.

Brendan Behan

I started reading *War and Peace* over ten years ago. Now I have to go back to the beginning again because I have forgotten how it starts.

Terry Wogan

Ted Hughes arrived in Hull, looking like a Christmas present from Easter Island.

Philip Larkin

I have known men come to London full of bright prospects and seen them complete wrecks in a few months through the habit of answering letters.

Oscar Wilde

Zola is determined to show that, if he has not got genius, he can at least be dull. How well he succeeds!

Oscar Wilde

It occurred to me that I would like to be a poet. The chief qualification, I understand, is that you must be born. Well, I hunted up my birth certificate and found I was alright on that score.

H.H. Munro

The first thing a writer has to do is find another source of income.

Ellen Gilchrist

Literature

Seneca writes as a boar doth pisse, by jerkes.

John Aubrey

To say that Agatha Christie's characters are cardboard cut-outs is an insult to cardboard cut-outs.

Ruth Rendell

Living and Family

Living and Family

There are few things more satisfying than seeing your children have teenagers of their own.

Doug Larson

Human beings are the only creatures on earth that allow their children to come back home.

Bill Cosby

One thing they never tell you about child-raising is that for the rest of your life, at the drop of a hat, you are expected to know your child's name and how old he or she is.

Erma Bombeck

All the men in my family were bearded, and most of the women.

W.C. Fields

I never want to become pregnant, ever. To me life is tough enough without having someone kick you from the inside.

Rita Rudner

I never saw my grandad because he was excellent at hiding.

Harry Hill

As a housewife, I feel that if the kids are still alive when my husband gets home from work, then hey, I've done my job.

Roseanne Barr

My teenage son is half man, half mattress.

Val Valentine

My parents used to beat the shit out of me. And, looking back on it, I'm glad they did. And I'm looking forward to beating the shit out of my own kids. For no reason whatsoever.

Denis Leary

The only thing I've ever been able to figure out about stove cleaning is to move house every couple of years.

P.J. O'Rourke

You're really old when your family talk about you in front of you. Where are we going to put Pop? We've got company coming over.

Rodney Dangerfield

When Mrs Thatcher said, 'We are a grandmother,' she was including Denis in her remarks.

James Prior

I slept like a baby. Every three hours I woke up looking for a bottle.

Liam O'Reilly

When you are eight years old, nothing is any of your business.

Lenny Bruce

I have a stepladder. It's a very nice stepladder but it's sad that I never knew my real ladder.

Craig Charles

Living and Family

An empty fridge is something you come to expect when you live through the locust phase of adolescence.

Ellen Goodman

My father had a philosophy in life. He used to say 'I brought you into being and if you do that again I'll take you out of it.'

Adrian Walsh

Tired mothers find that spanking takes less time than reasoning and penetrates sooner to the seat of memory.

Will Durant

I phoned my dad to tell him I had stopped smoking. He called me a quitter.

Steven Pearl

Of all my wife's relations I like myself the best.

Joe Cook

In spite of the cost of living, it's still popular.

Kathleen Norris

I think the delivery room should have traffic noise and pollution. The baby should then have the option to go back in.

Rita Rudner

To lose one parent, Mr Worthing, may be regarded as a misfortune; to lose both looks like carelessness.

Oscar Wilde

Living and Family

My idea of fatherhood is sending a telegram from Abyssinia saying 'Have you had your child yet, and what have you called it?'

Evelyn Waugh

My dad was a kind of father figure to me.

Alan Coren

For toddlers I suggest leaving their mittens on year-round, indoors and out. That way they can't get into aspirin bottles, liquor cabinets or boxes of kitchen matches. Also, it keeps their little hands clean for mealtimes.

P.J. O'Rourke

Never underestimate a child's ability to get into more trouble.

Martin Mull

Don't bother discussing sex with small children. They rarely have anything to add.

Fran Lebowitz

You may go into the fields or down the lane, but don't go into Mr McGregor's garden: your father had an accident there; he was put in a pie by Mrs McGregor.

Beatrix Potter

I advise you to go on living solely to enrage those who are paying your annuities. It is the only pleasure I have left.

Voltaire

Living and Family

It's hard to lose a mother-in-law. In fact it's almost impossible.

W.C. Fields

My eleven-year-old daughter mopes around the house all day waiting for her breasts to grow.

Bill Cosby

We had bad luck with our kids – they all grew up.

Christopher Morley

If this is dying, then I don't think much of it.

Lytton Strachey

The trouble with incest is that it gets you involved with relatives.

George S. Kaufman

I sometimes wish my father realised he was poor instead of being that most nerve-racking of phenomena, a rich man without money.

Peter Ustinov

Don't tell your kids you had an easy birth or they won't respect you. For years I used to wake my daughter up and say 'Melissa, you ripped me to shreds. Now go back to sleep.'

Joan Rivers

If you're killed, you've lost a very important part of your life.

Brooke Shields

The man who owns his own house is always just coming out of a hardware store.

Kin Hubbard

When I was a teenager, every Saturday night I'd ask my father for the car keys and he'd always say the same thing: 'All right, son, but don't lose them, because some day we may get a car'.

Yakov Smirnoff

My fiancé's father said to me, 'If you're going to be my son-in-law, you needn't go on calling me "Sir"... Call me "Field Marshal"'.

John Betjeman

John Crowne did have some genius but Crowne's mother and my father were very well acquainted.

John Dryden

They tell you that you'll lose your mind when you grow older. What they don't tell you is that you won't miss it very much.

Malcolm Crowley

I don't want to achieve immortality through my work – I want to achieve it through not dying.

Woody Allen

When Fortune empties her chamberpot on your head, smile and say, 'We are going to have a summer shower.'

John A. MacDonald

Living and Family

Housework is what a woman does that nobody notices unless she hasn't done it.

Evan Esar

When guests stay too long, try treating them like the rest of the family. If they don't leave then, they never will.

Martin Ragaway

Mom and Pop were just a couple of kids when they got married. He was 18, she was 16 and I was 3.

Billie Holiday

You know when you put a stick in the water and it looks like it's bent but it really isn't? That's why I don't take baths.

Steven Wright

When you have told anyone you have left him a legacy, the only decent thing to do is to die at once.

Samuel Butler

Blood is thicker than water and much more difficult to get out of the carpet.

Woody Allen

You're getting old when the girl you smile at thinks you're one of her father's friends.

Arthur Murray

We must believe in luck, for how else can we explain the success of those we don't like?

Jean Cocteau

I believe in large families; every one should have at least three husbands.

Zsa Zsa Gabor

I smoke ten to fifteen cigars a day – at my age I have to hold on to something.

George Burns

Our family was so poor we used to go to Kentucky Fried Chicken and lick other people's fingers.

Lenny Banks

My unhealthy affection for my second daughter has waned. I now despise all of my seven children equally.

Evelyn Waugh

Have you ever been in therapy? No? You should try it. It's like a really easy game show where the correct answer to every question is: 'Because of my mother'.

Robin Greenspan

No wonder people are so horrible when they start life as children.

Kingsley Amis

They were a tense and peculiar family, the Oedipuses, weren't they?

Max Beerbohm

It was one of those weddings where the bride's and groom's families stood out like opposing football teams, wearing their colours. All the decent hats were, thank God, on our side.

Barbara Trapido

Living and Family

Be kind to your mother-in-law, and if necessary, pay for her board at some good hotel.

Josh Billings

My mother-in-law is so fat, she has her own ZIP code.

Phyllis Diller

The only sense I can make out of having kids is that it's a good way to become a grandparent.

Ralph Noble

Try flying any plane with a baby if you want a sense of what it must have been like to be a leper in the fourteenth century.

Nora Ephron

I don't want to adopt. Not with my genes. I have award-winning genes.

Woody Allen

The Grand Canyon – what a marvellous place to drop one's mother-in-law.

Ferdinand Foch

I decided to have a vasectomy after a family vote on the matter. The kids voted for it eleven to three.

Bob Fraser

One Christmas things were so bad in our house that I asked Santa Claus for a yo-yo and all I got was a piece of string. My father told me it was a yo.

Brendan O'Carroll

The awe and dread with which the untutored savage contemplates his mother-in-law are amongst the most familiar facts of anthropology.

J.G. Frazer

Yes I did take money from children's piggy banks, but I always left my IOU.

W.C. Fields

It's not that I'm afraid to die. I just don't want to be there when it happens.

Woody Allen

No matter how old a mother is, she watches her middle-aged children for signs of improvement.

Florida Scott-Maxwell

I am not the head of our household – but I am the chairman of the fund-raising committee.

Don Foreman

The world is filled with willing people; some willing to work, the rest willing to let them.

Robert Frost

Induction of labour is an obstetric procedure which has brought considerable benefit to man as it reduces the number of duty staff required at week-ends and public holidays.

Don Foreman

Living and Family

Two can live as cheaply as one for half as long.

Howard Kandel

A Freudian slip is when you say one thing when you're really thinking about a mother.

Cliff Claven

Most human problems can be solved by an appropriate charge of high explosive.

Blaster Bates

I once bought my kids a set of batteries for Christmas with a note attached saying TOYS NOT INCLUDED.

Bernard Manning

The trouble with unemployment is that the minute you wake up in the morning, you're on the job.

Lena Horne

Even very young children need to be informed about dying. Explain the concept of death very carefully to your child. This will make threatening him with it much more effective.

P.J. O'Rourke

An optimist is just a guy who has never had much experience.

Don Marquis

I don't like work even when someone else does it.

Mark Twain

Laziness is nothing more than the habit of resting before you get tired.

Jules Renard

Dust is a protective coating for fine furniture.

Mario Buatha

Everyone seems to fear dying alone and I have never understood this point of view. Who wants to have to die and be polite at the same time?

Quentin Crisp

I don't have anything against work. I just figure, why deprive somebody who really enjoys it?

Dobie Gillis

You've got the brain of a four-year-old boy, and I bet he was glad to get rid of it.

Groucho Marx

Our terraced house was so small the mice walked about on their back legs.

Les Dawson

The longer I live the more I see that I am never wrong about anything and that all the pains I have so humbly taken to verify my notions have only wasted my time.

George Bernard Shaw

Why do we have to die? As a kid you get nice litle white shoes with white laces and a velvet suit with short pants and a nice collar and you go to college, you meet a nice girl and get married, work a few years and then you have to die! What is this shit? They never wrote that in the contract.

Mel Brooks

Living and Family

This year one third of the nation will be ill-nourished, ill-housed, and ill-clad. Only they call it summer vacation.

Joseph Salak

Observing the ancient housekeeper wrestling with the plantlife in the garden, I occasionally point out a weed and encourage her from the deckchair.

Arthur Marshall

Happiness is sitting down to watch some slides of your neighbour's vacation and finding out he spent two weeks in a nudist colony.

Johnny Carson

Parents are not interested in justice, they are interested in peace and quiet.

Bill Cosby

Any fool can criticise, condemn, and complain, and most of them do.

Dale Carnegie

The great comfort of turning forty-nine is the realisation that you are now too old to die young.

Paul Dickson

Heredity is what sets the parents of a teenager wondering about each other.

Laurence J. Peter

Lactomangulation is the act of manhandling the 'open here' spout on a milk carton so badly that one has to resort to using the 'illegal' side.

Rich Hall

Babies don't need a vacation but I still see them at the beach. I'll go over to a little baby and say, 'What are you doing here? You've never worked a day in your life.'

Steven Wright

Madam, there's no such thing as a tough child – if you boil them first for a few hours, they always come out tender.

W.C. Fields

The worst eternal triangle known is teenager, parent and telephone.

Lavonne Mathison

The family is the building block of society. If it did not exist it would have to be invented.

William Hague

Diana Barrymore, my daughter, is a horse's ass; quite a pretty one, but still a horse's ass.

John Barrymore

I've never really had any tough moments in my life, apart from when my granddad was dying when I was eight, and my mom took me to hospital to see him. She said, 'Make your granddad laugh, it'll help him get better,' but I couldn't so he died so she beat me. But apart from that I wasn't bullied or anything.

Emo Philips

Living and Family

When I was born, they threw away the mould. Of course some of it grew back.

Emo Philips

I'm not childless, darling. I am childfree.

Tallulah Bankhead

Handing over the Hoover to my mother was like distributing highly sophisticated nuclear weapons to an underdeveloped African nation.

Alan Bennett

The best substitute for experience is being sixteen.

Raymond Duncan

If somebody calls and says they'll be right over, throw everything down the clothes chute, including the kids.

Phyllis Diller

I have on occasion asked for whom the bell tolled and found it was not for me.

Robert Morley

Some believe the shin was invented for finding furniture in the dark. Others find the little toe much more effective for such activity.

Michael Hodgin

My husband will cook for the children while I'm watching television. He's the ideal woman I was looking for.

Ruby Wax

I have buried a lot of cooking in my back garden.

Phyllis Diller

There are three things you can predict in life: taxes, death and more meetings.

Mike Moore

Our family motto is 'no'.

Michael Grade

A wife is a person who does today what the rest of the family are going to do tomorrow.

Marilyn Morris

The basis of action is a lack of imagination. It is the last resource of those who know not how to dream.

Oscar Wilde

One of the best ways of avoiding necessary and even urgent tasks is to seem to be busily employed on things that are already done.

J.K. Galbraith

Without wives, all husbands would look like Norman Wisdom.

Pat Gilchrist

I'm getting old. When I squeeze into a tight parking space, I'm sexually satisfied for the day.

Rodney Dangerfield

Living and Family

For men obsessed with women's underwear, a course in washing, ironing and mending is recommended.

Charlotte Gilman

Boy, parents – that's a tough job. Damn easy job to get though. I think most people love the interview. You don't even have to dress for it.

Steve Bruner

My parents have been there for me, ever since I was about seven.

David Beckham

I grow increasingly impatient of holidays: they seem a wholly feminine conception, based on an impotent dislike of everyday life and a romantic notion that it will all be better at Frinton or Venice.

Philip Larkin

The only thing wrong with immortality is that it does tend to go on a bit.

Herb Caen

One day my father took me aside and left me there.

Jackie Vernon

I comfort myself by pretending that the number on my bathroom scales is my IQ.

Linda Iverson

I might give my life for my friend, but he had better not ask me to do up a parcel.

Logan Smith

What most persons consider as virtue after the age of forty is simply a loss of energy.

Voltaire

I'll never die in my sleep. I don't sleep that well.

Don Herold

Don't try to make your children to grow up to be like you or they will do it.

Russell Baker

Every day I beat my own previous record for the number of consecutive days I've stayed alive.

George Carlin

Some day we will look back on all this and plough into the back of a parked car.

Scott Adams

Give the woman in the bed more porter, give the man beside her water, and move over in the bed to make room for the lodger.

David Doyle

Her expression as she eyed my grubby brood implied that I had conceived them all in a drunken stupor with a series of nameless and unsuitable fathers.

Birna Helgadottir

People are not homeless if they are sleeping in the streets of their hometowns.

Dan Quayle

Living and Family

You can't take it with you. You never see a U-Haul following a hearse.

Ellen Glasgow

Those who survived the San Francisco earthquake said, 'Thank God, I'm still alive.' But of course, for those who died, their lives will never be the same.

Barbara Boxer

Whenever I mentioned to my father that I wanted a television set, his stock reply was: 'People in Hell want ice water.'

Garrison Keillor

The simplest toy, one which even the youngest child can operate, is called a grandparent.

Sam Levenson

Bruce Sutter has been around for a while and he's pretty old. He's thirty-five years old. That will give you some idea of how old he is.

Ron Fairley

I never thought I'd live to see the day of my death.

Samuel Goldwyn

I know, I know – you're a woman who has had a lot of tough breaks. Well, we can clean and tighten those breaks, but you'll have to stay in the garage all night.

Groucho Marx

One difference between outlaws and in-laws is that outlaws don't promise to pay it back.

Kin Hubbard

No need to worry about your teenagers when they're not at home. A national survey revealed that they all go to the place – 'out' – and they all do the same thing there – 'nothing'.

Bruce Lansky

Patience and restraint are what parents have when there are witnesses.

Franklin P. Jones

I believe you should live each day as if it was your last, which is why I don't have any clean laundry, because who wants to wash clothes on the last day of their life?

Jack Handey

I hate it at weddings when old relatives tell me, 'You'll be next, love.' I get my own back at funerals.

Mandy Knight

I know there's a balance; I see it every time I swing past.

John Mellencamp

When you wake up in the morning and nothing hurts, you can be sure you are dead.

Herbert Achternbusch

I try to take one day at a time, but sometimes several days attack me all at once.

Jenny Eclair

Living and Family

Atlas had a great reputation, but I'd like to have seen him carry a mattress upstairs.

Kin Hubbard

Age and treachery can always overcome youth and skill.

John Cleese

We are a grandmother.

Margaret Thatcher

It does not beggar well for the future.

Henry McLeish

Whatever happened to the good old days when children worked in factories?

Emo Philips

My father sincerely believed that any member of his own or his ex-wife's family who refused him a loan was genuinely of unsound mind and seldom hesitated to inform them of the fact – usually by telegram.

Robert Morley

My life is so full of surprises, nothing surprises me any more.

Kim Wilde

In obituaries, 'convivial' means a drunk; 'flamboyant' means an outrageous cottager; 'a great raconteur' means a crashing bore and 'relishing physical contact' describes a cruel sadist.

Vanora Bennett

When a kid turns thirteen, stick him in a barrel, nail the lid shut, and feed him through the knothole. When he turns sixteen, plug the hole.

Mark Twain

I wish I could tell you my age but I can't; it keeps changing all the time.

Greer Garson

The art of negotiation is learned from an early age. You'd be amazed how many teenagers get a car by asking for a motorcycle.

James Varley

I would not live forever, because we should not live forever, because if we were supposed to live forever, then we would live forever, but we cannot live forever, which is why I would not live forever.

Mariah Carey

To build is to be robbed.

Samuel Johnson

Little children's voices are like wasps' stings.

John Keats

Immortality is a long shot, I admit. But somebody has to be first.

Bill Cosby

No man is a hero to his undertaker.

Finley Peter Dunne

Living and Family

Any kid will run any errand for you if you ask at bedtime.

Red Skelton

You're probably a Red Neck if your family tree doesn't fork.

Jeff Foxworthy

I'm not a complete idiot. Some parts are missing.

Emo Philips

You know you are really a mother when:
You use your own saliva to clean your child's face
Your child throws up and you catch it.

Erma Bombeck

The trouble with women today is their excitement over too many things outside the home. A woman's home and her children are her real happiness. If she would stay there, the world would have less to worry about the modern woman.

Al Capone

Death is just life's way of telling you that you've been fired.

Richard Geiss

I believe in large families. Every woman should have at least three husbands.

Zsa Zsa Gabor

Why did Nature create Man? Was it to show that she is big enough to make mistakes, or was it just pure ignorance?

Holbrook Jackson

Hard work never kills anybody who supervises it.

Harry Bauer

My only problem with the death penalty is its name. We are all going to die, so it should just be called 'the early death penalty'.

John Malkovich

Marriage entitles women to the protection of a strong man who will steady the stepladder while they paint the kitchen ceiling.

Fran Lebowitz

Her house caught fire so often that she greeted the local fire brigade with a cry of 'Gentlemen, take your accustomed places'.

John Wells

Never take a cross-country trip with a kid who has just learned to whistle.

Jean Deuel

Most of our future lies ahead of us.

Denny Crum

Ma, I'm burnin.

Ferdy O'Halloran

I am as busy as a beaver with a new toothbrush.

Denis O'Leary

Coagulation is the only proof that blood is thicker than water.

Kathy Lette

Auntie did you feel no pain
Falling from that willow tree?
Could you do it please again?
'Cos my friend here didn't see?

Harry Graham

My second favourite household activity is ironing. My first is hitting my head on the top bunk bed until I pass out.

Erma Bombeck

I have a weight of twenty stone squeezed into a five-foot-eight-inch frame as a result of having been hit by a lift.

Harry Secombe

I've got two wonderful children. Well, two out of five isn't bad.

Henny Youngman

It is tragic that Howard Hughes had to die to prove he was alive.

Walter Kane

Never accept as a bunkmate anyone whose nickname is Fungus.

Johnny Carson

Trying is the first step towards failure.

Homer Simpson

A successful parent is one who raises a child so they can pay for their own psychoanalysis.

Nora Ephron

Our brave men who died in Vietnam, more than a hundred per cent of whom were black, paid the ultimate price.

Marion Barry

I was in hopes that Lord Illingworth would have married Lady Kelso. But I believe he said her family was too large. Or was it her feet? I forget which.

Oscar Wilde

Humans are the only animals that have children on purpose with the exception of guppies, who like to eat theirs.

P.J. O'Rourke

My mother-in-law was very depressed so I bought her one of those do-it-yourself suicide guides. It told her to place a gun just below her left breast and pull the trigger. She kneecapped herself.

Les Dawson

If I could take just two books to a desert island, I'd take a big inflatable book and 'How to make oars out of sand'.

Ardal O'Hanlon

My mother-in-law had just vanished, but I cannot give her description to the police. They'd never believe me.

Les Dawson

Living and Family

In March 1893 I took rooms at the Savoy Hotel and often spent the night there. I could not go home as I had forgotten the number of my house and I was not quite certain of the street, though I believe the district was Chelsea.

Oscar Wilde

When they put parents on a CD maybe then I'll listen.

Bart Simpson

I made a lot of mistakes with my children, but I have learned, finally, that spending time with one's own children is as important as spending time with children in refugee camps.

Vanessa Redgrave

You've got to understand why your wife pays more attention to the baby than you. The baby is a blood relation of your wife – he's her son. You're just some guy she met in a bar. She knows it, the kid knows it and I'm sure they have a good laugh about it when you're at work.

Gary Shandling

I believe in loyalty. When a woman reaches an age she likes, she should stick with it.

Eva Gabor

There isn't a child who hasn't gone out into the brave new world who eventually does not return to the old homestead carrying a bundle of dirty clothes.

Art Buchwald

When my mother-in-law was born, they fired twenty-one guns. The trouble was, they all missed.

Les Dawson

You are young only once, but you can stay immature indefinitely.

Clarence Darrow

I don't really have any enemies. It's just that some of my best friends are trying to kill me.

Emo Philips

If you are allowed to smack children you should be allowed to smack geriatrics as well, because they are just as much of a nuisance as children.

Jack Dee

I hope *The Times* has my obituary ready because I haven't been feeling very well recently.

Spike Milligan

Spike Milligan's death appears to me to be merely attention seeking.

Paul Whitehouse

My friend Winnie is a procrastinator. He didn't get his birthmark until he was eight years old.

Steven Wright

I'm nobody's fool – they couldn't find anybody to adopt me.

Emo Philips

Living and Family

Ambition is a poor excuse for not having enough sense to be lazy.

Charlie McCarthy

My formula for success is dress British, look Irish, think Jewish.

Murray Koffler

The one thing you will never find in a teenager's bedroom is the floor.

Bruce Lansky

Parents of today's teenagers are worried about their children's failing eyesight. Daughters cannot see anything to wear in a closet full of clothes and sons cannot see anything to eat in a fridge full of food.

Michael Hodgin

The bitterest of hatred is that of our near relatives.

Tacitus

At times I really wish I'd listened to what my mother told me. What did she tell me? I don't know; I never listened.

Douglas Adams

The only close bond Oliver Sachs mentions, outside of his immediate family, is with an octopus he kept for a time in the bath.

John Carey

Friends come and go, but enemies accumulate.

Chuck Swindoll

I told the police that I was sure that it was my mother-in-law's car that had knocked me down. I'd recognise that laugh anywhere.

Henny Youngman

> In Church your grandsire cut his throat;
> To do the job too long he tarry'd,
> He should have had my hearty vote,
> To cut his throat before he married.

Jonathan Swift

Life is like an enema; you get out of it what you put into it, plus a load of crap.

Ira Levin

Needing someone is like needing a parachute. If he isn't there the first time you need him, chances are you won't be needing him again.

Scott Adams

Most children threaten at times to run away from home. This is the only thing that keeps some parents going.

Phyllis Diller

Life is something that everyone should try at least once.

Henry Tillman

Never put anything on paper, my boy, and never trust a man with a small black moustache.

P.G. Wodehouse

Living and Family

I saw this car with a 'Baby on Board' sticker on the back. I wondered why don't they use a cushion?

Steven Wright

The best way to deal with a frying pan that has burnt food cemented to the bottom is to let it soak in soapy water for several days and then, when nobody is looking, throw it in the rubbish bin.

Dave Barry

I attribute my long life to the fact that I cancelled my trip on the *Titanic*.

George Burns

My new house is nothing but rooms.

Yogi Berra

February is the worst month of the year. It has only 28 days in it, usually, which means that if you rent an apartment you are paying for three full days you don't get. Try to avoid February wherever possible.

Steve Rubenstein

Living my life is a task so difficult it has never been attempted before.

Steven Wright

He who hesitates before he leaps is lost.

Patrick Murray

A day for decisions! Or is it?

Aaron Fuegi

He was a unique man and unique men are rare.

Eric Tully

Some people find me gruesome-looking.

Esther Rantzen

My dad worked in a mortuary, but he was fired. He was accused of having an intimate relationship with a corpse. The family was shocked – we thought it was purely platonic.

Bill Hicks

I worshipped the ground my wife Audrey walked upon. If only she lived in a better neighbourhood.

Billy Wilder

At my age getting a little action means your prune juice is working.

George Burns

I once made a great investment. I bought the mother-in-law a jaguar. It bit her leg off.

Chic Murray

A centenarian is a person who has lived to be a hundred years of age. He never smoked or he smoked all his life. He never drank whiskey or he drank whiskey for eighty years. He was a vegetarian or he wasn't a vegetarian. Follow these rules closely and you too can become a centenarian.

Stephen Leacock

Living and Family

Youth had been a habit of hers for so long that she could not part with it.

Rudyard Kipling

For pleasure, you cannot beat a small child, although the temptation is sometimes strong if there is a slipper handy.

Philip Howard

Whenever any one says 'theoretically', they actually mean 'not really'.

Dave Parnass

I'm going back a bit now to the days when it was sometimes necessary to work.

Jeffrey Bernard

Never count your blessings before they hatch.

John MacHale

It is one of the great urban myths that people get pregnant in order to have children.

Menzies Campbell

On my 88th birthday, I felt like a twenty year old. Unfortunately there wasn't one around.

Milton Berle

There is nothing so consoling as to find that one's neighbours' troubles are at least as great as one's own.

George Moore

You can live to be a hundred by giving up all of the things that make you want to live to be a hundred.

Woody Allen

Are you metabolically challenged? In other words, are you dead?

Nigel Rees

I want my children to have all the things I could never afford. Then I want to move in with them.

Phyllis Diller

Middle age is when a man chases a girl only if she's going downhill.

George Burns

Yo' Mamma's so fat she's got a smaller fat woman orbiting her.

Amanda Hugankiss

If you stand still, there's only one way to go, and that's backwards.

Peter Shilton

I don't think there is anybody bigger or smaller than Maradona.

Kevin Keegan

When your daughter is twelve years old, your wife buys her a splendidly silly article of clothing called a trainer bra. To train what? I never had a trainer jock.

Bill Cosby

Living and Family

I remember when outing meant a family picnic.

Rodney Dangerfield

People are still willing to do an honest day's work. The trouble is, they want a week's pay for it.

Joey Adams

The problem with the gene pool is that there is no lifeguard.

Steven Wright

Yo Momma's so fat it took me twenty minutes to download her picture from the Web.

Amanda Hugankiss

Hatred of domestic work is a natural and admirable result of civilisation.

Rebecca West

Objects are lost because people look where they are not instead of where they are.

Henry Miller

For every mile you jog, you add one minute to your life and this enables you, at eighty-five, to spend an additional five months in a nursing home at $5,000 a month.

Greta Garbage

Distant relatives are the best kind, and the further the better.

Kin Hubbard

Encourage independence in children by regularly losing them in the supermarket.

Erma Bombeck

You know you're trailer trash when you let your twelve-year-old daughter smoke at the dinner table in front of all her kids.

Greta Garbage

I share the same birthday as my twin sister Tracey.

Phil Neville

When I was a kid I got lost on the beach once and a cop helped me look for my parents. 'Do you think we'll find them?' I asked him. 'I don't know, kid,' he replied. 'There are so many places they can hide.'

Rodney Dangerfield

I am so wrinkled I can screw my hat on.

Phyllis Diller

My mother always said you could eat off her floor; you could eat off my floor too, there's so much food down there.

Elaine Boostler

I have no fear of death and am optimistic, if not convinced, that there will be some kind of after-life, which I look forward to as an interesting change from Hay-on-Wye.

Peggy Causton

Living and Family

I do enjoy life, I really do. Especially if I wake up the next day.

Elizabeth Taylor

As you grow old, you lose your interest in sex, your friends drift away, and your children often ignore you. There are many other advantages of course, but these would seem to me to be the outstanding ones.

Richard Needham

Is there any sound more terrifying on a Sunday afternoon than a child asking, 'Daddy, can we play Monopoly?'

Jeremy Clarkson

Children are immune to stress but are carriers.

John Fender

My parents didn't get divorced though I begged them to.

Woody Allen

I've seen aliens, so I had no problem witnessing the birth of my son.

Will Smith

Hope is the feeling you feel when you feel that the feeling you feel isn't going to be permanent.

Jean Kerr

Humphrey, your little son has just beaten me over the head with a large brass tray. Do you know what I am going to give Master Stephen Bogart for Christmas? A chocolate-covered hand grenade.

Noël Coward

I was such an ugly kid. When I played in the sandbox, the cat kept covering me up.

Rodney Dangerfield

I had ten years of being spoiled rotten before the squatters took up residence in our house – our children. I cannot wait to buy each of them a full set of luggage and wave them on their way.

Carlos Santana

I didn't want to move to the Midwest. I could never live in a place where the outstanding geographic feature is the horizon.

George Carlin

My own wife had a lot of children – eight if I remember rightly.

Frank Pakenham

In relation to Yogi Berra, our similarities are different.

Dale Berra

Wives are the only people who can make lump free beds.

Michael Saunders

Overtime is time spent doing the work in the evening you never quite got around to during the day.

John Kelly

I grew up with six brothers. That's how I learned to dance – waiting to get into the bathroom.

Bob Hope

Living and Family

If your children write their names in the dust on the furniture, don't let them put the year.

Phyllis Diller

You know you're getting old when you get winded playing cards.

George Burns

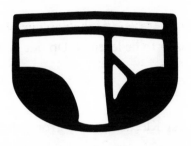

Love, Sex, Marriage, Men and Women

Love, Sex, Marriage, Men and Women

Women; can't live with them, can't bury them in the back yard without the neighbours seeing.

Sean Williamson

When authorities warn you of the dangers of sex, there is an important lesson to be learned. Do not have sex with the authorities.

Matt Groening

Men should be like Kleenex – soft, strong and disposable.

Cher

The three words you don't want to hear while making love are 'Honey, I'm home'.

Ken Hammond

An eighty-year-old friend of mine has just returned from his honeymoon with his eighteen-year-old bride. He described it as like trying to force a marshmallow into a piggy bank.

Keith Waterhouse

Everyone should be married. A bachelor's life is no life for a single man.

Sam Goldwyn

The time you spend grieving over a man should never exceed the amount of time you actually spent with him.

Rita Rudner

Don't have sex, man. It leads to kissing and pretty soon you've got to talk to them.

Steve Martin

Love, Sex, Marriage, Men and Women

Women complain about premenstrual syndrome, but I think of it as the only time of the month I can be myself.

Roseanne Barr

Like most men, I am consumed with desire whenever a lesbian gets within 20 feet.

Taki

She was so sweet that we just walked in the park and I was so touched by her that after fifteen minutes I wanted to marry her and, after half an hour, I completely gave up the idea of snatching her purse.

Woody Allen

If a woman insists on being called Ms ask her if that stands for miserable.

Russell Bell

Give a man a free hand and he'll run it all over you.

Mae West

You should always be missing some buttons. It's part of your boyish bachelor charm. Many a woman has sat down on the living-room couch to sew a button and has wound up doing something more interesting on another piece of furniture elsewhere in the room.

P.J. O'Rourke

Women asserted that they would not be dictated to but then went out and became stenographers.

G.K. Chesterton

Love, Sex, Marriage, Men and Women

I don't know the question, but sex is definitely the answer.

Woody Allen

They were not so much her private parts as her public parts.

Alan Bennett

Golf and sex are the only things you can enjoy without being any good at them.

Jimmy Demaret

There was not much wrong with Virginia Woolf except that she was a woman.

Germaine Greer

During my army medical, they asked me if I was homosexual. I said I wasn't but I was willing to learn.

Bill Murray

When I eventually met Mr Right, I had no idea his first name was 'Always'.

Rita Rudner

Under twenty-one women are protected by law; over sixty-five they're protected by nature; anything in between is fair game.

Cary Grant

There is at least one fool in every married couple.

Henry Fielding

Love, Sex, Marriage, Men and Women

Women are nothing but machines for producing children.

Napoleon Bonaparte

Sex is one of the most wholesome, beautiful and natural things that money can buy.

Steve Martin

When thou goest to woman, take thy whip.

Friedrich Nietzsche

You have to go back to the Children's Crusade in AD 1212 to find as unfortunate and fatuous attempt at manipulated hysteria as the Women's Liberation Movement.

Helen Lawrenson

I was asked if I would support the 18 compromise in the coming debate on the age of homosexual consent in the House of Lords, but I must have been reading the bill upside down because I thought it said 81, which did seem most unfair.

William Temple

The others were only my wives. But you, my dear, my fifth wife, will also be my widow.

Sacha Guitry

I had the upbringing a nun would envy. Until I was fifteen I was more familiar with Africa than my own body.

Joe Orton

My wife's hands are so beautiful that I'm going to have a bust made of them.

Sam Goldwyn

Love, Sex, Marriage, Men and Women

Any married man should forget his mistakes – no use two people remembering the same thing.

Duane Dewel

A married couple are well suited when both partners usually feel the need for a quarrel at the same time.

Jean Rostand

A man should be taller, older, heavier, uglier and hoarser than his wife.

Edgar W. Howe

If you cannot have your dear husband for a comfort and a delight, for a crosspatch, for a sofa, chair or a hotwater bottle, one can use him as a Cross to be Borne.

Stevie Smith

Another reason girls talk earlier than boys is breastfeeding. Boys would rather breastfeed than talk because they know they won't be getting that close again for another fifteen years.

Paul Seaburn

I wouldn't be caught dead marrying a woman old enough to be my wife.

Tony Curtis

You're getting old if you discuss the facts of life with your children and you get slapped by your wife when you attempt to try out some of the things they told you.

Russell Bell

Love, Sex, Marriage, Men and Women

Men have simple needs. They can survive the whole weekend with only three things: beer, boxer shorts, and batteries for the remote control.

Diana Jordan

When I was your age, I had been an inconsolable widower for three months, and was already paying my addresses to your admirable mother.

Oscar Wilde

Ask a toad what is beauty? A female with two great round eyes coming out of her little head, a large flat mouth, a yellow belly and a brown back.

Voltaire

A woman voting for divorce is like a turkey voting for Christmas.

Alice Glynn

Before we make love, my husband takes a painkiller.

Joan Rivers

If you want a good sex life the answer is communication. If you're making love to your partner, tell her.

Ivor Dembina

I have no boobs whatsoever. On my wedding night my husband said, 'Let me help you with those buttons' and I told him, 'I'm completely naked'.

Joan Rivers

Love, Sex, Marriage, Men and Women

Hanging on to a bad relationship is like chewing gum after the flavour is gone.

Rita Rudner

I have never married because I cannot mate in captivity.

Gloria Steinem

Conventional intercourse is like squeezing jam into a doughnut.

Germaine Greer

Breathes there a man with hide so tough,
Who says two sexes aren't enough?

Samuel Hoffenstein

Men carry their brains lower than women do, so when they're scratching their crotches, they're not being gross – they're just thinking.

Diana Jordan

The best way to remember your wife's birthday is to forget it once.

Joseph Cossman

Even the most respectable woman has a complete set of clothes in her wardrobe ready for a possible abduction.

Sacha Guitry

I would rather see a woman die, any day, than see her happy with someone else.

Pablo Picasso

Love, Sex, Marriage, Men and Women

There comes a moment in the day, when you have written your pages in the morning, attended to your correspondence in the afternoon, and have nothing further to do. Then comes the hour when you are bored; that's the time for sex.

H.G. Wells

After we made love he took a piece of chalk and made an outline of my body.

Joan Rivers

I'm all for women's rights – and for their lefts too.

Groucho Marx

To please my wife, I decided to get in touch with my feminine side. Now I've got a yeast infection.

Bob Delaney

You can tell how long a couple has been married by whether they are on their first, second or third bottle of Tabasco sauce.

Bruce R. Bye

Men aren't attracted to me by my mind. They are attracted to me by what I don't mind.

Gypsy Rose Lee

A sexagenarian, at his age, I think that's disgusting.

Gracie Allen

I save a fortune on plastic surgery. I just always turn the lights out.

Phyllis Diller

Love, Sex, Marriage, Men and Women

The secret of a successful marriage is not to be at home too much.

Colin Chapman

We have a saying in Russia, 'Women are like buses'. That's it.

Yakov Smirnoff

My girlfriend said to me in bed the other night, 'You're a pervert'. I said to her 'That's a big word for a girl of nine'.

Emo Philips

When I was told that by the year 2100 women would rule the world, I replied 'Still?'

Winston Churchill

In my house I'm the boss. My wife is just the decision maker.

Woody Allen

It was partially my fault that we got divorced. I tended to put my wife under a pedestal.

Woody Allen

Conrad Hilton gave me a very generous divorce settlement. I wound up with 5000 Gideon Bibles.

Zsa Zsa Gabor

The essential difference between men and women is that if you ask a woman how she feels, sooner or later you'll hear about every relationship she's ever been in. Ask a man what he feels and he'll tell you he feels like a pizza.

Diana Ford

Love, Sex, Marriage, Men and Women

Is sex dirty? Only if it's done right.

Woody Allen

Don't knock masturbation – it's sex with someone you love.

Woody Allen

Marrying for love is a very recent idea. In the old country, they didn't marry for love. A man married a woman because he needed an extra mule.

Woody Allen

The appropriate age for marriage is about eighteen for girls and thirty-seven for men.

Aristotle

A wise woman will always let her husband have her way.

Richard Brinsley Sheridan

I once read about a species of fish wherein the male is much smaller than the female, and when he mates with her, he becomes permanently stuck to her, and she sort of absorbs him until he is actually part of her body, just an appendage of the female, kind of like whoever is currently married to Elizabeth Taylor.

Dave Barry

I've finally figured out that being male is the same thing, more or less, as having a personality disorder.

Carol Shields

Love, Sex, Marriage, Men and Women

If thee marries for money, thee surely will earn it.

Ezra Bowen

Marriage is the most advanced form of warfare in the modern world.

Malcolm Bradbury

I asked her if she was doing anything on Saturday night and she told me she was committing suicide. So I asked her if she was doing anything on Friday night.

Woody Allen

I had a love-hate relationship with one of my husbands. He loved me, I hated him.

Zsa Zsa Gabor

Have I ever paid for sex? Only emotionally.

Lee Hurst

James Hunt used to write me love letters from all over the world. Well, not actually love letters. They were more like technical reports on his car.

Taormina Rich

Beware of the man who picks your dresses; he wants to wear them.

Erica Jong

A man and wife should never have it in their power to hang one another.

George Farquhar

Love, Sex, Marriage, Men and Women

I don't know if my first experience was heterosexual or homosexual because I was too polite to ask.

Gore Vidal

A lady, if surprised by melancholy, might go to bed with a chap, once; or a thousand times if consumed by passion. But twice, my dear fellow, twice, a lady might think she'd been taken for a tart.

Tom Stoppard

My wife doesn't care what I do when I'm away as long as I don't have a good time.

Lee Trevino

Marriage is a matter of give and take. You better give it to her, or she'll take it anyway.

Joey Adams

My wife got the house, the car, the bank account, and if I marry again and have children, she gets them too.

Woody Allen

'Tis safest in matrimony to begin with a little aversion.

Richard Brinsley Sheridan

Have you ever started dating someone because you were too lazy to commit suicide?

Judy Tenuta

I gave my beauty and youth to men. I am going to give my wisdom and experience to animals.

Brigitte Bardot

Love, Sex, Marriage, Men and Women

Women run everything. The only thing I have decided in my house over the last twenty years is to recognise Angola as an independent state.

Brian Clough

I believe it is possible to obtain a divorce in the United States on the grounds of incompatibility. If that is true, I am surprised there are any marriages left in the United States.

G.K. Chesterton

Joan Collins unfortunately can't be with us tonight. She's busy attending the birth of her next husband.

John Parrott

Women are called the opposite sex because when you want to do anything they want to do the opposite.

Corey Ford

Anyone making love to Germaine Greer should have his guide dog confiscated and be awarded the Victoria Cross.

Bernard Manning

It is relaxing to go out with my ex-wife because she already knows I'm an idiot.

Warren Thomas

I told my wife the truth. I told her I was seeing a psychiatrist. Then she told me the truth – she was seeing a psychiatrist, two plumbers and a bartender.

Rodney Dangerfield

Love, Sex, Marriage, Men and Women

Never marry a man with a big head. Because you're going to give birth to that man's child and you want a baby with a narrow head.

Jilly Goolden

A 'Bay Area Bisexual' told me I didn't quite coincide with either of her desires.

Woody Allen

Whatever else can be said about sex, it cannot be called a dignified performance.

Helen Lawrenson

I was so flat I used to put x's on my chest and write 'you are here'.

Joan Rivers

Zsa Zsa Gabor got married as a one-off and it was so successful she turned it into a series.

Bob Hope

My thirteenth wife cried and the judge wiped her tears with my chequebook.

Tommy Manville

I'm glad I'm not bisexual – I couldn't stand being rejected by men as well as women.

Bernard Manning

They kept mistresses of such dowdiness they might almost have been mistaken for wives.

Robertson Davies

Love, Sex, Marriage, Men and Women

'Tis better to have loved and lost than never to have lost at all.

Samuel Butler

There are three kinds of bachelors: the kind that must be driven into matrimony with a whip; the kind that must be coaxed with sugar; and the kind that must be blindfolded and backed into the shafts.

Helen Rowland

The only real argument for marriage is that it remains the best method for getting acquainted.

Heywood Brown

Alas! In choosing a husband, it seems that you've always got to decide between something tame and uninteresting like a goldfish and something wild and fascinating like a mountain goat.

Helen Rowland

It is not true that I had nothing on. I had the radio on.

Marilyn Monroe

I feel cheated, never being able to know what it's like to get pregnant, carry a child and breastfeed.

Dustin Hoffman

My true friends have always given me that supreme proof of devotion; a spontaneous aversion for the man I loved.

Colette

Love, Sex, Marriage, Men and Women

When I'm good, I'm very very good, but when I'm bad, I'm better.

Mae West

I like to wake up feeling a new man.

Jean Harlow

The difference between a man and a woman I cannot conceive.

John Mahaffy

I was introduced to a beautiful young lady as a man in his nineties. Early nineties, I insisted.

George Burns

My girlfriend turns twenty-one next week. In honour of the event I'm going to stop bathing her in the sink.

Jerry Seinfeld

Women, you can't live with them and sheep can't cook.

Emo Philips

There's nothing like good food, good wine and a bad girl.

Robin Williams

I'm not a breast man. I'm a breast person.

John Wilson

I hate a woman who seems to be hermetically sealed in the lower regions.

H. Allen Smith

Love, Sex, Marriage, Men and Women

When a man makes a woman his wife, it's the highest
compliment he can pay her, and it's usually the last.

Helen Rowland

Love is a painful but not a dignified malady, I think, like piles.

Cyril Connolly

My recipe for marital happiness is whenever you can, read
at meals.

Cyril Connolly

People ask me what my favourite colour is – I'd say blue.
But you certainly wouldn't want a girl to be that colour
after a bout of lovemaking. Who needs that again?

Emo Philips

Oh, yes, I've tried my hand at sex.

Emo Philips

I never speak of my ex-husbands except under hypnosis.

Joan Collins

Hell hath no fury like an ex-wife run to fat.

Tony Parsons

You can tell that a marriage is on the rocks when a couple
speak to each other rationally.

Leo Tolstoy

It doesn't matter how often a couple have sex as long as it is
the same number for both of them.

Marian Mills

Love, Sex, Marriage, Men and Women

My girlfriend and I almost didn't have the second date because on the first date I didn't open the car door for her. I just swam to the surface.

Emo Philips

Men who claw their way to the top don't get chastised for it. But look at the grief they gave Joan Rivers for clawing her way to the middle.

Ruth Batchelor

Radical feminists don't want an all-female society. Who would do the washing up for us?

Mandy Young

Sir Christopher Dilke kept his wife in one part of a very big bed and his mistress in another, and neither knew the other was there.

Tony O'Reilly

Glamour is that indefinable something about a girl with a big bosom.

Abe Burrows

The only way a woman can ever reform a man is by boring him so completely that he loses all possible interest in life.

Oscar Wilde

With my bum size, décolletage is my only hope. The theory is that men will be so mesmerised by my cleavage that they won't notice my bum.

Jane Owen

Love, Sex, Marriage, Men and Women

My wife is in league with the Devil. I don't know how much he pays her.

Emo Philips

You have no idea how difficult it has been being a closet heterosexual.

David Bowie

Asking me if I am homosexual or heterosexual is like asking a man crawling across the Sahara Desert if he would prefer Malvern or Perrier water.

Alan Bennett

My prescription for writer's block? Alimony – the world's greatest muse.

Dick Shaap

Being loved can never be a patch on being murdered. That's when someone really gives their all for you.

Quentin Crisp

After Oxford, Larkin's homosexual feelings evaporated and were henceforth seemingly confined to his choice of socks.

Andrew Motion

I have been intimate with the bride for many years and I can tell you that a finer woman never walked the streets.

Greville Janner

Intuition is the strange instinct that tells a woman she is right, whether she is or not.

Oscar Wilde

Love, Sex, Marriage, Men and Women

If men liked shopping, they would call it research.

Cynthia Nelms

Sex in marriage is like medicine. Three times a day for the first week. Then once a day for another week. Then once every three or four days until the condition clears up.

Peter De Vries

Speaking of rapists, even the most diehard feminist must admit that's one thing men do better than women.

Gabrielle Burton

My wife and I keep fighting about sex and money. I think she charges me too much, you know.

Rodney Dangerfield

We've been trying to have a kid. Well, she was trying. I just lay there.

Bob Saget

Marriage is not a man's idea. A woman must have thought of it. 'Let me get this straight, honey. I can't sleep with anyone else for the rest of my life, and if things don't work out, you get to keep half of my stuff? What a great idea.'

Bobby Shayton

'Happy marriage' is a contradiction in terms, like 'young poet'.

Philip Larkin

Love, Sex, Marriage, Men and Women

Lawrence was not in the slightest bit queer – later in life, possibly; even then he had Nancy Astor on the back of his motorbike.

Lowell Thomas

The old theory was: 'Marry an older man because they're more mature.' But the new theory is: 'Men don't mature. Marry a younger one.'

Rita Rudner

Marriage is like death. It may be inevitable, but you don't want anyone to start talking dates.

David Chater

I used to be a homosexual, but I had to give it up because it made my eyes water.

Michael Gambon

Marriage is a very good thing, but it's a mistake to make a habit of it.

Somerset Maugham

You can always surprise your husband on your anniversary by just mentioning it.

Al Schlock

What the hell is wrong with forty-year-old women? If our brains were a toy, the box would read 'batteries not included'.

Kathy Lette

Love, Sex, Marriage, Men and Women

To keep your marriage brimming,
With love in the loving cup,
Whenever you're wrong admit it;
Whenever you're right, shut up.

Ogden Nash

Apparently men rarely dream about getting married.
Women have a magazine called *Bride*, but there's no
magazine called *Groom*.

Mary Reinholz

Brevity is the soul of lingerie.

Dorothy Parker

I learned about sex the hard way – from books.

Emo Philips

After making love I said, 'Was it good for you too?' She
said, 'I don't think it was good for anybody.'

Gary Shandling

Save a boyfriend for a rainy day, and another in case it
doesn't rain.

Mae West

I have had the ashes of my late husband Dustin sewn into
my breast implants so he will always be close to my heart.

Sandi Canesco

Naomi Jacob's bold adoption of the male persona was so
successful that when Paul Bailey himself served her in
Harrods bookshop he mistook her for J.B. Priestley.

Michael Arditti

Love, Sex, Marriage, Men and Women

If brevity is the soul of wit, his penis was a riot.

Mae West

My wife was too beautiful for words, but not for arguments.

John Barrymore

Although Australian men don't go in much for 'foreplay', I never give my wife one without first asking if she's awake.

Les Patterson

I'm into bondage, I like to tie up my wife, gag her and go and watch a football game on TV.

Tom Arnold

Feminism was established to allow unattractive women easier access to the mainstream of society.

Rush Limbaugh

At seventy-eight, my favourite slow sex position is called 'The Plumber'. You stay in all day, but nobody comes.

John Mortimer

I don't believe in divorce. I believe in widowhood.

Carolyn Green

If diamonds are a girl's best friend and dogs are a man's, which sex is the dumber?

Rita Rudner

A man needs a mistress just to break the monogamy.

Robert Orben

Love, Sex, Marriage, Men and Women

In sex, nothing improves with age.

Steve Martin

Without lying there would be no sex.

Jerry Seinfeld

When my wife complained that I never told her I love her, I said, 'I told you I loved you when we got married and if I ever change my mind, I'll let you know.'

Liam O'Reilly

When I'm in a wig I'm pretty attractive. I stare at myself in mirrors because I'm my type.

Kevin McDonald

We've split up because the domestic violence got out of hand. I didn't fancy him with all the bruises.

Jackie Clune

Sex in the sixties is great, but it improves if you pull over to the side of the road.

Johnny Carson

This girl says to me, 'Do you want to double up?' I said, 'Sure,' so she kicks me in the groin.

Emo Philips

I had her in my bed gasping for breath and calling out my name. Obviously I didn't hold the pillow down long enough.

Emo Philips

Love, Sex, Marriage, Men and Women

Sex will outlive us all.

Samuel Goldwyn

The first thing I do when I wake up in the morning is to breathe on a mirror and hope it fogs.

Earl Wynn

Never trust anybody who says 'trust me'. Except just this once, of course.

John Varley

When I came into my hotel room last night I found a strange blonde in my bed. I gave her exactly twenty-four hours to get out.

Groucho Marx

Father Christmas advertisements must now be open to both male and female applicants. However, a female appointee must have whiskers, a deep voice, a big belly and a clearly discernible bosom. Children would be terrified of such a woman.

Simon De Bruxelles

Before accepting a marriage proposal take a good look at his father. If he's still handsome, witty and has all his teeth – marry his father instead.

Diane Jordan

Frenchmen hardly ever speak about their wives: they are afraid to do so in front of people who may know them better than they do.

Charles de Montesquieu

Love, Sex, Marriage, Men and Women

I wouldn't be marrying for the fifth time if it wasn't for keeps.

Joan Collins

Never ask a woman why she's angry at you. She will either get angrier at you for not knowing, or she'll tell you. Both ways, you lose.

Ian Scholes

I've been married seven times. I know nothing about marriage, but a lot about separation.

Artie Shaw

She is a peacock in everything but beauty.

Oscar Wilde

I bought a book called *A Hundred French Mating Positions*, but I never got past page one. I really hate chess.

Emo Philips

Friendship is more tragic than love. It lasts longer.

Oscar Wilde

Marriage is a ceremony in which rings are put on the finger of the lady and through the nose of the gentleman.

Herbert Spencer

Such is the Pastun obsession with sodomy – locals will tell you that birds fly over the city using only one wing, the other covering their posterior.

Tim Reid

Love, Sex, Marriage, Men and Women

Eye contact is a method utilised by a single woman to communicate to a man that she is interested in him. Many women find it difficult to look a man directly in the eyes, not because of shyness, but because a woman's eyes are not located in her chest.

Rita Rudner

Anniversaries are like toilets – men usually manage to miss them.

Jo Brand

There was a girl knocking on my hotel room door all night last night. I finally had to let her out of my room.

Henny Youngman

How marriage ruins a man! It's as demoralising as cigarettes, and far more expensive.

Oscar Wilde

Honey, anything I said seven or eight months ago is inadmissible in an argument. All comments become null and void after twenty-four hours.

Denis Leary

The way to girl's stomach is through her heart.

Philip Schwab

When God created two sexes, He may have been overdoing it.

Charles Smith

Love, Sex, Marriage, Men and Women

I've learned that you cannot make someone love you. All you can do is stalk them and hope they panic and give in.

Emo Philips

My daughter thinks I'm nosy. At least that's what she says in her diary.

Sally Joplin

Apparently man can be cured of drugs, drink, gambling, biting his nails and picking his nose, but not of marrying.

William Faulkner

Woman's first duty is to her dressmaker. What her second duty is no one has yet discovered.

Oscar Wilde

Some warning signs that your lover is getting bored are passionless kisses, frequent sighing and moved, left no forwarding address.

Matt Groening

Remember when I told you I didn't love you no more? Well, I lied.

Robert Cray

I knew absolutely nothing about bondage. I'd always presumed it was just an inventive way of keeping your partner from going home.

Kathy Lette

I have often wanted to drown my troubles, but I can't get my wife to go swimming.

Roy Brown

Love, Sex, Marriage, Men and Women

There is only one thing that keeps me from being happily married – my wife.

Henny Youngman

One reason people get divorced is that they run out of gift ideas.

Robert Byrne

Commitment is different in males and females. In females it is a desire to get married and raise a family. In males it means not picking up other women while out with one's girlfriend.

Rita Rudner

Spencer was searching for a woman interested in gold, inorganic chemistry, outdoor sex and the music of Bach. In short, he was looking for himself, only female.

Woody Allen

Madonna has beautiful skin. You can tell she isn't a scrubber.

Bernard Manning

Even if you could understand women, you still wouldn't believe it.

Frank Dane

Have you ever noticed how so many women's problems are due to men? For example, menstruation, menopause, guynaecology, himorrhoids, mental breakdown?

Joan Rivers

Love, Sex, Marriage, Men and Women

Don't fight over me, boys, there's plenty to go around.

Mae West

If you offer help to a woman, you're patronising. If you don't, you're a pig.

Donna McPhail

Remember the Seventies when there were hardly any black people on TV? My mum would shout up the stairs, 'Come quick, there's a black man on the telly,' but by the time you had run downstairs, he was already dead.

Wara

The telephone is an invention of the devil, which abrogates some of the advantages of making a disagreeable person keep his distance.

Ambrose Bierce

Gentlemen prefer blondes but take what they can get.

Don Herold

I am giving up marriage for Lent.

Brian Behan

I thought of him and the love bites on his mirror.

Kathy Lette

Sometimes a man just cannot satisfy all of a woman's desires. Which is why God invented dental floss.

Susanne Kollrack

Love, Sex, Marriage, Men and Women

Women and cats will do just as they please, so men and dogs should get used to the idea.

Robert Heinlein

If a couple walks along like the man was arrested, they're married.

Kin Hubbard

The trouble between my wife and me started during our marriage service. When I said, 'I do,' she said, 'Don't use that tone of voice with me.'

Roy Brown

If we did get a divorce, the only way my husband would find out about it is if they announced it on *Wide World of Sports*.

Joyce Brothers

I married my husband out of spite. I had been let down twice and I decided the next man who asked me would get it.

Daisy Attridge

The trouble about finding a husband for one's mistress is that no other man seems quite good enough.

William Cooper

A lot of guys think the larger a woman's breasts are, the less intelligent she is. I think the larger a woman's breasts are the less intelligent men become.

Anita Wise

Love, Sex, Marriage, Men and Women

A male gets very, very frustrated sitting in a chair all the time because males are biologically driven to go out and hunt giraffes.

Newt Gingrich

What do I know about sex? I'm a married man.

Tom Clancy

Adam and Eve had an ideal marriage. He didn't have to hear about all the men she could have married and she didn't have to hear about the way his mother cooked.

Kimberley Broyles

I don't want to say my girlfriend was loose. I think the term now is 'user-friendly'.

Emo Philips

The only thing that men really do better than women is peeing out a campfire.

Roseanne Barr

Dates used to be made days or even weeks in advance. Now dates tend to be made the day after. You get a phone call from someone who says, 'If anyone asks, I was out to dinner with you last night, okay?'

P.J. O'Rourke

Never assume that a guy understands that you and he have a relationship.

Dave Barry

Love, Sex, Marriage, Men and Women

I broke up with my girlfriend. She moved in with another guy and I draw the line at that.

Gary Shandling

Males cannot look at breasts and think at the same time.

Dave Barry

I think if people marry it ought to be for life; the laws are altogether too lenient with them.

Finley Peter Dunne

I've got to stop taking Viagra because I can't zip up my trousers.

Richard Harris

I practice safe sex. I use an airbag. It's a little startling at first when it flies out. Then the woman realises it's safer than being thrown clear.

Gary Shandling

I love men, even though they're lying, cheating scumbags.

Gwyneth Paltrow

A woman driver is one who drives like a man but gets blamed for it.

Patricia Ledger

Young man, if she asks you if you like her hair that way, beware; the woman has already committed matrimony with you in her heart.

Don Marquis

Love, Sex, Marriage, Men and Women

Not all men fancy eighteen-year-olds; no, many of them fancy sixteen-year-olds.

Kathy Lette

Personhole for manhole is not an acceptable de-sexed word.

Shirley Dean

Contrary to what many women believe, it's easy to develop a long-term, intimate and mutually fulfilling relationship with a male. Of course, the male has to be a Labrador retriever.

Dave Barry

Whenever you apologise to your spouse, the answer is always the same: 'It's too late now.' Anyway, it's always the wrong kind of apology.

Denys Parsons

There is some co-operation between wild creatures. The wolf and the stork work the same neighbourhood.

Alexander Woollcott

As soon as I get home, I'm going to rip my wife's bra off – the elastic is killing me.

Roy Brown

A long-forgotten loved one will appear soon. Buy the negatives at any price.

Emo Philips

Love, Sex, Marriage, Men and Women

The weather forecast reminded me of a typical married day of yesteryear. After a bright start it was going to be cold and dry. The evening would be chilly.

Jeffrey Bernard

Never despise a bow-legged girl. She may be on pleasure bent.

Billy Bennett

I proposed to Neil. It wasn't a question; it was an order.

Christine Hamilton

At least I can wear high heels now.

Nicole Kidman

No bird has a bill as big as the stork's.

Herbert Prochnow

The only real argument for marriage is that it's still the best method of getting acquainted.

Heywood Brown

My best chat-up line was: 'Shall I show you a few of my judo holds?'

Honor Blackman

Time and tide wait for no man, but time always stands still for the woman of thirty.

Robert Frost

There are perks to being flat chested. I can pass for fourteen in a blackout.

Jenny Eclair

Love, Sex, Marriage, Men and Women

At what age are men most attractive to women? Four years old.

Bill Vaughan

My divorce came as a complete surprise to me. That will happen when you haven't been home in eighteen years.

Lee Trevis

The only man who thinks Phyllis Diller is a ten is a shoe salesman.

Bob Hope

In lovemaking, what Tom Arnold lacked in size, he made up for in speed.

Roseanne Barr

Even a 747 looks small when it lands in the Grand Canyon.

Tom Arnold

Give me a sixteen-year-old and I'll return him when he's twenty-one.

Mae West

There are two theories about how to argue with a woman. Neither one works.

Walter Matthau

Poor Elizabeth Taylor – always the bride, never the bridesmaid.

Richard Curtis

Love, Sex, Marriage, Men and Women

If you could see my legs when I take my boots off, you'd form some idea of what unrequited affection is.

Charles Dickens

I still miss my ex-wife, but my aim is improving.

Henny Youngman

I genuinely do not believe in divorce.

Elizabeth Taylor

During lovemaking last night, Natasha called my name. I immediately ran into the bedroom to see what she wanted.

Karl McDermott

An engagement in war is a battle. In love it is the salubrious calm that precedes the real hostilities.

Gideon Wurdz

He kissed her hand with a sound like a mackerel being replaced clumsily on a fishmonger's slab, and withdrew.

J.B. Morton

I nearly had a psychic girlfriend once, but she left me before we met.

Steven Wright

Life with Zsa Zsa Gabor was like living on the slopes of a volcano. Very pleasant between eruptions.

George Sanders

I married Frank Sinatra because what would it have looked like if I didn't?

Ava Gardner

Love, Sex, Marriage, Men and Women

She said she would marry me over her dead body and I held her to that promise.

Emo Philips

The most important thing a woman can have – next to talent of course – is her hairdresser.

Joan Crawford

I once heard an alpha male say that sex with an older woman was like throwing a banana down Oxford Street.

Vanessa Wilde

If Mr Laughton is not a lady, why does he have breasts?

Igor Ustinov

In California, handicapped parking is for women who are frigid.

Joan Rivers

I am a drag queen trapped in a woman's body.

Kylie Minogue

Normally I have to keep the eager totty back with a shitty stick.

A.A. Gill

My marriage lasted just ten months. We still had wedding cake left.

Frank Skinner

My wife had half-a-dozen sex change operations, but couldn't find anything she liked.

Woody Allen

Love, Sex, Marriage, Men and Women

If Jeremy Clarkson came across a homosexual in his bath
he would jump on the loo seat holding his nightshirt tightly
at the knees and call in desperate falsetto for his wife to
come and deal with the huge hairy thing.

A.A. Gill

During sex, my wife often wants to talk to me. Just the
other night she called me from a motel.

Rodney Dangerfield

Oh, I'm so clever! I wish I could sleep with myself.

Philip O'Connor

Marriage is like having to stand on one leg for the rest of
your life.

Philip Larkin

I picked a pansy in the garden of love.

Sophie Tucker

There are some sure-fire ways to tell if your date is too young
for you. Can he fly for half-fare? Are his love letters to you
written in crayon? Do his pyjamas have feet? When you ask
him a question does he raise his hand before answering?

Phyllis Diller

It is okay to laugh in the bedroom so long as you don't point.

Will Durst

A wife is someone who gladly shares half your bed, but
claims her half in the middle.

William Tallon

Love, Sex, Marriage, Men and Women

A real woman has a special attitude to money. If she earns money, it is hers; if her husband earns it, it is theirs.

Joyce Jillsons

If a thing is worth doing it is worth doing slowly, very slowly.

Gypsy Rose Lee

I don't know anything about Jayne Mansfield except the common gossip I heard. When it comes to men, I hear she never turns anything down except the bedcovers.

Mae West

Media and Films

Media and Films

Go see it and see for yourself why you shouldn't see it.

Sam Goldwyn

When people run up to me these days, it's not to ask for my autograph, but to get a closer look at my wrinkles.

Elizabeth Taylor

I have never appeared as a centrefold in *Playboy* because I couldn't stand a staple through my navel.

Diana Rigg

The cable TV sex channels don't expand our horizons, don't make us better people, and don't come in clearly enough.

Bill Maher

Television is probably the least physically harmful of all the narcotics known to man.

Christopher Lehmann-Haupt

Julie Andrews has lilacs instead of pubic hairs.

Christopher Plummer

There are two good reasons why men will go to see Jane Russell.

Howard Hughes

Don't say yes until I've finished talking.

Darryl F. Zanuck

After *The Wizard of Oz* I was typecast as a lion, and there aren't all that many parts for lions.

Bert Lahr

The Russians love Brooke Shields because her eyebrows remind them of Leonid Brezhnev.

Robin Williams

Have you ever noticed how the best acting at the Academy Awards ceremony is done by losers congratulating the winners?

George Roberts

An editor is a person employed by a newspaper, whose business it is to separate the wheat from the chaff, and to see that the chaff is printed.

Kin Hubbard

I would rather play Hamlet with no rehearsal than TV golf.

Jack Lemmon

I read the newspaper avidly. It is my one form of continuous fiction.

Aneurin Bevan

The policy of the British film censor would seem to be 'inner labia are out, but outer labia are in!'

Christopher Tookey

Take a good look at Keith Richards' face. He's turned into leather. He's a giant suitcase. He has a handle on his head. That's how they move him around at the concerts.

Denis Leary

Media and Films

You can never hope to become a skilled conversationalist until you learn how to put your foot tactfully through the television set.

Dale Baughman

In a national survey in Britain most people thought that Lulu the singer was fictitious and that Alf Garnett was real.

Warren Mitchell

We don't want the television script good – we want it Tuesday.

Denis Norden

I have a face that is a cross between two pounds of halibut and an explosion in an old-clothes closet.

David Niven

The length of a film should be directly related to the endurance of the human bladder.

Alfred Hitchcock

You look at Ernest Borgnine and you think to yourself was there anybody else hurt in the accident?

Don Rickles

When I was a Sunday presenter on Classic FM I was not allowed to say goodbye to the listeners at the end of the programme in case they thought the station was closing down.

Tom Conti

Any movie that resorts to a talking tortoise has serious problems.

Simon Rose

I'm all for a free press. It's the newspapers I can't stand.

Tom Stoppard

A James Cagney love scene is where he lets the other guy live.

Bob Hope

The mike boom appears more often in this film than some of the actors.

Simon Rose

As long as there are sex-mad teenagers swimming in the nude at night, there will be a *Friday the 13th* movie.

Simon Rose

Life doesn't imitate art – it imitates bad television.

Woody Allen

Lust in the Dust features the gargantuan transvestite Divine, with Hunter searching for some gold, guided only by a map that has been tattooed on a couple of pairs of buttocks; sadly, after this refined start, it becomes rather cheap and tawdry.

Simon Rose

The best that can be said about Norwegian television is that it gives you the sensation of a coma without the worry and inconvenience.

Bill Bryson

This film cost $31 million. With that I could have invaded some country.

Clint Eastwood

It's the old old story. A diplomat's wife falls for a chimpanzee and is astounded at how stuffy and narrow-minded people can be.

Simon Rose

Depressingly, *Drop Dead Fred* became popular in America, but then so did serial killing.

Christopher Tookey

Burt Reynolds sings like Dean Martin with adenoids and dances like a drunk killing cockroaches.

John Barbour

George Mair was such a fastidious journalist, he once telephoned a semicolon from Moscow.

James Bone

My tears stuck in their little ducts, refusing to be jerked.

Peter Stack

People who are funny and smart and return phone calls get much better press than people who are just funny and smart.

Howard Simons

In Russia we had only two TV channels. Channel One was propaganda. Channel Two consisted of a KGB officer telling you, 'Turn back at once to Channel One.'

Yakov Smirnoff

In Hollywood, if you don't have happiness, you send out for it.

Rex Reed

Johnny, keep it out of focus. I want to win the foreign picture award.

Billy Wilder

In a moment, we hope to see the pole vault over the satellite.

David Coleman

Every director bites the hand that lays the golden egg.

Samuel Goldwyn

If it wasn't for Baird, the inventor of television, we'd still be eating frozen radio dinners.

Johnny Carson

It was once a rather half-hearted consumer programme, one of those don't-read-in-bed-with-a-blow-torch consumer progammes.

A.A. Gill

Animal rights activists demanded that the film-makers remove a scene in which a wolf attacks a man, describing it as an 'anti-wolf statement'.

Simon Rose

Media and Films

I cannot sing, dance or act – what else would I be but a talk-show host?

David Letterman

If you want to see a comic strip, you should see me in the shower.

Groucho Marx

Hollywood is the only place where an amicable divorce means each one gets fifty per cent of the publicity.

Lauren Bacall

Sean Connery's amazing array of accents includes Russian-Scottish, Irish-Scottish, Spanish-Scottish, Arabian-Scottish, and English-Scottish.

Simon Rose

Television's idea of an uplifting programme is one about brassieres.

Patrick Murray

I want you to put more life into your dying.

Samuel Goldwyn

John Ford shot a retake only if one of the horses misbehaved.

Maureen O'Hara

I'll give you a definite maybe.

Samuel Goldwyn

Cheech and Chong look like Abbott and Costello on drugs.

John Simon

How did I get to Hollywood? By train.

John Ford

My parents finally realise that I'm kidnapped and they snap into action immediately; they rent out my room.

Woody Allen

The worst movie I ever saw was *The Three Stooges Relax*.

Richard Lewis

Groucho isn't my real name – I'm just breaking it in for a friend.

Groucho Marx

Menabilly was full of dry rot. The only reason the building still stood was that the woodworm obligingly held hands.

Daphne Du Maurier

Bogart's a helluva nice guy until 10.30 p.m. After that he thinks he's Bogart.

David Chasen

Winning a Golden Rose of Montreux is a non-event because for as long as I can remember British Television has always won all of them. Even Hale and Pace got one, through in what category I can't begin to imagine. It must be so dispiriting being an Andorran comedy writer.

A.A. Gill

Media and Films

I don't have ulcers; I give them.

Harry Cahn

The career of Sylvester Stallone is more of a mystery than cot death.

Rex Reed

Epitaph for a Hollywood actress:
She Sleeps Alone At Last.

Robert Benchley

What do I think of Dustin Hoffman? It taught me never to work with any actor smaller than his Oscar.

Larry Gelbart

Sylvester Stallone's latest film *Cobra* is like being run over by a convoy of manure trucks.

Michael Pye

Let's have some new clichés.

Samuel Goldwyn

If Greta Garbo really wants to be alone, she should come to a performance of one of her films in Dublin.

Hugh Leonard

It's always been my ambition to go get hold of a video camera and to go round to Jeremy Beadle's house disguised as a mad axe-man, just for a laugh, and kill him.

Paul Merton

Journalists are people who take in another's washing and then sell it.

Marjorie Eldershaw

I didn't direct Mae West and W.C. Fields. I merely refereed the movie between them.

Eddie Cline

Film directors are people too short to become actors.

Josh Greenfield

Popcorn is the last area of the movie business where good taste is still a concern.

Mike Barfield

After Schwarzenegger, Dolph Lundgren is a bit of a disappointment. At least Arnie looks as if he comes supplied with batteries.

Adam Mars-Jones

A celebrity is any well-known TV or movie star who looks like he spends more than two hours working with his hair.

Steve Martin

The chat show is where a disc-jockey plays a few of his friends.

Frank Muir

In Hollywood, if a guy's wife looks like a new woman, she probably is.

Dean Martin

Media and Films

Having your book turned into a movie is like seeing your oxen turned into bouillon cubes.

John Le Carré

Women reporters are just trying to prove their manhood.

Ronald Reagan

I wish to be cremated. One tenth of my ashes shall be given to my agent, as written in our contract.

Groucho Marx

I've been accused of vulgarity. I say that's bullshit.

Mel Brooks

If the NBA was on Channel 5 and a bunch of frogs were making love on Channel 4 I'd watch the frogs, even if they were coming in fuzzy.

Bobby Knight

One day someone will join two Terry Christians together and make one long plank.

Rory Bremner

Elizabeth Taylor has more chins than the Chinese telephone directory.

Joan Rivers

I thought *Deep Throat* was a movie about a giraffe.

Bob Hope

Acting on television is like being asked by the captain to entertain the passengers while the ship goes down.

Peter Ustinov

A movie theatre manager in Seoul, South Korea, decided that the running time of *The Sound of Music* was too long. He shortened it by cutting out all the songs.

Bruce Felton

In Hollywood it's not enough to have a hit. Your best friend should also have a failure.

Peter Bogdanovich

My only advice to young actors is to stay out of jail.

Alfred Hitchcock

Hear no evil, see no evil and speak no evil – and you'll never get a job working for a tabloid.

Phil Pastoret

Raquel Welch is silicone fron the knees up.

George Masters

What do BBC weathermen do with their clothing allowance?

Mitchell Symons

A script of *Brideshead Revisited* needs an intravenous dose of syrup of figs or just a bullet.

A.A. Gill

Media and Films

It is a politician's right to refuse to speak to a journalist though he may afterwards find ways of penalising you.

Gerald Kaufman

The secret of successful journalism is to make your readers so angry they will write half your paper for you.

C.E.M. Joad

My grandfather and I used to sit for hours in front of the television watching it intently. Eventually he would say, 'Will we switch it on?'

Kevin McAleer

It is difficult to produce a television documentary that is both incisive and probing when every twelve minutes one is interrupted by twelve dancing rabbits singing about toilet paper.

R. Serlking

The one luxury I would take to a desert island is a television set that does not work.

Robert Mark

My movie *Assassins* is an existential action film – screenplay by Sartre and dialogue by Camus.

Sylvester Stallone

Every improvement in communication makes the bore more terrible.

Frank Moore Colby

Patrick Lichfield had more cameras than a pawnbroker.

Dirk Bogarde

I would wring Claudette Colbert's neck, if she had one.

Noël Coward

Clint Eastwood has two expressions on camera: sullen and angry. Off camera, he has one: very, very rich.

Don Siegel

The other day a woman came up to me and said, 'Didn't I see you on television?' I said, 'I don't know. You can't see out the other way.'

Emo Philips

The conscience of an editor is purely decorative.

Oscar Wilde

An actress I met assured me her real ambition was to be a waitress at a coffeehouse.

Woody Allen

Saul is a frequent broadcaster who never speaks but is constantly mentioned by those who do: Goodbye from Saul here in the studio.

Fritz Spiegl

Joan Crawford had perfect posture, but it was rather intimidating. She looked as if she had swallowed a yardstick.

Glenn Ford

Media and Films

As an effective means of communicating complex arguments, the television discussion programme ranks somewhere between smoke signals and interpretive dance.

Liam Fay

Clark Gable – the best ears of our lives.

Milton Berle

Merle Oberon had so much plastic surgery done that she had to sleep with her eyes open.

James Agate

I make a most thoughtful, symmetrical and admirable argument. But a Michigan newspaper editor answered, refuted it, and utterly demolished it by saying I was in the constant habit of horse whipping my great grandmother.

Mark Twain

That Jack Ford, he yells real loud. He'd make a great director.

Carl Laemmle

Beverly Hills is very exclusive. For example, their fire department won't make house calls.

Woody Allen

Some publishers are honest and never rob their clients of more than 200 per cent.

Miles Franklin

Brando now appears on movie sets naked from the waist down so that cameramen have to keep their lenses trained on his face, thereby avoiding filming his sumo-sized belly.

Joe Joseph

The hand of God, reaching down into the mire, couldn't elevate a newspaperman to the depths of degradation.

Ben Hecht

Paul Newman's hockey movie *Slap Shot*, retitled to appeal to Japanese audiences, was released in Tokyo as *The Cursing Roughhouse Rascal Who Plays Dirty*.

William Marsano

I haven't had a hit film since Joan Collins was a virgin.

Burt Reynolds

We live in far too permissive a society. Never before has pornography been this rampant. And those films are lit so badly.

Woody Allen

The BBC operates a policy of employing female reporters with cute faces, cute bottoms and nothing in between.

Kate Adie

Anne Robinson is about as cuddly as a cornered ferret.

Lynn Barber

What actresses have I slept with? Well, most of my work was in westerns with donkeys and brood mares. But some of them were pretty damn attractive.

Robert Mitchum

Media and Films

On television today you can say you've pricked your finger but not the other way around.

George Carlin

Anne Robinson is a smirking gnome.

Germaine Greer

On the television programme *Call My Bluff*, I was aptly nicknamed 'the portly sunbeam'.

Arthur Marshall

I was in a supermarket and I saw Paul Newman's face on the salad cream and the spaghetti sauce; I thought he was missing.

Bob Saget

To get a man's attention, just stand in front of the TV and don't move. He'll talk to you, I promise.

Tim Allen

The plot of many old films can be summarised as follows – 'Separated at birth for a crime he did not commit.'

Des MacHale

Reading something edited by an editor is like kissing a girl through a veil.

Abe Hirschfield

Rolf Harris is a difficult man to hate, though that doesn't mean we shouldn't try.

A.A. Gill

I couldn't hit a wall with a six-gun, but I can twirl it on my finger and it looks good on the screen.

John Wayne

I've been up and down so many times that I feel as if I'm in a revolving door.

Cher

I've got my faults, but living in the past is not one of them. There's no future in that.

Sparky Anderson

And don't forget – on Sunday, you can hear the two-minute silence here on Radio One.

Steve Wright

Mother Teresa never reads the newspaper, never listens to the radio and never watches television so she's got a pretty good idea of what's going on in the world.

Malcolm Muggeridge

Watching the movie I thought, 'I bet Paul Newman is the murderer.' Then I realised that Paul Newman wasn't even in the movie. And then I thought, 'What an alibi.'

Steven Wright

People laugh at Mickey Mouse because he's so human. That's the secret of his popularity.

Walt Disney

Media and Films

Madonna wouldn't let me interview her because I was too famous.

Martin Amis

When we grab Osama bin Laden, we should put him on my show. That would be a taste of hell.

Jerry Springer

I belong to the Gérard Depardieu school of nudity: just drop 'em. Whether you are fat or old or ugly or sagging, just get it over.

Helen Mirren

TV news can present only the bare bones of a story; it takes a newspaper, with its capability to present vast amounts of information, to render the story truly boring.

Dave Barry

Operator, we seem to have drifted into a position of somewhat redundant intimacy.

Alan Bennett

A mini series is an Australian fillum that doesn't know when to stop.

Barry Humphries

They cannot censor the gleam in my eye.

Charles Laughton

Arnold Schwarzenegger is a living example of what a person starting from nothing can achieve.

Christian Joksch

Media and Films

The *Toronto Sun*'s summary of Perry Como's Christmas Special read as follows: 'The members of a Greek family are murdered systematically in a bizarre fashion.'

William Marsano

The only qualities for real success in journalism are rat-like cunning, a plausible manner and a little literary ability. The capacity to steal other people's ideas and phrases – the one about rat-like cunning was invented by my colleague Murray Sayle – is also invaluable.

Nicholas Tomalin

Needless to say, the film *Farinelli: Il Castrato* ended on a high note.

Tony Clayton-Lea

Some of my early TV shows were low budget. The set shook, as did most of the actors.

John Mitchum

I always say that if you've seen one Gentleman of the Press having delirium tremens, you've seen them all.

P.G. Wodehouse

My worst awards ceremony was when I presented the award for Best Linoleum with an Adhesive Underside.

Tony Hawks

You'd think with all that money, Minnie Driver could afford a bigger car.

Bill Bailey

Media and Films

American motion pictures are written by the half-educated for the half-witted.

St John Ervine

Until Ace Ventura, no actor had considered talking through his ass.

Jim Carrey

David Lynch, you want me to give you a job? You're a madman! You're in.

Mel Brooks

Never throw away the *Radio* or *TV Times*. They'll come in handy next year.

Harold Wilson

If you don't like the news, buy a gun and go out and make your own.

W.C. Fields

If a person is not talented enough to be a novelist, not smart enough to be a lawyer, and his hands are too shaky to perform operations, he becomes a journalist.

Norman Mailer

No news is good news; no journalists is even better news.

Nicholas Bentley

Michael Parkinson has a mouth on him like the wrong end of a plucked fowl and he wouldn't last ten seconds in my wife's kitchen because she'd be up his gob with a handful of sage and onions.

Les Patterson

No female director would ever fall in love with an actor. They are stupid and ignorant and don't know how to follow instructions.

Catherine Breillat

You fail to overlook the critical point.

Samuel Goldwyn

CNN editorial policy would appear to be: 'If it bleeds, it leads.'

M.D. Kavanaic

Television is the haunted goldfish bowl.

Kathy Lette

Just because someone's in a wheelchair doesn't make them a better person. So in our films we usually portray them as bastards. We think that helps to humanise them.

Peter Farrelly

If John Huston weren't the son of my beloved friend, Walter Huston, and if he weren't a brilliant writer, a fine actor and a magnificent director – he'd be nothing but a common drunk.

Gregory Ratoff

The *Daily Telegraph* is top as the paper that readers specially choose to buy – but research shows they don't want their friends to know they read it.

Brian MacArthur

Media and Films

Megalomania is the vocational disease of newspaper proprietors. The symptoms are egocentricity and the illusion of infallibility. There is no known cure.

Lord Cudlipp

The worst thing that can happen to you as a journalist is for the President of the United States to choke on a piece of meat and for you not to be there.

Mel Elfin

It's just gone seventeen minutes past four. That's the time by the way.

Paul Jordan

I do not mean to be the slightest bit critical of TV news people, who do a superb job, considering that they operate under severe time restraints and have the intellectual depth of hamsters.

Dave Barry

Most of what you read in the papers is lies. And I should know, because a lot of the lies you see in the papers are mine.

Max Clifford

Why is the slum set so dirty? That set cost a lot of money. It shouldn't look like just an ordinary dirty slum.

Samuel Goldwyn

If it must be true because it's in the newspapers, what about my horoscope?

George Thomas

Trying to be a first-rate reporter on the average American newspaper is like trying to play Bach's Saint Matthew Passion on the ukulele. The instrument is too crude for the work, for the audience and for the performer.

Ben Bagdikian

Jeremy Clarkson's lift doesn't go all the way to the top.

Geoffrey Bowman

Newspapers have degenerated. They may now be absolutely relied upon.

Oscar Wilde

I began my humour column because I was too old for a paper route, too young for social security and too tired for an affair.

Erma Bombeck

Newspapermen meet many interesting people, most of them other newspapermen.

Frederick Klein

There's a new service that lets you test your IQ over the phone. It costs $3.75 a minute. If you make the call at all, you're a moron. If you stay on hold for over three minutes, you're a complete idiot.

Jay Leno

The filmmakers Bobby and Peter Farrelly are known for their brazen political incorrectness and inventive uses for bodily fluids.

Ed Potton

Media and Films

When two or more television presenters are gathered together, and the subject of Anne Robinson comes up, the air grows green and acrid with spite and envy.

Esther Rantzen

Acting with Woody Allen was like kissing the Berlin Wall.

Helena Bonham Carter

And the award goes to Rosie Millard for the best-supported dress.

Michael Buerk

Currently, the death toll is estimated at 5,000, but this figure is expected to rise sharply as volunteer helpers reach outlying villages.

William Marsano

I don't know if anyone has ever seen a parson with a nose like a chicken's arse, but surely they must have hit the crossbar when they cast Karl Malden as the priest in *On the Waterfront*.

Allan Miller

The first reference to TV is in Shakespeare: 'What light through yonder window breaks? It speaks, yet says nothing.'

Marshall McLuhan

In Hollywood the woods are full of people that learned to write but evidently can't read. If they could read their stuff they'd stop writing.

Will Rogers

I would rather clean toilet bowls than make another film with Sharon Stone.

Paul Verhoeven

Mr Verhoeven and I have a love-hate relationship: he loves me and I hate him.

Sharon Stone

Some Like it Hot was my favourite movie. *Sunset Boulevard* was a nice little movie too, but I didn't have a share of the gross.

Billy Wilder

Richard Harris once told me he would love to work with me, which surprised me as we had starred together in *Camelot*.

Robert Morley

If you cannot see a digital clock on your TV screen, that's because there isn't one.

Murray Walker

The secret of a great photo call is to smile and mouth the word 'sex'.

Norman Wisdom

For some reason I'm more appreciated in France than I am back home. The subtitles must be incredibly good.

Woody Allen

If I had known I was going to win a Bafta award I would have bleached my moustache.

Eileen McCallum

Media and Films

The demise of Ally McBeal can be blamed on collapsing
ratings, poor reviews and plots thinner than the star
herself.

Katty Kay

Joan Bakewell is the thinking man's crumpet.

Frank Muir

I have never seen *Jaws 4* but by all accounts it is terrible.
However, I have seen the house that I bought with the
money I got for doing it and it is terrific.

Michael Caine

The only animal hurt while making *Stagecoach* was a press
agent who got in the way of a posse. Fortunately, there's
no society for the prevention of cruelty to press agents.

John Ford

When the Academy phoned me I thought they were going
to ask me to return the Oscar I won for *Annie Hall*. I
panicked because the pawnshop has been out of business
for ages.

Woody Allen

I became a film director because I was hungry.

John Ford

Not a single human being has asked me about the selection
process – only journalists.

Frank Dobson

Darling, if I get excited during this bedroom scene, please forgive me. And if I don't get excited, please forgive me.

Tom Berenger

Look, Orson, if you'll just say yes to doing a picture with me I'll give you a blanket cheque right now.

Samuel Goldwyn

I wouldn't piss on Joan Crawford if she were on fire.

Bette Davis

I have never been present to accept an Oscar. Once I went fishing. Another time there was a war on. And on another occasion, I remember, I was suddenly taken drunk.

John Ford

The standing ovation I got at the Oscar ceremony made up for the strip search.

Woody Allen

Big Brother – we should, apparently, enjoy being in the company of people whose only skill is blinking.

Jeremy Clarkson

Joan Crawford slept with every male on the MGM lot except Lassie.

Bette Davis

You know you're trailer trash when you watch Jerry Springer because it's the only chance you get to see your extended family.

Greta Garbage

Media and Films

Vanessa Feltz has just brought out a new fitness video guaranteed to make you lose weight. She does a striptease and you run a mile.

Billy Connolly

I am not a speed-reader, but I turn the TV channels very fast.

Gil Stern

The English language is a stream beside which a few patient fishermen wait, while newspapers and the BBC shovel effluent into the water upstream.

Cyril Connolly

My television contribution went down like a cup of warm Dettol with a hair in it.

Hugh Leonard

A lot of people think I don't know the meaning of the word 'hip'. But I do, and I hope to have it replaced soon.

Terry Wogan

The girls on the top floor had a television set that gave you quite a good picture if you hit it with a clenched fist at the right angle.

Clive James

David Lean's *Dr Zhivago* does for snow what his *Lawrence of Arabia* did for sand.

John Simon

At a time when religion needs all the help it can get, John Huston's *The Bible* may have set its cause back a couple of thousand years.

Rex Reed

The inaccuracies in *Mary of Scotland* must have involved tremendous research.

Robert Stebbins

Orson Welles' *Macbeth* is a famous – or infamous – attempt to film Shakespeare in twenty-one days in papier mâché settings running with damp; further hampered by the use of a form of unintelligible bastard Scots.

Leslie Halliwell

I was thinking the other night how the standard of TV had improved. Then I realised that my wife had rearranged the furniture and I was looking at the fish tank.

Benjamin Beare

Television is a medium that uses up innovation faster than an Egyptian package tour uses loo roll.

A.A. Gill

I have been accused by the media of one in a bed romps.

Steve Davis

You could have swung a scythe five feet six inches above the ground all around California in the 1930s and not done any damage to the head of a major motion picture company.

Philip French

Media and Films

We were so long shooting the film that when anyone asked my children what their father did for a living, they invariably replied *Spartacus*.

Peter Ustinov

Television has improved my mind a lot – it has raised my level of taste to the point where I no longer watch it.

Woody Allen

When I get a script in the post, I ask only two things: 'Do I get wet or have to ride a horse?' If the answer to both was in the negative, I would do the film.

Alice Terry

The crew on Tom Cruise's latest film have been ordered not to make eye contact with him. That should be easy – all they have to do is remember not to look down.

Martina Devlin

In case of a nuclear attack, go directly to RKO – they haven't had a hit in years.

David Niven

As he ages, Mickey Rooney gets even shorter.

George Carlin

My first TV programme attracted worse viewing figures than a party political broadcast on behalf of the No Chinese Takeaways Without Dinner Suits Movement.

Bill Tidy

I became a newspaperman. I hated to do it, but I couldn't find honest employment.

Mark Twain

The only things you can believe in a newspaper are the date and the lighting up times, and even these should be checked against a diary.

Josh Billings

Medicine and Doctors

Medicine and Doctors

The only people who have the right to use the editorial 'we' are presidents, editors and people with tapeworm.

Mark Twain

As she lay there dozing next to me, one voice inside my head kept saying, 'Relax, you are not the first doctor to sleep with one of his patients,' but another kept reminding me, 'Howard, you are a veterinarian.'

Dick Wilson

My teeth stuck out so far, I used to eat her kids' candy bars by accident.

Rita Rudner

The patient is not likely to recover who makes the doctor his heir.

Thomas Fuller

A mild heart attack is one you remember.

Jim Caffrey

It is a statistical fact that women who wear suspenders and stockings are less likely to suffer from gout, rickets or loneliness.

Craig Charles

Some people think you should eat human placenta because that's what animals do. Well, animals also lick their own balls. Do we have to do that too?

Denis Leary

My obstetrician was so dumb that when I gave birth he forgot to cut the cord. For a year that kid followed me everywhere. It was like having a dog on a leash.

Joan Rivers

Early to rise and early to bed,
Makes a male healthy, wealthy and dead.

James Thurber

Suicide is a real threat to health in a modern society.

Virginia Bottomley

A test for paranoia: if you cannot think of anything that's your fault, you've got it.

Robert Hutchins

If I had known I was going to live so long, I would have taken better care of myself.

George Burns

I cannot fight to the death, doctor's orders. I have an ulcer and dying is one of the worst things for it.

Woody Allen

Half of the patients who call the doctor in the middle of the night are suffering from wind.

Francis Young

My plastic surgeon told me my face looked like a bouquet of elbows.

Phyllis Diller

Medicine and Doctors

In the old days it was called voodoo and you used to stick needles into a doll. Now it is called acupuncture and you just stick them straight into the person.

Cathy Hopkins

The definition of an orthopaedic surgeon is someone with the strength of an ox but half the brain.

John Dorgan

Being ill is one of the greatest pleasures of life, provided one is not too ill and is not obliged to work until one is better.

Samuel Butler

I did consider liposuction at one point, but then I heard they can accidentally vacuum out internal organs that you're using.

Rita Rudner

Health nuts are going to feel stupid some day, lying in hospitals dying of nothing.

Red Foxx

It was not until I attended a few post-mortems that I realised that even the ugliest exteriors may contain the most beautiful viscera, and was able to console myself for the facial drabness of my neighbours in omnibuses by dissecting them in my imagination.

J.B.S. Haldane

Carl Llewellyn is so optimistic he would give himself a fifty-fifty chance after a decapitation.

Richard Edmondson

Medicine and Doctors

My dentist told me recently to spend more time with my gums.

Rita Rudner

Aneurin Bevan is a thrombosis – a bloody clot that undermines the constitution.

Winston Churchill

Whenever I fill in an application, it says 'In case of emergency, notify ...'. I put 'Doctor'. What the hell would my mother do in an emergency?

Steven Wright

Dying can damage your health. Every coffin contains a Government Health Warning.

Spike Milligan

The last time I saw anything like you, the whole herd had to be destroyed.

Eric Morecambe

The practice of medicine is a thinker's art, the practice of surgery a plumber's.

Martin Fischer

These modern analysts, they charge so much. In my day for five marks Freud himself would treat you. For ten marks he would treat you and press your pants. For fifteen marks Freud would let you treat him – that included a choice of any two vegetables.

Woody Allen

Medicine and Doctors

Blood! That should be on the inside.

Woody Allen

One of the minor pleasures of life is to be slightly ill.

Harold Nicolson

I've been smoking for thirty years now and there's nothing wrong with my lung.

Freddie Starr

I learned why they are called wonder drugs – you wonder what they'll do to you.

Harlan Miller

People wish their enemies dead, but I do not; I say give them the gout, give them the stone!

Mary Montagu

It requires a great deal of faith for a man to be cured by his own placebos.

John McClenahan

Garry Maddox has turned his life around. He used to be depressed and miserable. Now he's miserable and depressed.

Harry Kalas

No one can feel as helpless as the owner of a sick goldfish.

Kin Hubbard

I refused to have an operation on the grounds that I already had two operations and found them painful. They were having my hair cut and sitting for my portrait.

Richard Brinsley Sheridan

In hospital, bleeding to death takes second place to filling in forms.

Bill Dana

Cystitis is a living death, it really is. Nobody ever talks about it, but if I was faced with a choice between having my arms removed and getting cystitis, I'd wave goodbye to my arms quite happily.

Louise Wesner

A bottle of sleeping tablets I have just bought bears the label 'WARNING – MAY CAUSE DROWSINESS'.

Peter Orr

My genitals are like a sort of travel version of Linford Christie's.

Frank Skinner

I'm not as normal as I appear.

Woody Allen

Physicians of the Utmost Fame
Were called at once, but when they came
They answered, as they took their fees,
'There is no cure for this disease.'

Hilaire Belloc

Medicine and Doctors

Physicians of all men are most happy; what good success soever they have, the world proclaimeth, and what faults they commit, the earth covereth.

Francis Quarles

No doctor takes pleasure in the health even of his friends.

Montaigne

To really really lose weight playing golf, the best place to play is Mexico. Go to any Mexican golf course, stop at every hole, and drink water. Within a week you'll be down to your desired weight.

Buddy Hackett

The trouble with being a hypochondriac these days is that antibiotics have cured all the good diseases.

Caskie Stinnet

Boot's cough syrup for children bears a notice saying DO NOT DRIVE CAR OR OPERATE MACHINERY. AVOID ALCOHOLIC DRINKS.

Robin Young

Advice to expectant mothers: you must remember that when you are pregnant, you are eating for two. But you must remember that the other one of you is about the size of a golf ball, so let's not go overboard with it. A lot of pregnant women eat as though the other person they're eating for is Orson Welles.

Dave Barry

The genitals themselves have not undergone the development of the rest of the human form in the direction of beauty.

Sigmund Freud

It's a good idea to obey all the rules when you're young just so you'll have the strength to break them when you're old.

Mark Twain

Exercise is just a short cut to the cemetery.

John Mortimer

Here is a health warning: be suspicious of any doctor who tries to take your temperature with his finger.

David Letterman

Tell me your phobias and I'll tell you what you're afraid of.

Robert Benchley

I was in analysis for years because of a traumatic childhood; I was breast-fed through falsies.

Woody Allen

People who feel well are sick people neglecting themselves.

Jules Romains

When I go to the dentist, he's the one that has to have the anaesthetic.

Phyllis Diller

Medicine and Doctors

When I was forty my doctor advised me that a man in his forties shouldn't play tennis. I heeded his advice carefully and could hardly wait until I reached fifty to start again.

Hugo Black

First the doctor told me the good news – I was going to have a disease named after me.

Steve Martin

In Hollywood people are going for plastic surgery at twenty-three. Personally I'm going to wait until there is enough spare skin to make a handbag and matching gloves.

Pam Ferris

When going to Paris for the first time, I asked my mother if she would like me to bring her back a present. She requested a bottle of Chanel Number 5, but if that was too expensive, Number 4 would do.

Alan Bennett

I am not paranoid. I prefer to call it galloping sensitivity.

Timothy West

Professor Toad used to play Bach on an odd sort of pianola contrivance not because he was particularly enamoured of the fugues, but because the exercise of pedalling was good for constipation.

Beverly Nichols

When she was in Greece she had diarrhoea for a fortnight solid.

Fritz Spiegl

I had an asthmatic attack the other night. An asthmatic jumped me as I went round a corner. Always carry pollen.

Emo Philips

I like BBC2. It's nice and warm and smells of wee.

Kathy Burke

Poor Lou Gehrig – died of Lou Gehrig's disease. How the hell did he not see that coming? We used to tell him, 'Lou, there's a disease with your name all over it, pal.'

Denis Leary

Men and children have 'flu in bed. Women have it at the kitchen sink.

Catherine Murray

A medical statistician is somebody who goes into a ward and takes the average temperature of all the patients.

Shimon Peres

I am still buying books. It is like getting pregnant after the menopause; it's not supposed to happen.

Louis Szathmary

I think any guy who films his wife giving birth ought to allow her to be able to film his haemorrhoid surgery later on. 'Look, girls, Tony is totally dilated. What a trouper he was.'

Jeff Foxworthy

Being married or single is a choice we all have to make, but it's not a great choice. It's sort of like when the doctor goes, 'Ointment or suppositories.'

Richard Jeni

Medicine and Doctors

When I die, I wish to be buried in the no smoking section of the cemetery.

David Stry

If you are inserting a suppository last thing at night, always take your socks off first and if you are inserting a suppository in the morning, always ensure that your socks are on first. Bending over can cause the thing to fly out with great velocity and there is always the danger of a ricochet. Once I broke a holy statue.

Hugh Leonard

Psychiatry is a waste of good couches. Why should I make a psychiatrist laugh, and then pay him?

Kathy Lette

Never go to a dentist with blood in his hair.

William Ruskin

Never accept a drink from a urologist.

Erma Bombeck

If I had as many love affairs as the media have given me credit for, I would now be speaking to you from a jar in the Harvard Medical School.

Frank Sinatra

Breastfeeding should not be attempted by fathers with hairy chests, since they can make the baby sneeze and give it wind.

Mike Harding

The best-kept medical secret is that everything gives white mice cancer.

Marvin Kitman

I do not have a psychiatrist and I do not want one, for the simple reason that if he listened to me long enough, he might become disturbed.

James Thurber

The kind of doctor I want examining me is one who when he's not examining me is home studying medicine.

George Kaufman

At the breakfast table Kingsley would look dreamy and say, 'If they shut all the hospitals in London, we could have two Trident submarines.'

Martin Amis

You know it's time to stop facelifts when you have that permanently surprised look.

Joan Rivers

She thinks she's ill, but she's nothing but a hypodermic.

Yogi Berra

My psychiatrist was both a Freudian and a Behaviourist. He liked sex with electric shocks.

Emo Philips

Never, under any circumstances, take a sleeping pill and a laxative on the same night.

Dave Barry

Medicine and Doctors

It is very important to die in good health.

Jeanne Moreau

Not only was she having a nervous breakdown, but she was having a tough time mentally, too.

Simon Bates

Health is merely the slowest possible rate at which one can die.

Martin Fischer

Guillain-Barré syndrome. When they name any disease after two guys, it's got to be terrible.

Mario Puzo

He is in hospital suffering from a nervous breakdown, but no doubt he will soon be better and running around like a maniac.

Simon Bates

Doctors say only heirs pay really well.

Nicholas Chamfort

A patient of mine was admitted to hospital with a whole cucumber in his rear end. His rather innocent wife asked me how it had got there, so I said to her, 'Ma'am, your husband needs to chew his food better.'

Jeff Kimball

The Royal Family doesn't understand hugging. The Queen once tried hugging patients in a hospital. Unfortunately it was a Burns Unit.

Armando Iannucci

Of course Osama bin Laden should be put out of action, but not until he reveals his slimming secret.

Jo Brand

In the mid-Eighties I had breast enlargement to quiet that noise in my head and fill the gaping hole in my self-esteem.

Iman

A bad cold wouldn't be so annoying if it weren't for the advice of our friends.

Kin Hubbard

No one is sicker than a man who is sick on his day off or a child on a day when there is no school.

E. W. Howe

A hospital in Woolwich has set up a 'comedy room' and is appealing for old Morecambe and Wise videos, Railtrack timetables and Tory Party manifestos.

Richard Morrison

Finding the virus was as difficult as finding a Volkswagen in a haystack.

Elaine De Freitas

I joined a health club last year and spent about £400. I didn't lose a pound. Apparently, you have to show up.

Jo Brand

The easiest job in the world has to be a pathologist. You perform surgery on dead people. What's the worst thing that could happen? Maybe once in a while you'd get a pulse.

Dennis Miller

Medicine and Doctors

There is a history of heart disease in my family. My grandmother had a little vagina.

Yogi Berra

Anyone living in Los Angeles who says they don't need a psychiatrist, needs a psychiatrist.

Kathy Lette

I asked my girlfriend what she wanted for a present so she said, 'Surprise me; just give me something crazy and expensive I won't even need.' So I signed her up for radiation treatment.

Emo Philips

There is a very fine line between 'hobby' and 'mental illness'.

Dave Barry

My girlfriend is saving up for a breast reduction. I told her that two is the normal number.

Steven Wright

My friend George is weird because he has false teeth with braces on them.

Steven Wright

My teeth are all my own – I've just finished paying for them.

Ken Dodd

Psychoceramics – the study of crackpots.

Benny Hill

You know you've really got a problem when you cannot remember the word 'Alzheimer'.

Paul Erdos

Doctors say it's okay to have sex after a heart attack, provided you close the ambulance door.

Phyllis Diller

We all have our hang-ups, but unfortunately mine is hanging down.

Spike Milligan

Did he die a natural death or was the doctor sent for?

Charles Rogers

Although so far there is no known treatment for death's crippling effects, still everyone can acquaint himself with the three early warning signs of death: one, rigor mortis; two, a rotting smell; three, occasional drowsiness.

Henry Gibson

There is no use holding a post mortem on something that is dead.

Gordon Duddridge

I am as bald as he is and the only thing that distinguishes the two of us is that I have slightly more hair between my two parts.

Henry McLeish

If this is what viral pneumonia does to one, I really don't think I shall bother to have it again.

Gladys Cooper

Medicine and Doctors

The most terrifying phrase in the English language is 'uh, oh!'. As when the specialist looks at your X-rays and says 'uh, oh!'.

H. Allen Smith

I have a touch of pantomime poisoning.

Yogi Berra

Why fear Taliban terrorist reprisals? Women who are having cosmetic surgery are waging chemical and germ warfare on themselves at £250 a pop.

Kathy Lette

Suicide is cheating the doctors out of a job.

Josh Billings

If you were to open up a baby's head – and I am not suggesting for a moment that you should – you would find nothing but this enormous drool gland.

Dave Barry

At my army medical examination the doctor said to me, 'Get your clothes off.' I said, 'Shouldn't you take me out to dinner first?'

Spike Milligan

Where do all the sick people of Lourdes go to?

Tom Shields

He was off work, choked up with diarrhoea.

Tom Shields

My brother-in-law must be the unluckiest man in the world. He had a kidney transplant and he got one from a bed-wetter.

Roy Brown

You should never say anything to a woman that even remotely suggests you think she is pregnant unless you can see an actual baby emerging from her at that moment.

Joan Rivers

I have evidence that the government is planning to have me certified by psychiatrists.

Ian Paisley

I picked my nose as a child – in consultation with the plastic surgeon.

Emo Philips

I smoke eight to ten cigars a day – I drink five martinis a day and surround myself with beautiful women. And what does my doctor say? Nothing. My doctor is dead.

George Burns

He's got the icepack on his groin there so it's possibly not the old shoulder injury.

Ray French

I like having colonic irrigation because sometimes you find old jewellery.

Jim Carrey

Medicine and Doctors

What is it like to be in a coma? How the **** do I know? I was in a coma.

Evel Knievel

One more face-lift and Zsa Zsa Gabor will have pubic hair on her chin.

Virginia Graham

I'm on so many pills now, I'll need a childproof lid on my coffin.

Paul O'Grady

I cannot stand whispering. Every time a doctor whispers in the hospital, next day there's a funeral.

Neil Simon

When on a diet and weighing yourself, take all your clothes off; remove glasses, body jewellery, make up and prosthetics; cut your nails, squeeze your spots, cut your hair, shave your legs and clean your ears.

Michael Powell

A doctor is a person who has his appendix, tonsils and gall bladder.

Herbert Prochnow

I saw this really annoying TV commercial. A woman takes a laxative and then goes hiking. What idiot would take a laxative and then hike up a mountain? What is more stupid is people hiking behind her.

Jay Leno

One man's meat is another man's meat, after seventy-two hours of pioneering surgery.

Michael Powell

There are two types of doctor – the specialist who has trained his patients to become ill only during office hours and the general practitioner who may be called off the golf course at any time.

Ambrose Bierce

Jewish Alzheimer's is forgetting everything except a grudge.

Maureen Lipman

I told my doctor that when I woke up in the morning I couldn't stand looking at myself in the mirror. He said, 'At least we know your vision is perfect.'

Rodney Dangerfield

I am not a hypochondriac, but my gynaecologist firmly believes I am.

Rodney Dangerfield

I should go and see my doctor today, but I don't like to because I am not feeling very well. I care to see doctors only when I am in perfect health; then they comfort one, but when one is ill, they are most depressing.

Oscar Wilde

My early flirtation with a Charles Atlas course terminated when the instructions mentioned self-administered enemas.

Bill Tidy

Medicine and Doctors

After reading *GP* for twenty-five years, I feel qualified to hang out my shingle as a bogus doctor, and I could remove a fishhook from an exotic dancer's bosom in under two hours.

Bill Tidy

Come back next Thursday with a specimen of your money.

Groucho Marx

TB or not TB that is the congestion.

Woody Allen

Because of the danger of gas, Red Adair and his men were forced to evacuate.

Fritz Spiegl

Music

Music

I can't open my eyes when I'm singing because the words are written on the back of my eyelids.

Christy Moore

I went to watch Pavarotti once. He doesn't like it when you join in.

Mick Miller

I can't listen to that much Wagner. I start getting the urge to conquer Poland.

Woody Allen

Madame, I have cried only twice in my life; once when I dropped a wing of truffled chicken into Lake Como, and once when for the first time I heard you sing.

Gioacchino Rossini

I don't think the orchestra as we know it will survive. The future lies with the chamber orchestra of highly professional soloids.

Thomas Beecham

I bought an audio cleaning tape. I'm a big fan of theirs.

Kevin Gildea

A trombone is a quaint and antique drainage system applied to the face.

Thomas Beecham

Modern music is just noise with attitude.

Patrick Murray

Jerry Lee Lewis has been married twenty times. He gets married on a Tuesday, they find his wife dead in a swimming pool on Thursday. Maybe if you married someone who's old enough to swim next time, OK, Jerry?

Denis Leary

I like to conduct ballet music at a very fast tempo. That makes the buggers hop.

Thomas Beecham

A piano is a piano is a piano.

Gertrude Steinway

Talking of Toscanini, I hear he is in some trouble with his eyes and has therefore to conduct from memory. It is indeed a double affliction when you consider how many years he has been practically tone-deaf.

Thomas Beecham

The upright piano is a musical growth found adhering to the walls of most semi-detached houses in the provinces.

Thomas Beecham

I am a rock music producer. It is an honour and a privilege to be in the same business as Wagner and Elgar.

Pete Waterman

I love Wagner, but the music I prefer is that of a cat hung up by its tail outside a window and trying to stick to panes of glass with its claws.

Charles Baudelaire

Music

Going to the opera, like getting drunk, is a sin that carries its own punishment with it.

Hannah More

Jazz is the most degraded form of human aberration.

Thomas Beecham

If a literary man puts together two words about music, one of them will be wrong.

Aaron Copland

The singers think they are going to be heard. It is the duty of the orchestra to make sure they are not.

Thomas Beecham

I know two kinds of audience only – one coughing and one not coughing.

Artur Schnabel

The harpsichord is a birdcage played with a toasting fork.

Thomas Beecham

Of course we've all dreamed of reviving the castrati and I have drawn up a list of well-known singers I'm sure would benefit. It's only a matter of getting them to agree.

Henry Reed

No opera plot can be sensible for in sensible situations people do not sing.

W.H. Auden

Music

I am very fond of women, but in an orchestra if they're not good-looking – and often they're not and they always look worse when they're blowing – it puts me off, while if they are good-looking it puts me off a damn sight more.

Thomas Beecham

There's a fellow, John Lennon. He wanted peace and he got it.

Bernard Manning

I have just seen Niagara Falls – fortissimo at last.

Gustav Mahler

All music is folk music – I ain't ever heard no horse sing.

Louis Armstrong

Because of its famous echo, British composers should all endeavour to have their works performed in the Royal Albert Hall; they will thus be assured of at least two performances.

Thomas Beecham

The concert is a polite form of self-imposed torture.

Henry Miller

How is it possible for Bob Dylan to play the harmonica, professionally, for thirty years and still show no sign of improvement?

David Sinclair

The organ of Winchester Cathedral is audible at five miles, painful at three, and lethal at one.

Thomas Beecham

Music

Ladies and gentlemen, in upwards of fifty years of concert-giving, it has seldom been my good fortune to find the programme correctly printed. Tonight is no exception to the rule, and therefore, with your kind permission, we will now play you the piece which you think you have just heard.

Thomas Beecham

A piano is a parlour utensil for subduing the impenitent visitor. It is operated by depressing the keys of the machine and the spirits of the audience.

Ambrose Bierce

Harpists spend half their life tuning and the other half playing out of tune.

Thomas Beecham

Every supermarket has a dungeon housing a staff of deaf and dumb troglodytes especially trained to make random selections of cassettes for playing during business hours.

George Crosby

When you have nothing to say, sing it.

David Ogilvy

Can't you read? The score demands *con amore*, and what are you doing? You are playing it like married men.

Arturo Toscanini

The difference between a bass and a cello is that a bass burns longer.

Thomas Beecham

He was a fiddler and consequently a rogue.

Jonathan Swift

My biggest regret in life is that I didn't hit John Denver in the mouth while I had the chance.

Denis Leary

Michael Jackson looks like a Barbie doll that has been whittled by a malicious brother.

Thomas Sutcliffe

Once you're dead, you're made for life.

Jimi Hendrix

Mick Jagger is about as sexy as a pissing toad.

Truman Capote

Cole Porter sang like a hinge.

Ethel Merman

How thankful we ought to feel that Wordsworth was only a poet and not a musician. Fancy a symphony by Wordsworth! Fancy having to sit it out! And fancy what it would have been if he had written fugues!

Samuel Butler

Bernstein uses music merely as an accompaniment to his conducting.

Oscar Levant

Music

All the good music has already been written by people with wigs and stuff.

Frank Zappa

Frank Sinatra's game is fine – but I still prefer golf.

Arnold Palmer

The approach of Frankie Lane to the microphone is that of an accused man pleading with a hostile jury.

Kenneth Tynan

A homeless musician is one without a girlfriend.

Dave Barry

It's bad when they don't perform your operas – but when they do, it's far worse.

Camille Saint-Saëns

I spent many years laughing at Harry Secombe's singing until somebody told me it wasn't a joke.

Spike Milligan

The *Glasgow Herald* once carried a classified ad which read 'Bagpipes, used only once, for sale, owing to bereavement.'

Billy Connolly

For three hundred years flautists tried to play in tune. Then they gave up and invented vibrato.

George Barrère

The Sydney Opera House looks like a typewriter full of oyster shells, like a broken Pyrex casserole dish in a brown cardboard box.

Clive James

If only James had stuck to music, we might have made some money.

Nora Joyce

I don't like piccolo playing even if it's good.

Franklin P. Adams

When conducting an orchestra, if you as much as look at the brass instruments, they will play too loudly.

Richard Strauss

Australia was the first country not to require that women play the cello side-saddle.

John Thompson

They all laughed when I sat down at the piano, but oh!, when I began to play, they laughed even more.

John Caples

The typewriting machine, when played with expression, is no more annoying than the piano when played by a sister or near relation.

Oscar Wilde

Barry Manilow's voice sounds like a bluebottle caught in the curtain.

Jean Rook

Music

Whoever wrote the British entries for the Eurovision Song Contest knew how to keep them simple. Knew the sort of rhythm the Laplanders could assimilate and teach their dog teams.

Robert Morley

My favourite opera is *La Bohème* because it is the shortest.

King George V

Next to listening to the minutes of a previous meeting, there is nothing as dull as a highbrow concert.

Kin Hubbard

Getting in the key of C sharp is like an unprotected female travelling on the Metropolitan Railway, and finding herself at Shepherd's Bush without quite knowing where she wants to go. How is she ever going to get safely back to Clapham Junction?

Samuel Butler

Any request to have the canned music turned down in a restaurant leads to it being turned up.

Ken Lake

I feel really guilty having to put my name on my songs because I write them, compose them and score them, but it's really the work of God.

Michael Jackson

I don't like country music, but I don't mean to denigrate those who do. And for people who like country music, 'denigrate' means 'put down'.

Bob Newhart

I'm going to play a piece by a well-known Danish composer – Mozart, Hans Christian Mozart.

Victor Borge

Adrian Boult came to see me this morning positively reeking of Horlicks.

Thomas Beecham

I want you to sound like twenty-two women having babies without chloroform.

John Barbirolli

The Rolling Stones suffered a great loss with the death of Ian Steward, the man who had for so many years played the piano quietly and silently with them on stage.

Andy Peebles

My second hit was a complete flop.

Shakin' Stevens

In Blues, 'adulthood' means being old enough to get the electric chair if you shoot a man in Memphis.

Paul Cloutman

I cannot explain why Americans dropped the last cha in cha-cha-cha. It was either laziness or a lack of rhythm.

Omar Torres

There are just two kinds of conductor – too fast and too slow.

Camille Saint-Saëns

Music

I can hold a note as long as the Chase National Bank.

Ethel Merman

The music of Stravinsky is just Bach on the wrong notes.

Sergei Prokofiev

Opera is the coming together of music, theatre, design, people and coughing in the greatest synthesis of art.

Armando Iannucci

You got to have smelt a lot of mule manure before you can sing like a hillbilly.

Hank Williams

My music is not modern, it is merely badly played.

Arnold Schoenberg

Do I play any other musical instrument? Well, I have another piano.

Victor Borge

The phonograph is an irritating toy that restores life to dead noises.

Ambrose Bierce

I like to go to the opera whether I need the sleep or not.

Henny Youngman

Have you heard about the bagpiper who parked his car with the windows open, forgetting that he had left his bagpipes on the backseat? He rushed back to the car but it was too late – somebody had already put another set of bagpipes in the car.

E.K. Kruger

If you play it twice then it isn't a mistake.

Kevin Johnsrude

The Steinway people have asked me to announce that this is a Baldwin piano.

Victor Borge

When a piano piece gets difficult, make faces.

Artur Schnabel

One can always count on Gilbert and Sullivan for a rousing finale, full of words and music, signifying nothing.

Tom Lehrer

Gershwin asked me if his music would be played in a hundred years' time. I told him that it would be if he was still around.

Oscar Levant

'Middle of the road' music can be dangerous. While listening to one of those albums, I almost got hit by a truck.

Yakov Smirnoff

Thank heaven there are no nightingales in the countryside to ruin the music of the stillness with their well-meant, but ill-produced voices.

Oscar Wilde

Music

Business was so bad in a club I worked in last week that the orchestra was playing 'Tea for One'.

Henny Youngman

The trouble with a folk song is that once you have played it through there is nothing much you can do except play it over again and play it rather louder.

Constant Lambert

Boléro is a piece for orchestra without music.

Maurice Ravel

A man with male pattern baldness ain't the blues. A woman with male pattern baldness is.

Paul Cloutman

The world's greatest optimist is a banjo player with a pager.

Fred Metcalf

Denis Norden's voice was like a heron with its leg caught.

Frank Muir

Handel is so great and simple that no one but a professional musician is unable to understand him.

Samuel Butler

The only sanction contemplated against Israel is forcing them to take part in the Eurovision Song Contest.

George Galloway

How can you tell if there is a banjo player at the door? He can't find the key and he doesn't know when to come in.

Tom Shields

Better not listen to Debussy's music; you risk getting used to it and then you would end up liking it.

Nikolai Rimsky-Korsakov

It is a good thing that Parry died when he did; otherwise he might have set the whole Bible to music.

Frederick Delius

John Lennon's first girlfriend was named Thelma Pickles. Which explains why Lennon was the one guy who thought Yoko Ono was a perfectly fine name.

Randy Horn

I knew that Malcolm Sargent had been knighted, but I didn't know he'd been doctored.

Thomas Beecham

I seldom mention Elvis Presley unless I stub my toe.

Groucho Marx

Jazz is a terrible revenge by the culture of the Negroes on that of the whites.

Jan Paderewski

'Aria' is Italian for 'a song that will not end in your lifetime'.

Dave Barry

Music

The number of women in the musical profession has been increasing steadily in the last thirty years or so. As the art of music is in a state of hopeless decadence, this phenomenon is inevitable.

Thomas Beecham

Carmen Silvera had a trained voice, but at some stage it escaped and reverted to the wild.

Gordon Kaye

I have not been to see Irving in *Faust*. I go to the pantomime only at Christmas.

W.S. Gilbert

You can be sure that at the end of most operas, there will be work for the undertaker.

St John Peskett

The first of the three acts of *Parsifal* occupied three hours and I enjoyed that in spite of the singing.

Mark Twain

English singers cannot sing. There is only one I know who can walk on the stage with any grace. The others come on like a duck in a thunderstorm.

Thomas Beecham

Hang Irish harpers wherever found.

Queen Elizabeth I

Contemporary music is like drinking a quinine cocktail and having an enema simultaneously.

Philip Larkin

I sing only to punish my children.

David Feherty

Music is the most expensive of all noises.

Oscar Wilde

Operas have a plot that is roughly as complex as *The Magic Roundabout,* only louder obviously.

Joe Joseph

The Spice Girls are threatening to make a comeback. Can't we just pay them what they want?

Alan Aitchison

As for operas, they are essentially too absurd and extravagant to mention. I look upon them as a magic scene contrived to please the eyes and the ears at the expense of the understanding.

Lord Chesterfield

It was pathetic to see the lengths most of the foreign contestants at the Eurovision Song Contest would go to in order to disguise their musical inadequacy; some even had children lisping the unintelligible lyrics; others relied on cleavage or gimmickry such as backing groups imitating cowbells.

Robert Morley

Nationalities and Places

Nationalities and Places

Gaiety is the most outstanding feature of the Soviet Union.

Joseph Stalin

I once stayed in a German hotel which displayed the notice BREAKFAST IST OBLIGATORY.

Derek Nimmo

This Scottish fellow had a hip replacement operation. He asked the surgeon if he could have the bone for his dog.

Frank Carson

Of course, travelling is much easier today than it used to be. A hundred years ago, it could take you the better part of a year to get from New York to California; whereas today, because of equipment problems at O'Hare, you can't get there at all.

Dave Barry

I went to Naples to see Vesuvius and would you believe it, the bloody fools had let it go out.

Spike Milligan

A Dublin marriage proposal often goes like this: would ya like to go halves on a baby?

Brendan Behan

I like the Irish but I cannot quite understand how when I say 'I'm from London', in a Dublin pub, this tends to be heard as 'I am Oliver Cromwell'.

Jo Brand

Nationalities and Places

The English may not like music, but they absolutely love the noise it makes.

Thomas Beecham

In Anglo-Saxon countries men prefer the company of other men. In England twenty-five per cent of the men are homosexual.

Edith Cresson

New York City is perfectly safe if you follow certain commonsense safety rules such as:
1 Always walk at at least 30 miles per hour
2 Always keep your money and other valuables in a safe place, such as Switzerland
3 Avoid unsafe areas, such as your hotel bedroom
4 Never make eye contact. This is asking to be mugged. In the New York court system, a mugger is automatically declared not guilty if the defence can prove the victim has a history of making eye contact.

Dave Barry

In Ethiopia when a father turns to his son and says, 'Whaddya want to do when you grow up?' nine times out of ten the kid says 'Eat'.

Denis Leary

I don't like abroad. I've been there.

King George V

I am not wanting to make too long speech tonight as I am knowing your old English saying 'Early to bed and up with the cock!'

Yakov Smirnoff

Nationalities and Places

I saw the new Italian navy. Its boats have glass bottoms so they can see the old Italian navy.

Peter Secchia

An Iranian moderate is one who has run out of ammunition.

Henry Kissinger

The Race Relations Board concentrated their fire some years ago on a fellow who was selling Irish coffee mugs which had the handle on the inside. He turned out to be a native of Cork.

Stan Gebler Davies

We had gone out there to pass the beautiful day of high summer like true Irishmen – locked in the dark snug of a public house.

Brendan Behan

Poland is now a totally independent nation, and it has managed to greatly improve its lifestyle thanks to the introduction of modern Western conveniences such as food.

Dave Barry

Waiting for the verb in German is the ultimate thrill.

Flann O'Brien

The Swiss are not a people so much as a neat, clean, quite solvent business.

William Faulkner

It profits a man nothing to give his soul for the whole world – but for Wales?

Thomas More

The Germans – if they can't stuff it into an animal casing they won't eat it.

Tim Allen

There must be at least 500 million rats in the United States; of course, I am speaking only from memory.

Edgar W. Nye

My mind is like a Welsh railway – one track and dirty.

Dylan Thomas

When asked by an anthropologist what the Indians called America before the white man came, an Indian said simply 'Ours'.

Vine Deloira

Eating in Germany is easy because there is basically only one kind of food, called the 'wurst'. This is a delicious item made by compressing random pig parts until they have reached the density of bowling balls, then serving them in long brown units that don't look at all like large bowel movements, so just put that thought right out of your mind.

Dave Barry

On entering the United States I was given a form to fill in by the Immigration Authority. To the question 'Is it your intention to overthrow the government of the US by force', I gave the written answer 'Sole purpose of visit'.

Gilbert Harding

Nationalities and Places

The English are a pacifist race – they always hold their wars in someone else's country.

Brendan Behan

England were beaten only in the sense that they lost.

Dickie Davis

England had Thatcher. We had Reagan. But at least we have one thing we can hold over England's head. We tried to kill Reagan.

Denis Leary

The Englishwoman is so refined.
She has no bosom and no behind.

Stevie Smith

In Ireland schizophrenics are treated not by one psychiatrist but by two.

Barry Took

German is a language which was developed solely to afford the speaker the opportunity to spit at strangers under the guise of polite conversation.

P.J. O'Rourke

If I were a cassowary
On the plains of Timbuctoo,
I would eat a missionary
Cassock, band, and hymn-book too.

Samuel Wilberforce

Poor Mexico, so far from God and so close to the United States.

Porfiris Diaz

A Russian and a Polish labourer repairing a derelict house chanced upon a horde of gold. The Russian said eagerly 'We will share it like brothers'. 'No,' replied the Pole, 'fifty-fifty'.

Peter Ustinov

Practically every game played internationally today was invented in Britain, and when foreigners became good enough to match or even defeat the British, the British quickly invented a new game.

Peter Ustinov

In a restaurant, the average Englishman would much prefer poor food, poor service and a good complaint to the manager and maybe even a letter to the *Times* rather than enjoy a good meal.

Malcolm Muggeridge

Montreal is the only place on earth where a good French accent isn't a social asset.

Brendan Behan

The Welsh have overrun the country with nonconformity and lust.

Evelyn Waugh

Here is the difference between Dante, Milton and me. They wrote about Hell and never saw the place. I wrote about Chicago after looking the town over for years and years.

Carl Sandburg

Nationalities and Places

Lichtenstein and Luxembourg are not European nations. They are minor characters in William Shakespeare's famous play *Hamlet II: The Next Day.*

Dave Barry

I went to the United States for one purpose only; to continue my lifelong search for naked women in wet mackintoshes.

Dylan Thomas

She's not dead, sir, she's English.

Cathy Hopkins

The French are sawed-off sissies who eat snails and slugs and cheese that smells like people's feet. They are utter cowards who force their own children to drink wine and they gibber like baboons even when you try to speak to them in their own wimpy language.

P.J. O'Rourke

New Zealanders will bet on anything that moves, and, if it doesn't move, they will kick it and bet on when it will move.

Robin Oakley

Californication.

James Montgomery

Americans will put up with anything provided it doesn't block traffic.

Dan Rather

Last week I went to Philadelphia, but it was closed.

W.C. Fields

Natives who beat drums to drive off evil spirits are objects of scorn to Americans who blow horns to break up traffic jams.

Mary Ellen Kelly

There is nothing at all primitive about European medical care except that in some countries they practise it in foreign languages, meaning you run the risk of entering hospital complaining of an inflamed appendix and coming out as a member of a completely different gender.

Dave Barry

One of the cardinal rules of travel is 'stay the hell out of Paraguay'.

Dave Barry

The French and the English are such good enemies that they can't resist being friends.

Peter Ustinov

My father never lived to see his dream come true of an all Yiddish-speaking Canada.

David Steinberg

If you are not in New York you are camping out.

Thomas Dewing

The Spanish Civil War was not a war at all. It was a comic opera with an occasional death.

Georges Kopp

Nationalities and Places

Texas used to be the largest state, but because of Alaska, it no longer is. Texans are still very touchy about this, so you should be sensitive when you discuss it with them. 'What a large state this is, despite being nowhere near as large as Alaska!' is a sensitive remark you might want to make.

Dave Barry

Two out of five Irish women prefer alcohol to sex and it's just my luck to have gone out with both of them.

Joseph O'Connor

The Germans are a cruel race. Their operas last for six hours and they have no word for fluffy.

Rowan Atkinson

Scotsmen wear kilts because sheep can hear zippers a mile away.

Blanche Knott

You can have no concept of the vastness and emptiness of the outback of Australia until you have seen the dress circle of a Sydney theatre on a Saturday afternoon.

Robert Morley

'Vacation' is the word Americans use to describe going someplace different to have fun and get away from all their trials and tribulations. The English call it 'holiday'. In Russia it's known as 'defecting'.

Yakov Smirnoff

Many people are surprised to hear we have comedians in Russia, but they are there. They are dead, but they are there.

Yakov Smirnoff

I have recently been all round the world and have formed a very poor opinion of it.

Thomas Beecham

Finland has produced so many brilliant distance runners because back home it costs $2.50 a gallon for gas.

Esa Tikkannery

John Kenneth Galbraith and Marshall McLuhan are the two greatest modern Canadians that the US has produced.

Anthony Burgess

I have just returned from a weekend in Paris and all I can say is that sex in Ireland is only in its infancy.

Patrick Kavanagh

The Welsh are said to be so remarkably fond of cheese, that in cases of difficulty their midwives apply a piece of toasted cheese to the *janua vitae* to attract and entice the young Taffy, who on smelling it makes the most vigorous efforts to come forth.

Francis Grose

There's a store in New York called Bonjour Croissant. It makes me want to go to Paris and open a store called Hello Toast.

Fran Lebowitz

Nationalities and Places

Hoover's slogan was 'a chicken in every pot' but Gorbachev has a new slogan: a chicken in every time zone.

Johnny Carson

These two Irishmen were passing a pub – well, it could happen.

Frank Carson

We are now approaching Belfast Airport. Please fasten your seatbelts, extinguish your cigarettes and put your watches back three hundred years.

Niall Toibin

I had this prejudice against the British until I discovered half of them were female.

Ray Floyd

An Englishman, even if he is quite alone, forms an orderly queue of one.

George Mikes

The English instinctively admire any man who has no talent and is modest about it.

James Agee

My first rule of travel is never to go to a place that sounds like a medical condition and Critz is clearly an incurable disease involving flaking skin.

Bill Bryson

Everything you ever need to know about the Germans' innate sense of romance, lyricism, eroticism and indeed their tender feelings for the fairer sex is encapsulated in their word for nipple. The German word is *brustwarze*, a breast wart.

A.A. Gill

I am moving to Switzerland because I am devoted to chocolate.

Noël Coward

Intelligence governs our universe except in certain parts of New Jersey.

Woody Allen

Another innocent bystander was shot in New York yesterday. You just stand around in this town long enough and be innocent and somebody is going to shoot you.

Will Rogers

What annoys me about Britain is the rugged will to lose.

William Camp

Beautiful city of Glasgow I now conclude my muse,
And to write in praise of thee my pen does not refuse;
And, without fear of contradiction, I will venture to say
You are the second grandest city in Scotland at the
    present day.

William McGonagall

Britain has invented a new missile. It's called the civil servant – it doesn't work and it can't be fired.

Walter Walker

Nationalities and Places

A gifted person ought to learn English (barring spelling and pronouncing) in thirty hours, French in thirty days, and German in thirty years.

Mark Twain

Niagara Falls is simply a vast unnecessary amount of water going the wrong way and then falling over unnecessary rocks.

Oscar Wilde

An Irishman will always soften bad news, so that a major coronary is no more than 'a bad turn', and a near-hurricane that leaves thousands homeless is 'good drying weather'.

Hugh Leonard

All culture corrupts, but French culture corrupts absolutely.

Laurence Durrell

In the Dublin of the 1930s to get enough to eat was regarded as an achievement. To get drunk was a victory.

Brendan Behan

The two sides of industry have traditionally always regarded each other in Britain with the greatest possible loathing, mistrust and contempt. They are both absolutely right.

Auberon Waugh

In America you can always find a party. In Russia, the party always finds you.

Yakov Smirnoff

Nationalities and Places

One thing I will say for the Germans, they are always perfectly willing to give anybody's land to somebody else.

Will Rogers

Lord I will go wherever you want me to. But not India.

St Thomas

Only one arrest was made at the Belgium v. Ireland match in Brussels. It was an Irishman with a painted moustache who attempted to kiss a police horse.

Patrick Murray

The great thing about Glasgow now is that if there's a nuclear attack it'll look exactly the same afterwards.

Billy Connolly

I see the customs authorities in England searched the round-the-world fliers when they landed. I guess they thought the boys had smuggled over a couple of baby grand pianos.

Will Rogers

You always know a sick Irishman is on the mend when you see him blowing the froth off his medicine.

Brendan Behan

There'll always be an England, even if it's in Hollywood.

Bob Hope

The Irish are excellent timekeepers because they are used to working with watches that are an hour fast and ten minutes slow.

Patrick Murray

Nationalities and Places

The English think that incompetence is the same thing as sincerity.

Quentin Crisp

To hear a German struggling with language is like watching a deep sea diver disappearing under the water before finally emerging with the verb between his teeth.

Mark Twain

Saloons in Philadelphia were closed at twelve o'clock on Saturday night and opened at one minute past midnight on Sunday.

W.C. Fields

Three ducks were flying over Belfast. The first duck said 'quack', the second duck said 'quack' and the third duck said 'Look, I'm going as quack as I can'.

Frank Carson

It is part of the unwritten British Constitution that all major events have to be presented by a Dimbleby.

Jeremy Paxman

He created a man who was hard of head, blunt of speech, knew which side his bread was buttered on, and above all took no notice of women. Then God sent him forth to multiply in Yorkshire.

Reginald Hill

Polar exploration is at once the cleanest and most isolated way of having a bad time which has been devised.

Apsley Cherry-Garrard

The importance of a country is inversely proportional to the length of its national anthem.

Allen Otter

All Englishmen talk as if they've got a bushel of plums stuck in their throats, and then after swallowing them get constipated from the pits.

W.C. Fields

Of all noxious animals, the most noxious is a tourist. And of all tourists, the most vulgar, ill-bred, offensive and loathsome is the British tourist.

Francis Kilvert

What I look forward to most on returning from a long tour of India is a dry fart.

Phil Edmonds

In parts of India they have a law that if a man is married and is unfaithful to his wife, her family can take him out and publicly shoot him. There is no trial or anything – it's just their religious and state custom. If that was the custom in America, I would take every cent I make and put it into an ammunition factory.

Will Rogers

I do not dislike the French for their vulgar antipathy between neighbouring nations, but for their insolent and unfounded airs of superiority.

Horace Walpole

Nationalities and Places

In an underdeveloped country, don't drink the water; in a developed country, don't breathe the air.

Jonathan Raban

Italian men and Russian women don't shave before a race.

Eddy Ottoz

The Irish treat you like royalty before and after a game, and kick you to pieces during it.

Jeff Probyn

French bread is so long so they can dip it in the sewer.

Blanche Knott

On my first day in New York a guy asked me if I knew where Central Park was. When I told him I didn't he said, 'Do you mind if I mug you here?'

Paul Merton

I bought a Korean kitchen knife. The label read: WARNING – KEEP OUT OF CHILDREN.

Robin Young

I was in a pub in Glasgow the other night. What a rough joint it was – they had a pig on the counter as an air freshener.

Stan Boardman

They say if you stop smoking you'll get your sense of smell back. I live in New York City – why do I want my sense of smell back?

Bill Hicks

Have you heard about the Irishman who reversed into a car boot sale and sold the engine?

Frank Carson

A motto for New Jersey – Not as bad as you might have expected.

Calvin Trillin

We used to play a game in Liverpool called forwards, backwards, sideways. You'd hit a fellow on the head with a shovel and guess which way he'd fall.

Stan Boardman

Foreign tourists should realise that in England they are encouraged to take a piece of fruit, free of charge, from any open-air stall or display.

Michael Lipton

I don't mind dictatorships abroad provided they are pro-American.

George Wallace

In the Soviet Army it takes more courage to retreat than to advance.

Joseph Stalin

The only English words I saw in Japan were Sony and Mitsubishi.

Bill Gullickson

Boy George is all England needs: another Queen who can't dress.

Joan Rivers

Nationalities and Places

I hate two towns. Edmonton and Aswan. I've enjoyed all the rest. Even New Zealand.

John Cleese

Visitors to England should be informed that London barbers are delighted to shave patrons' armpits.

Gerard Hoffnung

An Aborigine is a non-speaking character actor in an Australian movie.

Mike Barfield

I swear I saw a road sign in Ireland which said: WARNING! THIS IS A ONE WAY CUL-DE-SAC AT BOTH ENDS.

Spike Milligan

A Canadian is someone who knows how to make love in a canoe.

Pierre Berton

Boy, those French – they have a different word for everything.

Steve Martin

The curtain rises on a vast primitive wasteland, not unlike certain parts of New Jersey.

Woody Allen

The Middle Eastern states aren't nations; they're quarrels with borders.

P.J. O'Rourke

My dear Oscar, you are not clever enough for us in Dublin. You had better run over to Oxford.

John Mahaffy

Very big, China.

Noël Coward

It was wonderful to find America, but it would have been still more wonderful to miss it.

Mark Twain

France has neither winter nor summer nor morals – apart from these drawbacks it is a fine country.

Mark Twain

Welsh Nationalists are a political group successful in having secured extra work for indigneous traffic-sign writers.

Mike Barfield

A family of my acquaintance in Glasgow had their father badly burnt in a fire so they demanded half price at the crematorium.

Michael Munro

Since both of Switzerland's national products, snow and chocolate, melt, the cuckoo clock was invented solely in order to give tourists something solid to remember it by.

Alan Coren

Nationalities and Places

I think one of the highest compliments ever paid to Australia was the imminent Japanese invasion. To think the Japanese would actually think of coming to Australia to live! They did change their mind, with a little persuasion.

Barry Humphries

Fifteen years ago, Britain was a great country in which to have a heart attack in the street.

John Le Carré

I knew Daniel Day Lewis before he was Irish.

Stephen Frears

In Dublin you are worse off if you have written books than if you are illiterate.

Patrick Kavanagh

It seems that the only three letters in the Basque alphabet are X, K and X again. Everyone, even in the Basque hill towns, prefers to use Spanish, despite the lisping and the spitting.

Jeremy Clarkson

If the English could only learn to believe in fairies, there wouldn't ever have been any Irish problem.

W.B. Yeats

The people of Zaire are not thieves. It merely happens that they move things, or borrow them.

Sese Mobuto

Poor countries enjoy two basic rights: to sell cheap and to buy dear.

Julius Nyerere

Nationalities and Places

The Rhine is drying up – it has apparently something to do with the failure of the Swiss to provide enough snow on the Alps.

Robert Morley

To disagree with three-fourths of the British public on all points is one of the first elements of sanity, one of the deepest consolations in moments of spiritual doubt.

Oscar Wilde

Advertising men are the Robbing Hoods of America.

Will Rogers

My father had four brothers in the war – one on the Confederate side who was killed. Two on the Union side, and one who was on both sides – he got two pensions.

John Ford

Vernon Duke speaks with a monocle in his throat.

Oscar Levant

Anyone who ventures south of the Trent is likely to contract an incurable disease of the vowels; it's a disease to which for some reason weather forecasters are particularly prone to and lecturers in sociology.

Alan Bennett

I never have any trouble getting a table in a Vienna restaurant. All I have to do is have my name paged and half the diners leave.

Simon Wiesenthal

Nationalities and Places

The United States will never be a civilized country until we spend more money on books than we do on chewing gum.

Elbert Hubbard

The most important advice I would give a writer going from Harvard to Oxford is to pack lots of long underwear.

T.S. Eliot

My luggage trolley at Singapore airport had a notice saying: 'Not to be Removed from Crewe Station.'

Clive James

Australian women look pleasantly attractive, the ones who do not have skin cancer.

Clement Freud

Chambers Dictionary defines the word 'Taghairm' as 'divination in the Scottish Highlands, especially inspiration sought by lying in a bullock's hide behind a waterfall'.

Brian Greer

I told the Frenchman in French. He said he could not understand me. I repeated. Still he did not understand. He appeared to be very ignorant of French.

Mark Twain

To the Irishman there are only two ultimate realities: Hell and the United States.

Evelyn Waugh

I wonder if people in Australia call the rest of the world 'Up Over'.

George Carlin

Dealing with Ulster is like handling a fight in a bar. It is a stupid local row between people who just aren't American enough.

Bill Clinton

If you liked Beirut, you'll love Mogadishu.

Smith Hempstone

In Canberra, even the mistakes are planned by the National Capital Development Commission.

Alan Fitzgerald

By the year 2050 half the people living in Moscow will have their own private jets. This will be particularly useful when they hear that potatoes are available in St. Petersburg – they will be able to get to the head of the queue.

Christie Davies

Swedes are just fake Norwegians.

Greg d'Alessio

Gentlemen, a toast: I give you Canada because I don't want it myself.

Artemus Ward

The word 'Toxteth' it appears is a combination of 'toxic' and 'death'.

Paul Hoggart

Nationalities and Places

Even today, well-brought-up English girls are taught to boil all vegetables for at least a month and a half, just in case one of the guests comes without his teeth.

Calvin Trillin

For the past eleven years, American students have scored lower on standardised tests than European students, Japanese students and certain species of elk.

Dave Barry

In England they've got Valium in the water supply, which is why the place moves about as fast as a snail with piles.

Barry Humphries

The global importance of the Middle East is that it keeps the Near East and the Far East from encroaching on each other.

Dan Quayle

I have never seen such a place for wanton women as Northampton.

George Borrow

United States planes have the capability to penetrate deep into the Soviet soil.

John Rogers

Why should Irishmen stand with their arms folded and their hands in their pockets when England called for aid?

Thomas Myles

Nationalities and Places

Australia is an outdoor country. People go indoors only to use the toilet and that's just a recent development.

Barry Humphries

Niagara Falls would be much more impressive if they flowed the other way.

Oscar Wilde

I find the word 'Brit', a recent and I suspect Irish coinage, objectionable, as it lumps us with the Scots and Welsh, with a suggestion of football hooliganism thrown in.

Paul Johnson

French troops arrived in Afghanistan last week. They are acting as advisors to the Taliban, to teach them how to surrender properly.

Jay Leno

The Irish humour of John Ford in his Cavalry Trilogy made me wish that Oliver Cromwell had done a more thorough job.

James Agate

At the hospitals and churches in Venice, where it is not allowed to applaud in the same manner as at the Opera, they cough, hem and blow their noses to express admiration.

Charles Burney

The Great Wall of China is certainly a very great wall.

Richard Nixon

Nationalities and Places

Indiana produces more first-rate second-class men than any other state in the union.

Thomas Marshall

Like the Irish Census, I am broken down by age, sex and religion.

Sean MacReamoinn

Half of the American people never read a newspaper. Half never voted for the President. One hopes it is the same half.

Gore Vidal

The English have but three vegetables, and two of them are cabbage.

Walter Page

Every third German is a motorcar.

Martin Allwood

Headline of the Year 2001: 'Man Found Guilty of Indecency with Welsh Lamppost.'

David Randall

I come from a state where gun control is just how steady you hold your weapon.

Alan Simpson

Diaries are full of indispensable information, such as the recommended tyre pressures for North Korea.

Leslie Mallory

Fall is my favourite season in Los Angeles, watching the birds change colour and fall from the trees.

David Letterman

Into the face of the young man had crept a look of furtive shame, the shifty, hangdog look which announces that an Englishman is about to talk French.

P.G. Wodehouse

We English don't have a lot to be proud of but we are proud of our mustard. On the Continent mustard is used to bring out the flavour of meat, but English mustard really makes your nose bleed.

Jack Dee

Argentina is a true democracy – everybody eventually becomes president.

Joe Duffy

When it's Fall in New York, the air smells as if someone's been frying goats in it, and if you are keen to breathe, the best plan is to open a window and stick your head into a building.

Douglas Adams

British women dance as though they were riding on donkeys.

Heinrich Heine

I am investigating the possibility of taking legal action to restrain the BBC from broadcasting discouraging weather forecasts for the Weston-Super-Mare area.

George Brenner

Nationalities and Places

I told someone in the US that I was getting married and they said, 'Have you picked a date yet?' I said, 'Wow, you can bring a date to your own wedding?' What a country!

Yakov Smirnoff

Because of their cuisine, Germans don't consider farting rude. They'd certainly be out of luck if they did.

P.J. O'Rourke

If people looked like their passport photographs, very few countries would let them in.

Doug Larson

Americans are so overwhelmed by their children that they will do anything for them except stay married to their co-producer.

Katharine Whitehorn

Surely, after twenty days of trial by fire, the Australians must now realise that God never really intended this enormous tinderbox to be used for human habitation.

Jeremy Clarkson

If the French were really intelligent, they would speak English.

Wilfrid Sheed

If all of the people in China – more than one billion of them – were to hold hands around the equator, more than half of them would drown.

Steven Wright

Nationalities and Places

Will all the snakes who wish to remain in Ireland please raise their right hands.

Brendan Behan

I was born in Louisiana, but I get to lots of overseas places like Canada.

Britney Spears

For Scotland, one should be an amphibian.

D.H. Lawrence

It gives me great pleasure to declare that the English, as a people, are very little inferior to the Scots.

Christopher North

The roaches are that big in some parts of Australia they help with the washing up.

Barry Humphries

How come the winner of the Miss Universe contest is always from Earth? I think it is rigged.

Rick Hall

In the war in Serbia, Germany is fighting on the right side for the first time in its history.

Joschka Fischer

In England an elevator is called a lift, a mile is called a kilometre and botulism is called a steak and kidney pie.

Greg Daniels

Nationalities and Places

A person is not a real New Yorker if going home for the holidays involves leaving the city.

Naomi Miller

There was great controversy in antiquity as to whether the Isle of Man should belong to Britain or Ireland. Eventually, it was decided that, since it supported poisonous reptiles, it should belong to Britain.

Gerald of Wales

Anybody can act. Most people in England do nothing else.

Oscar Wilde

One swell thing about the United States is that the newspapers can print whatever stories they want. Another one is that nobody has to read them.

Dave Barry

The first white man to sail near Australia was the world's most useless explorer, a Dutchman called Abel Tasman. In a three-year voyage he found Fiji, Tasmania and New Zealand, but in one of the most inept pieces of navigation ever, he completely missed the big bit in the middle.

Jeremy Clarkson

Switzerland has produced nothing except theologians and waiters.

Oscar Wilde

Finding that the Vatican gardens were open only to the Bohemian and Portuguese pilgrims, I at once spoke both languages fluently, explaining that my English dress was a form of penance.

Oscar Wilde

He can't speak Turkey, but you can tell he's delighted.

Kevin Keegan

The only winter sport at which the British excel is phoning in sick.

Ronald White

The Scots invented golf – which could also explain why they invented Scotch.

James Dent

West Wickham fire station is situated in a road which is blocked at both ends.

Frank Ruler

A friend of mine sent me a postcard with a satellite photo of the entire planet on it and on the back he wrote, 'Wish you were here.'

Steven Wright

In Milan, traffic lights are instructions. In Rome they are suggestions. But in Naples, they are Christmas decorations.

Antonio Martino

Yorkshire born, Yorkshire bred,
Strong in the arm ...

Ken Dodd

Nationalities and Places

Britain doesn't win any medals at the Winter Olympics for one simple reason – we don't have any snow. Now if they had a wet-weather Olympics we would definitely take gold in the twenty-yard dash with a Sainsbury's bag on the head.

A.A. Gill

I cannot see the sense of becoming a Commander of the British Empire. They might as well make me a Commander of Milton Keynes – at least that exists.

Spike Milligan

We do not go to war with France because her prose is perfect.

Oscar Wilde

Inverkip is so rough they put a date stamp on your head when they mug you so they don't do you twice in the one day.

Chic Murray

In Hollywood a romantic man is one who talks to you after sex.

Kathy Lette

Australian beaches are not dangerous. We've lost only one Prime Minister to sharks in living memory.

Barry Humphries

Australia was discovered by Captain James Cook who stepped off his ship, sniffed the air and declared, 'Yes. This would make a fantastic prison.'

Jeremy Clarkson

Nationalities and Places

As St Patrick said when he was driving the snakes out of Ireland, 'Are ye alright there in the back lads?'

Patrick Murray

I don't object to foreigners speaking a foreign language, I just wish they'd all speak the same foreign language.

Billy Wilder

The second sight possessed by the Highlanders in Scotland is actually a foreknowledge of future events. I believe they possess this gift because they don't wear trousers.

Georg C. Lichtenberg

The continent of Nigeria.

George W. Bush

Halfghanistan.

Jay Leno

When the Japanese arrived in her Shanghai garden during the war, Sylvia successfully ordered them off the grass.

John Wells

Here we are in the Holy Land of Israel – a Mecca for tourists.

David Vine

Historians have now definitely established that Juan Cabrillo, the discoverer of California, was not looking for Kansas, thus setting a precedent that continues to this day.

Wayne Shannon

Nationalities and Places

Australia's in the big league now. We've got organised crime, racial prejudice, cable TV, AIDS, disabled toilets, and underage drug abuse, second to none.

Barry Humphries

Africa is God's country and He can have it.

Groucho Marx

The action takes place in Poland; in other words, nowhere.

Alfred Jarry

When it comes to attaching clothes pegs to your face, we British still rule the world.

Edward McKenna

Harpo Marx was driving his battered car which, he asserted, was his town car. 'And the town is Pompeii,' I added.

Alexander Woollcott

There is so much sand in North Africa that if it were spread out it would completely cover the Sahara Desert.

Alan Turing

I once saw this sign on an Irish lift: 'Please do not use this when it is not working.'

Spike Milligan

Pageantry is the sort of thing the British overdo so well.

Noël Coward

Nationalities and Places

It is the perpetual boast of the Englishman that he never brags.

Wyndham Lewis

With the Euro-Disney World soon to be built in Paris, British Theme Parks will just seem like Mickey Mouse affairs.

Neil Walker

Football hooligans are a compliment to the English martial spirit.

Alan Clark

No other British institution can quite touch the hotel in its single-minded devotion to the interests of those who work there and its complete indifference to those who are guests there.

Kingsley Amis

You learn not to make jokes at the European Parliament. Otherwise you find the Germans getting it ten minutes after the Swedes.

Glenys Kinnock

I killed more Indians than Custer, Beecher and Chivington all put together.

John Ford

The only way to solve the New York City traffic problem is to put all the lights on red and keep them that way.

George Kaufman

Nationalities and Places

If all of the salmon caught in Canada in one year were laid end to end across the Sahara Desert, the smell would be terrible.

Alan Fleming

Tracking through the Amazon, avoiding crocodiles and snakes, pales into insignificance compared to going to Liverpool by train.

John Blashford-Snell

Some hate me because I am not a Tory, some because I am not a Whig, some because I am not a Christian, and all because I am a Scotsman.

David Hume

I know only two words of Spanish. One is mañana, which means tomorrow. The other is pyjama, which means tonight.

Woodrow Wyatt

Visiting the Millennium Dome felt like an enforced six-hour stopover at a second-rate German airport.

Martin Amis

Dangerous foreigners begin at Calais and don't stop until you get to Bombay, where they speak English and play cricket.

Clement Attlee

Las Vegas is full of all kinds of gambling devices – dice tables, slot machines and wedding chapels.

Joey Adams

Cannibals found the French delicious, by far the best. The English came next. The Dutch were dull and stodgy and the Spaniards so stringy, that they were hardly a meal at all, even boiled.

Felipe Fernandez-Armesto

The citizens of Griggsville invited me to give them a lecture on aesthetics. I began by advising them to change the name of their town.

Oscar Wilde

English coffee tastes like water that has been squeezed out of a wet sleeve.

Fred Allen

There are ways out of everything, apart from the city of Oxford's one-way system.

Simon Mayo

Unfortunately the infrared night goggles were made in Russia – which is another way of saying 'badly made by someone who's drunk'.

Jeremy Clarkson

It had never occurred to him that one foreign language could be translated into another. He had assumed that strange tongues existed only by virtue of their not being English.

Tom Stoppard

The trouble with the French is that they don't have any word for entrepreneur.

George W. Bush

Nationalities and Places

The Basques are said to understand one another, but I don't believe a word of it.

Nicolas Scalinger

'Accelerato' is the Italian word for a train stopping at every station and going very slowly in between, so as not to overshoot.

Clive James

Never criticise the Americans. They have the best taste that money can buy.

Miles Kington

A Mexican straight flush is any five cards and a gun.

Hugh Leonard

I have no A-levels and the last time I asked for directions in Paris, I inadvertently gave the man my mother's recipe for baked Alaska.

Jeremy Clarkson

Much of the contemporary English polite comedy writing suggests a highly polished and very smooth billiard table with all the necessary brightly polished cups, but without the balls.

George Nathan

In France one must adapt oneself to the fragrance of the urinal.

Gertrude Stein

The average American Southerner has the speech patterns of someone slipping in and out of consciousness.

Bill Bryson

The German – as opposed to the human – mind.

William James

The Welsh are not meant to go out in the sun. They start to photosynthesise.

Rhys Ifans

I love Germany so much I hope there will always be two of them.

François Mauriac

Spain is a country that can be saved only by a series of earthquakes.

Cyril Connolly

Edinburgh is the Reykjavik of the South.

Tom Stoppard

Islington is about as far as you can get from London without needing yellow-fever jabs.

A.A. Gill

If Scotland ever discover that football is a team game, the rest of us will have to watch out.

John Adams

Nationalities and Places

Rochdale have supporters travelling from all over the country – one from London, one from Newcastle, one from Brighton ...

David Kilpatrick

Rugby League is so popular in Auckland because every town must have its sewer.

James Baxter

I don't think the Israelis should give back the land they won from the Arabs. I think they should sell it back.

Woody Allen

Never try to make Americans or foreigners feel at home – had they wished to feel at home, they would have remained in their own country.

Rose Heaton

Why do the Dutch people have two names for their country – Holland and the Netherlands – neither of which includes the word 'Dutch'?

George Carlin

I'm starting a campaign to have Finland removed as a country. We don't need it.

George Carlin

One of Canada's most serious needs is some lesser nation to domineer over and shame by displays of superior taste.

Robertson Davies

To live in Manchester is a totally incomprehensible decision for any free human being to make.

Melford Stevenson

I must say I like Newcastle. It's all vomit and love-bites.

Alan Bennett

The inn at Bristol was so bad that Boswell wished he was in Scotland.

Samuel Johnson

The state of deprivation in Glasgow is appalling. There is a waiting list of two years to vandalise a phone box.

Arnold Brown

Irishmen are so busy being Irish that they don't have any time to be anything else.

Beverley Nichols

In the United States of America there are no trappings, no pageants, and no gorgeous ceremonies. I saw only two processions: one was the Fire Brigade preceded by the Police, the other was the Police preceded by the Fire Brigade.

Oscar Wilde

Only one part of the body must not move during an Irish dance – the bowels.

Jack McHale

My ex-girlfriend was very sexy. She reminded me of the Sphinx because she was very mysterious and eternal and solid and her nose was shot off by French soldiers.

Emo Philips

Nationalities and Places

In Germany last year I had only to raise my hand to have my tricycle mended every day.

Flann O'Brien

Dublin snobbery – all fur coats and no knickers.

Jimmy O'Dea

Politics

Politics

It is no exaggeration to say that the undecideds could go one way or the other.

George Bush

I've read about foreign policy and studied – I know a number of continents.

George Wallace

It was but a few weeks since he had taken his seat in the House of Lords; and this afternoon, for want of anything better to do, he strayed in and sat in it.

Max Beerbohm

Thank God W.C. Fields was a comic. Had he been a statesman he would have plunged the world into total war.

Will Rogers

We'd all like to vote for the best man but he's never a candidate.

Kin Hubbard

In 1932 President Herbert Hoover was so desperate to remain in the White House that he dressed up as Eleanor Roosevelt. When FDR discovered the hoax in 1936, the two men decided to stay together for the sake of the children.

Johnny Carson

Consider the Vice-President, George Bush, a man so bedevilled by bladder problems that he managed, for the last eight years, to be in the men's room whenever an important illegal decision was made.

Barbara Ehrenreich

We expect the Salvadorean officials to work towards the extermination of human rights.

Dan Quayle

Hey, you guys, get up! Reagan is President. Call the Betty Ford Centre. We shoulda known, man. They let us do all the drugs and have unlimited sex so we would forget to vote. They caught us with our pants down.

Denis Leary

Do you remember the good old days when sleeping with the President meant you attended a cabinet meeting?

P.J. O'Rourke

Members of Parliament are the blind leading the people who can see.

G.K. Chesterton

Gerald Ford can't fart and chew gum at the same time.

Lyndon B. Johnson

I can think of no better step to signalise the inauguration of the National Health Service than that Aneurin Bevan who so obviously needs psychiatric attention should be among the first of its patients.

Winston Churchill

Politics

The War Office kept three sets of figures; one to mislead the public, another to mislead the Cabinet and a third to mislead itself.

H.H. Asquith

The only safe pleasure for a member of parliament nowadays is a bag of boiled sweets.

Julian Critchley

I have opinions of my own – strong opinions – but I don't always agree with them.

George Bush

Let the Democratic Party try winning and see what it feels like. If we don't like it, we can go back to our traditions.

Paul Tsongas

Any political party that includes the word 'democratic' in its name, isn't.

Patrick Murray

For twenty years Herbert Asquith has held a season ticket on the line of least resistance and has gone wherever the train of events has carried him, lucidly justifying his position at whatever point he has happened to find himself.

Leo Amery

If capitalism depended on the intellectual quality of the Conservative Party, it would end about lunchtime tomorrow.

Tony Benn

Sir Anthony Eden was half mad baronet and half beautiful woman.

R.A. Butler

The quickest way to become a left winger in the Labour Party today is to stand still for six months.

Dave Nellist

Any American citizen can become President of the United States, just as long as he's a millionaire.

Patrick Murray

Margaret Thatcher went to Venice only because somebody told her she could walk down the middle of the street.

Neil Kinnock

No man is regular in his attendance at the House of Commons until he is married.

Benjamin Disraeli

We shoot JFK, we shoot RFK but when it comes to Teddy we go, 'Ah, leave him alone, he'll screw it up himself, no problem, you know'. He's the biggest target in the whole goddamn Kennedy family – and nobody takes a shot at him. He weighs about 7,000 pounds. You could shoot a bullet in Los Angeles and hit him in the ass in Boston five minutes later.

Denis Leary

Never believe anything in politics until it has been officially denied.

Otto Von Bismarck

Politics

Corruption is nature's way of restoring our faith in democracy.

Peter Ustinov

Anybody who enjoys being in the House of Commons probably needs psychiatric help.

Ken Livingstone

The typical Socialist is a prim little man with a white-collar job, usually a secret teetotaller and often with vegetarian leanings, with a history of Nonconformity behind him, and, above all, with a social position which he has no intention of forfeiting.

George Orwell

There were so many candidates on the Democratic platform that there were not enough promises to go round.

Ronald Reagan

Ronald Reagan doesn't dye his hair, he's just prematurely orange.

Gerald Ford

The peace process is like a wedding night in a minefield.

Shimon Peres

I am not a politician, and my other habits are good.

Artemus Ward

Trust J. Edgar Hoover as much as you would a rattlesnake with a silencer on its rattle.

Dean Acheson

Most British statesmen have either drunk too much or womanised too much. I never fell into the second category.

George Brown

How the hell would I know why there were Nazis? I don't even know how a can opener works.

Woody Allen

I hope I stand for anti-bigotry, anti-racism and anti-Semitism.

George Bush

The President is going to lead us out of this recovery.

Dan Quayle

Tony Blair has pushed moderation to extremes.

Robert MacLennan

An election is coming. Universal peace is declared, and the foxes have a sincere interest in prolonging the lives of the poultry.

George Eliot

The members of Congress never open their mouths without subtracting from the sum of human knowledge.

Thomas Reed

At the reunion at a Washington party a few weeks ago there were three ex-Presidents, Carter, Ford and Nixon: See no Evil, Hear no Evil and Evil.

Bob Dole

Politics

My dog Millie knows more about foreign policy than those two bozos Clinton and Gore.

George W. Bush

In a democracy everyone has the right to be represented, including the jerks.

Chris Patten

The world 'liberty' in the mouth of Daniel Webster is like the word 'love' in the mouth of a courtesan.

Ralph Waldo Emerson

Facts are stupid things.

Ronald Reagan

A politician is an arse upon which everyone has sat except a man.

e.e. cummings

Calvin Coolidge slept more than any other President, whether by day or by night. Nero fiddled, but Coolidge only snored.

H.L. Mencken

I have always said about Tony Benn that he immatures with age.

Harold Wilson

People that are really very weird can get into sensitive positions and have a tremendous impact on history.

Dan Quayle

Politics would be a helluva good business if it weren't for the goddamned people.

Richard Nixon

It's not the voting that's democracy, it's the counting.

Tom Stoppard

Haven't we got all the fools in town on our side? And ain't that a big enough majority in any town?

Mark Twain

The House of Commons is the longest running farce in the West End.

Cyril Smith

President Johnson was a real centaur – part man and part horse's ass.

Dean Acheson

The largest turnout at elections is always where there is only one candidate.

Peter Ustinov

That one never asks a question unless he knows the answer is basic to parliamentary questioning.

John Diefenbaker

You might be interested to know that the scriptures are on our side in relation to the arms build-up.

Ronald Reagan

Politics

Sir Anthony Eden was not only a bore; he bored for England.

Malcolm Muggeridge

It is often said that the central lobby in the House of Commons is the third easiest place in Europe to pick people up after Funland in Leicester Square and the arrival lounge at Rome airport.

Alan Clark

Winston Churchill devoted the best years of his life to preparing his impromptu speeches.

F.E. Smith

Joseph McCarthy is the only major politician in the country who can be labelled 'liar' without fear of libel.

Joseph Alsop

Politicians are interested in people in the same way that dogs are interested in fleas.

P.J. O'Rourke

No diet will remove all the fat from your body because the brain is entirely fat. Without a brain you might look good, but all you could do is run for public office.

Covert Bailey

I have nothing against Kinnock. I just think it's a shame her husband is such a spineless dork.

Kit Hollerbach

I enjoy American political debates more than Soviet political debates because there are twice as many people involved – two instead of one.

Yakov Smirnoff

In the US Civil War, they were cutting each other's throats because one half of them prefer hiring their servants for life, and the other by the hour.

Thomas Carlyle

Most politicians look like people who have become human by correspondence course.

A.A. Gill

Giving money and power to the government is like giving whiskey and car keys to teenage boys.

P.J. O'Rourke

No man ever listened himself out of a job.

Calvin Coolidge

If elected, I will win.

Pat Paulsen

Why talk with the monkey when you can talk with the organ grinder?

Winston Churchill

Nothing was ever done so systematically as nothing is being done now.

Woodrow Wilson

Politics

I wear the pants in our house but I also wash and iron them.

Denis Thatcher

The House of Lords is a second chamber elected by the whips – a seraglio of eunuchs.

Michael Foot

I will sit on the fence if it is strong enough.

Cyril Smith

When Henry Kissinger won the Nobel Peace Prize, I gave up satire on grounds of unfair competition.

Tom Lehrer

The ship of state is the only known vessel that leaks from the top.

James Reston

They say everyone remembers what he was doing when Kennedy was shot. I'd love to ask Lee Harvey Oswald what he was doing.

Paul Merton

I can always tell how well I stand politically by the number of fingers Lady Londonderry offers me at her receptions.

Austin Chamberlain

Who drinks more, the House or the Senate? I believe the House drinks more because it has 531 members and the

Senate has only 96. But if the Senate had about two more members they would go ahead of them.

Will Rogers

Who is responsible for the riots? The rioters!

Dan Quayle

When Clinton says 'Attorney General', he means the first semi-qualified woman he could find without a criminal record.

Mort Sahl

I can't say I've ever got visually, artistically or sexually excited by any of the women MPs. They all look as though they're from the Fifth Kiev Stalinist machine-gun parade.

Nicholas Fairbairn

Frankly, I'd like to see the government get out of war altogether and leave the whole field to private industry.

Joseph Heller

That son of a bitch MacArthur isn't going to resign on me. I want him fired.

Harry S. Truman

Henry VIII perhaps approached as nearly to the ideal standard of perfect wickedness as the infirmities of human nature will allow.

James Mackintosh

Politics

Margaret Beckett looks like a woman resigned to walk home alone to an empty bedsit after Grab-a-Granny night at the local disco.

Richard Littlejohn

If you give Congress a dollar of unnecessary taxes, they'll spend about 1.75 dollars and that's inflationary. Inflation is unAmerican, therefore tax avoidance is patriotic.

William Donoghue

The most terrifying words in the English language are, 'I'm from the government and I'm here to help.'

Ronald Reagan

The honourable member for Bourke has committed every crime in the calendar – except the one we could so easily have forgiven him – suicide.

Henry Parkes

I have nothing against Nicholas Ridley's wife or family, but I think it is time he spent more time with them.

Philip Goodhart

I have seen better-looking faces than Alec Douglas-Home's on pirate flags.

John Agar

We've never had a President named Bob. I think it's about time we had one.

Bob Dole

I still play the saxophone because I don't have much job security.

Bill Clinton

A man that would expect to train lobsters to fly in a year is called a lunatic; but a man that thinks men can be turned into angels by an election is a reformer and remains at large.

Finley Peter Dunne

The first mistake in politics is the going into it.

Benjamin Franklin

Prayer never seems to work for me on the golf course. I think this has something to do with my being a terrible putter.

Billy Graham

I often think how much easier the world would have been to manage if Herr Hitler and Signor Mussolini had been to Oxford.

Lord Halifax

Jimmy Hoffa's most valuable contribution to the American labour movement came at the moment he stopped breathing on July 3, 1975.

Dan Moldea

John Major makes George Bush seem like a personality.

Jackie Mason

Politics

Democracy is that system of government under which the people having 35,717, 342 native-born adult whites to choose from, including thousands who are handsome and many of whom are wise, pick out Coolidge as head of state.

H.L. Mencken

Australian communists are pathological exhibits, human scum, paranoics, degenerates, morons, bludgers, pack of dingoes, industrial outlaws and political lepers, ratbags. If these people went to Russia, Stalin wouldn't even use them for manure.

Arthur Caldwell

Progress in the Foreign Service is either vaginal or rectal. You either marry the boss's daughter or you crawl up his bottom.

Nicholas Monsarrat

I am being frank about myself in this book. I tell of my first mistake on page 850.

Henry Kissinger

Many MPs never see the London that exists beyond the wine bars and brothels of Westminster.

Ken Livingstone

You can always get the truth from an American statesman after he has turned seventy, or given up all hope of the Presidency.

Wendell Phillips

Public speaking is very easy.

Dan Quayle

It is said that Mr Gladstone could persuade most people of most things, and himself of anything.

W.R. Inge

John Major is the only man who ran away from the circus to become an accountant.

Edward Pearce

Lady Astor told me that if I were her husband, she would put poison in my tea. I retorted by saying that if I were her husband, I would drink it.

Winston Churchill

I want loyalty. I want him to kiss my ass in Macy's window at high noon and tell me it smells like roses.

Lyndon B. Johnson

I seldom think of politics more than eighteen hours a day.

Lyndon B. Johnson

A Conservative is a statesman who is enamored of existing evils, as distinguished from the Liberal, who wishes to replace them with others.

Ambrose Bierce

Spiro Agnew's library burned down and both books were destroyed – and one of them hadn't even been coloured in.

Mort Sahl

Politics

There's always room at the top – after the investigation.

Oliver Herford

John Tyler has been called a mediocre man; but this is unwarranted flattery. He was a politician of monumental littleness.

Theodore Roosevelt

I think I can say, and say with pride, that we have some legislatures that bring higher prices than any in the world.

Mark Twain

I am against vice in every form, including the Vice Presidency.

Morris K. Udall

Bill Clinton is the only politician in the world who can distract people's attention from one sex scandal by becoming involved in another.

Matthew Campbell

The biggest danger for a politician is to shake hands with a man who is physically stronger, has been drinking and is voting for the other fellow.

William Proxmire

I stand by all the misstatements I've made.

Dan Quayle

For a working man or woman to vote Republican this year is the same as a chicken voting for Colonel Sanders.

Walter Mondale

The rhinoceros is an animal with a hide two feet thick, and no apparent interest in politics. What a waste.

James Wright

The Democratic Party is like a mule. It has neither pride of ancestry nor hope of posterity.

Ignatius Donnelly

Sales of sleeping pills drop alarmingly during party political broadcasts.

Mitchell Symons

It is not a lie, it's a terminological inexactitude.

Alexander Haig

Asked if they would have sex with President Clinton, 90 per cent of American women replied 'Never again.'

Albert Roge

Edwina Currie has done about as much for the Tory Party as King Herod did for babysitting.

Andrew MacKay

If Jeanne Kirkpatrick were George Bush's running mate, at least there would be some macho on the ticket.

Graham Jones

A zebra cannot change his spots.

Dan Quayle

Bill Clinton operates from the Oral Office in the White House.

Albert Roge

Politics

In the House of Commons Peter Snape accused Transport Secretary Nicholas Ridley of being 'a hypocrite' and 'an old Etonian twerp.' He was immediately asked by the speaker to withdraw the word 'hypocrite'.

Graham Jones

A low voter turnout is an indication that fewer people are going to the polls.

Dan Quayle

Now and then an innocent person is sent to the legislature.

Mark Twain

Receiving support from Ted Heath in a by-election is like being measured by an undertaker.

George Gardiner

John Major collects political jokes – in fact he's got a whole Cabinet full of them.

Graham Jones

If one morning I walked on top of the water across the Potomac River, the headline that afternoon would read PRESIDENT CAN'T SWIM.

Lyndon B. Johnson

The Secret Service have orders to protect Hillary because if she is shot, Bill becomes President.

Bill Casey

I am not politically incorrect. I am just politically challenged.

Matt Bloom

Oswald Mosley was a cross between a demented Terry Thomas and Bill Clinton.

David Aaronovitch

Henry Campbell-Bannerman is remembered chiefly as the man about whom all is forgotten.

Nicholas Bentley

Mr Macmillan is the best Prime Minister we have.

R.A. Butler

Harold Macmillan and I exchanged many frank words in our respective languages.

Peter Cook

I always wanted to get into politics, but I was never light enough to make the team.

Art Buchwald

Citizens should not lie. Lying is the prerogative of the government.

Plato

I am a loyal republican. I support Ronald Reagan when he's right – and I just keep quiet the other 95 per cent of the time.

John LeBoutiller

Harry Truman loved politicians – even Republicans.

Margaret Truman

Politics

We have a presidential election coming up. And the problem is, of course, that one of those candidates is going to win.

Barry Crimmins

A sample of a thousand Scottish people were asked if they spoke Gaelic; ninety-two per cent said no, four per cent said yes, and four per cent said they didn't know.

Tom Shields

When someone with a rural accent says, 'I don't know anything about politics,' zip up your pockets.

Donald Rumsfeld

He who lives by the sword shall perish by the champagne cocktail.

Saul Alinsky

Henry Cabot was as cool as an undertaker at a hanging.

H.L. Mencken

It is not true that I am surrounded by yes-men. When I say no everybody says no.

Joseph Stalin

IPolitical satire died the moment Henry Kissinger received the Nobel Peace Prize.

Tom Lehrer

I do not often attack the Labour Party. They do it so well themselves.

Edward Heath

For six years the profound silence of the Coolidge administration was mistaken for profound wisdom.

Alben Barkley

I am now celebrating the twentieth anniversary of the first request for my resignation. I look forward to many more.

Richard Darman

I will not upset the apple tart.

Bertie Ahern

Minister Michael Smith's solemn intonation is like that of a monsignor on a bad line from Medjugorje.

Pat Rabbitte

All the contact I have had with politicians has left me feeling as though I had been drinking out of spittoons.

Ernest Hemingway

There are two kinds of truth – the real truth and the made-up truth.

Marion Barry

Corruption is the most infallible system of constitutional liberty.

Edward Gibbon

The way to beat Osama bin Laden is through humiliation. The CIA should kidnap him, give him a sex change operation and send him back to Afghanistan.

Sean Moncrieff

Politics

Any politician who lies to the American people should resign.

Bill Clinton

It would be rude to say that Boris Johnson looks as if he dresses at a charity shop because no charity shop would accept stuff in that condition.

Simon Hoggart

When I introduce myself to an old age pensioner as her local Conservative candidate, she replies, 'Oh, my dear, I know just how you feel. I'm a Jehovah's Witness.'

Juliet Peck

Look, Al, they've discovered a few hundred extra votes over in Florida and they're all yours. Would you like to come over here and take them immediately?

George W. Bush

So long as governments set the example of killing their enemies, private citizens will occasionally kill theirs.

Elbert Hubbard

Points are for appearance only, just like a politician's family.

Drew Carey

They say, 'If you want a friend in Washington, buy a dog,' but I didn't need one because I have Barbara.

George Bush

If Ross Perot runs, that's good for us. If he doesn't run it's good for us, too.

Dan Quayle

What right does congress have to go around making laws just because they deem it necessary? The nerve of some people!

Marion Barry

If you vote for me, not alone will I return Northern Ireland to the Republic, but I'll get back Gibraltar and Hong Kong as well.

John Reidy

What do I think about polls? Well, I have a lot of respect for them, especially the way they drink vodka.

Thelonius Monk

More bad news for the Taliban. Remember how they are promised 72 virgins when they die? Turns out it is only one seventy-two-year-old virgin.

Jay Leno

The public perceive party politics as mud wrestling.

Robin Cook

If somebody's gonna stab me in the back, I want to be there.

Allan Lamport

Politics

This afternoon I slept for two hours in the Library of the House of Commons. A deep House of Commons sleep – rich, deep and guilty.

Henry Channon

The Democratic Party has succeeded so well that many of its members are now Republicans.

Tip O'Neill

The Vice-President is a man who sits in the outer office of the White House, hoping to hear the President sneeze.

H.L. Mencken

Verbosity leads to unclear inarticulate things.

Dan Quayle

Solutions are not the answer.

Richard Nixon

Politics is a choice of enemas. You're going to get it up the ass, no matter what you do.

George Higgins

Votes are like trees if you are trying to build a forest. If you have more trees than you have forests, then at that point the pollsters will probably say you will win.

Dan Quayle

I've left parliament to spend more time on politics.

Tony Benn

There is only one party in this coalition.

Henry McLeish

Britain voted for Margaret Thatcher in a series of regular involuntary spasms throughout the Eighties.

Armando Iannucci

When they call the roll in the Senate, the senators do not know whether to answer 'present' or 'not guilty'.

Theodore Roosevelt

Look, I'm not interested in agriculture – missile silos and stuff. I want to hear about the military stuff.

William Scott

If Senator Donovan can get a resurrection clause into his death penalty bill, I will be willing to give it a second look.

Hugh Carey

Being Vice-President means you get all the French fries the President can't get to.

Al Gore

A newspaper found that fewer than one in twenty people could explain the government's third way. Some thought it was a religious cult, others a sexual position, and one man asked if it were a plan to widen the M25.

Keith Waterhouse

If we open the Pandora's box of the Council of Europe, you never know what Trojan Horses will jump out.

Ernest Bevin

Politics

Richard Milhouse Nixon was the first US President whose name contained all the letters of the word "criminal". The second was William Jefferson Clinton.

Peter Johnson

Crime does not pay as well as politics.

Alfred E. Neumann

Anybody who thinks that the Liberal Democrats are a racist party is staring the facts in the face.

Paddy Ashdown

I'm not a politician; I just play one on TV – kind of like George W. Bush.

Bradley Whitford

We need a President who is fluent in at least one language.

Buck Henry

I don't really want to go to my cake-decorating class, but we're electing a new secretary and it's like everything else: if the rank and file don't go, the militants take over.

Alan Bennett

My friends, no matter how rough the road may be, we can and we will never, never surrender to what is right.

Dan Quayle

I want to make sure that everybody who has a job wants a job.

George W. Bush

Politics is the entertainment branch of industry.

Frank Zappa

Politics is the systematic organisation of hatreds.

Henry Adams

I'm not going to have some reporters pawing through our papers. We are the President.

Hillary Clinton

We have learned from Al Gore that you can be Vice-President during America's most prosperous period, run against a dumb guy, get more votes, and still lose.

David Letterman

The first black President will be a politician who is black.

Douglas Wilder

Jimmy Carter is a great ex-President. It's a shame he couldn't have gone directly to the ex-Presidency.

Thomas Mann

I'm convinced there's a small room in the attic of the Foreign Office where future diplomats are taught to stammer.

Peter Ustinov

I have never concealed that, in my youth, I was a Conservative, but never, in the depth of my ignorance or degradation, was I a Liberal.

James Maxton

Politics

I oppose the plan to reform the House of Lords. I will be sad, if I look down after my death and don't see my son asleep on the same benches on which I slept.

Lord Onslow

Haig offered me a job explaining US foreign policy to the Chinese – one by one.

Henry Kissinger

David Steel has passed from rising hope to elder statesman without any intervening period whatsoever.

Michael Frost

The average Australian politician wouldn't know a tram was up him unless the bell rang.

Les Patterson

Two hundred years from now, they will probably go, 'And that's why we always castrate the President when he gets elected.'

John Hockenberry

As Margaret Thatcher is partly responsible for the Channel tunnel, why not erect her statue at the French end? If that doesn't deter immigrants, nothing will.

R. Smith

Ever since the Republican landslide on 8 November, it's been getting dark outside a little earlier every day. You notice that?

Mario Cuomo

Voting Tory is like being in trouble with the police. You'd rather the neighbours didn't know.

Charles Kennedy

There is but one way for a newspaperman to look at a politician and that is down.

Frank Simonds

A week is a long time in politics and three weeks is twice as long.

Rosie Barnes

The street was in a rather rough neighbourhood. It was near the Houses of Parliament.

Oscar Wilde

A politician is a fellow who will lay down your life for his country.

Texas Guinan

I'm not going back into government, even if I'm asked.

Peter Mandelson

There are liars, damn liars and politicians.

Will Rogers

I've had a tough time learning how to be a Congressman. Today I accidentally spent some of my own money.

Joseph P. Kennedy II

Politics

Tony Blair has pushed moderation to extremes.

Robert MacLennan

Liberals think that goats are just sheep from broken homes.

Malcolm Bradbury

I don't intend to write a book until Northern Ireland settles down a bit.

Albert Reynolds

Florida Secretary of State Katherine Harris has announced that she is running for congress. Though she may run unopposed, many believe it will be an extremely dirty campaign.

Jimmy Fallon

George Bush's lips are where words go to die.

Garrison Keillor

The Conservative establishment has always treated women as nannies, grannies and fannies.

Teresa Gorman

I have done the public. Some service! And they know it.

Charles J. Haughey

Politicians feel an enormous sexual pull towards mirrors.

Richard Condon

Republicans have been accused of abandoning the poor. It's the other way around. They never vote for us.

Dan Quayle

For seven-and-a-half years I've worked alongside President Reagan. We've had triumphs. Made some mistakes. We've had some sex ... uh, setbacks.

George Bush

I am motivated thirty per cent by public service, forty per cent by sheer egomania and thirty per cent by disapproval of swankpot journalists.

Boris Johnson

How do you tell a communist? Well, it's someone who reads Marx and Lenin. And how do you tell an anti-communist? It's someone who understands Marx and Lenin.

Ronald Reagan

Democracy means that anyone can grow up to be President, and anyone who doesn't grow up can be Vice-President.

Johnny Carson

We must resist the Tallybin.

John Prescott

With the money I spent to have JFK elected I could have elected my chauffeur.

Joe Kennedy

Politics

Dukakis never became President because his name was too much of a mouthful.

Bill Clinton

Mr Heath envies me two things. First, I have a first-class honours degree. Second, I am a gentleman.

Quentin Hogg

I hope my phone is still tapped. It's my only remaining link with the establishment.

Tony Benn

Conor Cruise O'Brien has done more to unify public opinion than any other person in Irish history. Thousands of people who disagree on absolutely everything else are united in their hatred of the Cruiser.

Fergus Lawlor

If there is anything a public servant hates to do it's doing something for the public.

Kin Hubbard

You know what they say – don't get mad get angry.

Edwina Currie

Tony Blair is just Bill Clinton with his zip done up.

Neil Hamilton

The difference between Christianity and Communism is that Christians believe in life after death whereas Communists believe in posthumous rehabilitation.

Timothy Ash

He was having sexual intercourse with a woman who, in the middle of the proceedings, announced that she voted Conservative. It offended his socialist principles so deeply that he threw her out of his bed and into the street.

Jeffrey Bernard

I was wondering what dreadful things I must have done in a previous life to end up as Sports Minister in this one.

Tony Banks

Everyone has a skeleton in the closet. The difference between Bill Clinton and myself is that he has a walk-in closet.

Pat Buchanan

Don't buy a single vote more than is necessary. I'll be damned if I'm going to pay for a landslide.

Joseph Kennedy

Anyone in Nelson Mandela's position needs to be whiter than white.

Jill Knight

If Richard Nixon was second-rate, what in the world is third-rate?

Joseph Heller

The President doesn't want yes-men around. When he says no, we all say no.

Elizabeth Dole

Politics

At an election meeting an old woman in the crowd called me a bastard. I replied, 'Mother, I told you to stay at home.'

F.E. Smith

How can the Republican Party nominate Thomas Dewey, a man who looks like the bridegroom on a wedding cake?

Alice Longworth

The EU Summit in Barcelona was a joy as ever.

Tony Blair

At the photo call, Baroness Thatcher said I should be on her right. I replied that this would be difficult.

Edward Heath

All of the black people are screwing up my democracy.

Ian Smith

Ronald Reagan was an actor and after-dinner speaker.

Barry Phelps

Albert Einstein held that nothing could move faster than light. I beg to differ. He never saw anybody reach for the TV remote control when a Party Political broadcast comes on the screen.

Des MacHale

I've wanted to be President for a long time and the year 2000 is looking like my opportunity.

Dan Quayle

I would never do anything to deride the profession of politics – although I think it is a form of madness.

Alec Douglas-Home

Character is a journey, not a destination.

Bill Clinton

Michael Heseltine canvassed like a child molester hanging around the lavatories.

Norman Lamont

Sometimes in politics you just have to lie and I think we should tell the truth about that.

Charles Kennedy

The crunch time for tolerance in this country will be when gays and lesbians can openly admit they are Conservatives.

Philip Levy

Flying the Union Jack is a bit like a eunuch being given his nuts back for a few days to wear as earrings.

Julie Burchill

This measure is unparalysed in the history of the state of Texas.

Gib Lewis

Are you labouring under the impression that I read those memoranda of yours? I can't even lift them.

Franklin D. Roosevelt

Politics

An elector is one who enjoys the sacred privilege of voting for the man of another man's choice.

Ambrose Bierce

The French have all the gifts except that of running their country.

James Cameron

John Major flashed the sort of practised smile that comes from a thousand meetings with Prime Ministers of countries most people thought were just anagrams.

Jeremy Paxman

The trap was so big I have seen Middle East wars started over smaller areas of sand.

David Feherty

The British are the first race in the world and the more of it we rule, the better it is for the world.

Cecil Rhodes

I am not accusing Mrs Thatcher of lying. I am merely suggesting that she has what psychologists call 'selective amnesia'.

Denis Healey

I wouldn't put Jimmy Carter and his party in charge of snake control in Ireland.

Eugene McCarthy

Stamps are adorned with kings and presidents that we may lick their hinder parts and thump their heads.

Howard Nemerov

Politics

There is no way in this world you're going to make a
political party respectable unless you keep it out of office.

Will Rogers

Nothing can be said about politics that hasn't already been
said about haemorrhoids.

Denis Leary

Religion

Religion

I've always fancied being a monk – drinking mead, tending gardens and making honey.

Vic Reeves

If there is no Hell, a good many preachers are obtaining money under false pretences.

William Sunday

More people are driven insane through religious hysteria than by drinking alcohol.

W.C. Fields

I admire the Pope. I have a lot of respect for anyone who can tour without an album.

Rita Rudner

In the beginning there was nothing and God said 'Let there be light', and there was still nothing, but everybody could see it.

Dave Thomas

Those characters in the Bible who rent their garments – wouldn't it have been less expensive to buy them in the first place?

Paul Merton

The good Lord never gives you more than you can handle. Unless you die of something.

Steve Martin

I am half-Catholic and half-Jewish. When I go to confession, I bring my lawyer with me.

Ed Mann

One half of the world does not believe in God and the other half does not believe in me.

Oscar Wilde

He stopped sinning suddenly – he died.

Elbert Hubbard

So my dear brethren which would you prefer, to be in the light with the five wise virgins or in the dark with the five foolish virgins?

Alan Bennett

Being a Catholic doesn't stop you from sinning. It just stops you from enjoying it.

Cleveland Amory

In some copies of the article 'The Power of the Papacy' the Pope was described as His Satanic Majesty. This should have read The Roman Antichrist.

Ian Paisley

Sailors ought never to go to church. They ought to go to hell, where it is much more comfortable.

H.G. Wells

I don't think God gets enough recognition for what He does.

Mandy Smith

I do not accept the word of the slanderous bachelor who lives on the banks of the Tiber.

Ian Paisley

Religion

The merit claimed for the Anglican Church is that, if you let it alone, it will let you alone.

Ralph W. Emerson

If absolute power corrupts absolutely, where does that leave God?

George Deacon

I have four children, which is not bad considering I am not a Catholic.

Peter Ustinov

God in his goodness gave us brains so that we would have the wisdom to know when not to use them.

Hugh Leonard

There can hardly be a town in the South of England where you could throw a brick without hitting the niece of a bishop.

George Orwell

I never pray on a golf course. Actually, the Lord answers my prayers everywhere except on the course.

Bill Graham

The one thing father always gave up for Lent was going to church.

Clarence Day

Merit, indeed! We are come to a pretty pass if they talk of merit for a bishopric.

Lord Westmorland

Religion

Almost all religions agree that God is fond of music, sometimes of dancing and always of processions.

Robert Morley

As the poet said, 'Only God can make a tree,' probably because it's so hard to figure out how to get the bark on.

Woody Allen

I dislike blasphemy on purely rational grounds. If there is no God, blasphemy is stupid and unnecessary; if there is, it's damned dangerous.

Flann O'Brien

Florence Nightingale felt towards God as she might have felt towards a glorified sanitary engineer; and in some of her speculations she seems hardly to distinguish between the Deity and the Drains.

Lytton Strachey

The day the Catholic and Protestant churches combine, it's the end of all drinking. I'll have to go to Rome to sabotage the affair.

Brendan Behan

The primary function of a priest is to keep his congregation awake.

Peter Ustinov

My friends in Christian Coalition, no matter how rough the road may be, we can and we will never, never surrender to what is right.

Dan Quayle

Religion

If God had intended us to fly, he would have made it easier to get to the airport.

Jonathan Winters

And God said, 'Let there be light'; and there was light, but the Electricity Board said He would have to wait until Thursday to be connected. And God saw the light and it was good; He saw the quarterly bill and that was not good.

Spike Milligan

The Book of Mormon is chloroform in print.

Mark Twain

If ever I come face to face with my maker, I shall say 'God, why did you make the evidence for your existence so insufficient?'

Bertrand Russell

I read the Book of Job last night – I don't think God comes well out of it.

Virginia Woolf

I hear Glenn Hoddle has found God. That must have been one hell of a pass.

Bob Davies

One goldfish told another that he intended to become an atheist. 'Don't be crazy,' the other goldfish replied, 'of course there's a God – who do you think changes the water every day?'

Richard Needham

Eternal nothingness is fine if you happen to be dressed for it.

Woody Allen

At the moment I'm working on a non-fiction version of the Warren Report.

Woody Allen

In 1969 I published a small book on Humility. It was a pioneering work which has not, to my knowledge, been surperseded.

Frank Longford

I shall walk, nay I shall run, through the Valley of Death.

Woody Allen

A survey revealed that 96 per cent of Americans believe in God, 90 per cent pray regularly, 71 per cent believe in an afterlife, and 41 per cent attend church once a week. Another poll found that 3 per cent believe they are God.

James Adams

The Lord created the universe in seven days but the Lord had the wonderful advantage of being able to work alone.

Kofi Annan

The average minister should be unfrocked immediately and prevented, by force if necessary, from communicating any ideas to persons under thirty-five.

W.C. Fields

Religion

A sixty-two-year-old friend of mine went to bed at night and prayed, 'Please God give me skin like a teenager's'. Next day, she woke up with acne.

Phyllis Diller

If you're going to sin, sin against God, not the bureaucracy. God will forgive you but the bureaucracy won't.

Hyman Rickover

An Anglican clergyman is invisible six days a week and incomprehensible on the seventh.

Dean Inge

On one occasion when the Reverend Laurence Chaderton had been preaching for over two hours, he is said to have shown signs of flagging. The congregation then cried out, with one voice: 'For God's sake, Sir, go on!'

Henry Button

Walking in a churchyard I have often asked myself, 'Where are all the bad people buried?'

Charles Lamb

Between projects, I go into the park and bite the grass and wail, 'Why do You make me aware of the fact that I have to die one day?' God says, 'Please, I have Chinese people yelling at me, I haven't time for this.' I say all right. God is like a Jewish waiter, he has too many tables.

Mel Brooks

No mention of God. They keep him up their sleeve for as long as they can, vicars do. They know it puts people off.

Alan Bennett

Religion

Methodism is not really a religion – it's just a sort of insurance policy in case there does turn out to be a God.

Peter Barr

Most of your parishioners will meet you on only three occasions. The first and last, baptism and burial, they are not conscious at all. And the middle one, holy matrimony, they are barely half conscious, if that.

Kenneth Haworth

As luck would have it, Providence was on my side.

Samuel Butler

She believed in nothing. Only her scepticism kept her from being an atheist.

Jean-Paul Sartre

Woody Allen has a face that convinces you that God is a cartoonist.

Jack Kroll

I have always been amazed that women are allowed to enter churches. What sort of conversations can they have with God?

Charles Baudelaire

Every human being commits 630,720,000 sins by the age of thirty.

Augustus Toplady

Religion

There is not the least use in preaching to anyone unless you chance to catch them ill.

Sydney Smith

Lest O Lord this prayer be too obscure, permit thy servant to illustrate it with an anecdote.

Allan Laing

I dreamt last night I was in hell: It was just like a missionary meeting – I couldn't get near the fire for parsons.

Samuel Wilberforce

Satan, who has during all time maintained the imposing position of spiritual head of four-fifths of the human race and political head of the whole of it, must be granted the possession of executive abilities of the loftiest order.

Mark Twain

If it turns out that there is a God, I don't think that he's evil. But the worst you can say about him is that he's an underachiever.

Woody Allen

What a pity that Noah and his party didn't miss the boat.

Mark Twain

I have a fear that there is an afterlife but no one will know where it's being held.

Woody Allen

There are three sorts of country parson in my diocese. Those who have gone out of their minds. Those who are going out of their minds. And those who have no minds to go out of.

Edward King

To you I'm an atheist; to God, I'm the loyal opposition.

Woody Allen

If God can do anything, can He make a stone so heavy that He cannot lift it?

A.A. Milne

His was the sort of career that made the Recording Angel think seriously about taking up shorthand.

Nicholas Bentley

In the beginning, the universe was created. This has made a lot of people very angry, and is generally considered to be have been a bad move.

Douglas Adams

The Bible doesn't forbid suicide. It's a Catholic directive, intended to slow down their loss of martyrs.

Ellen Blackstone

I'd love to see Christ come back to crush the spirit of hate and make men put down their guns. I'd also like just one more hit single.

Tiny Tim

Giving away a fortune is carrying Christianity too far.

Charlotte Bingham

Religion

Serving God is doing good to man, but praying is thought an easier service and therefore more generally chosen.

Benjamin Franklin

It is the function of vice to keep virtue within reasonable bounds.

Samuel Butler

I'm going to take a moment to contemplate most of the Western religions. I'm looking for something soft on morality, generous with holidays, and with a very short initiation period.

David Addison

Mohammed is one of the most common Christian names in the world.

David Jensen

I know God will not give me anything I can't handle. I just wish that He didn't trust me so much.

Mother Teresa

I once asked a man what he thought would happen to him after he died. He replied that he believed he would inherit eternal bliss, but he didn't wish to talk about such unpleasant subjects.

F. W. Myers

A lie is a very poor substitute for the truth, but the only one known to date.

Ambrose Bierce

Lutherans are like Scottish people, only with less frivolity.

Garrison Keillor

Only a vegan nun who has taken a vow of silence lives without hurting anyone.

Tim Rayment

Of course heaven forbids certain pleasures, but one finds means of compromise.

Molière

There is a charm about the forbidden that makes it unspeakably desirable.

Mark Twain

Everybody has a God-given right to be an atheist.

Michael Patton

December 10, 1777 Jas. Soaper hanged for stealing a nail.
December 14, 1777 Jas. Soaper found to be innocent.
December 17, 1777 Jas. Soaper dug up and removed to Consecrated Ground.

Michael Green

I can discern no difference in behaviour between English Protestant and English atheist.

Cyril Connolly

Bless me father for I have sinned. I'm just in here to develop the film.

Emo Philips

Religion

I want to introduce you to my mother. We have founded a society for the suppression of virtue.

Oscar Wilde

After washing twelve pairs of such feet, the crucifixion must have been a pushover.

Alan Bennett

As the Bible says, it is easier for a rich man to get through the eye of a needle than for a camel to get into heaven.

Andy Mulligan

Honesty consists not in never stealing but in knowing where to stop stealing, and how to make good use of what one steals.

Samuel Butler

Originality is no longer possible, even in sin.

Oscar Wilde

I don't have a religion – I am an Irish protestant.

Oscar Wilde

The Catholic Church is for saints and sinners. For respectable people the Anglican Church will do.

Oscar Wilde

The Church of England is constituted so that its members can really believe anything, but of course almost none of them do.

Alan Bennett

I looked as out of place as a Presbyterian in hell.

Mark Twain

The legend of Saint Denis, who carried his severed head for six miles after his execution, teaches us that the distance is not important; it is only the first step that is difficult.

Marquise Du Deffand

Greater love no man hath than to attend the Episcopal Church with his wife.

Lyndon B. Johnson

You can tell a lot about a person's personality if you know his sign; Jesus: born on 25 December; fed the 5,000; walked on water – typical Capricorn.

Harry Hill

Do not be led astray into the paths of virtue.

Oscar Wilde

How holy people look when they are seasick.

Samuel Butler

This fellow in the theatre asked me 'Is this seat saved?' I said, 'If Aquinas reasoned that even animals have no souls, how much less chance does an inanimate object like a chair have of gaining salvation?'

Emo Philips

Blessed are they who can laugh at themselves, for they shall never cease to be amused.

Fulton J. Sheen

Religion

I would suggest the following rider to the Ten Commandments: candidates should not attempt more than six of these.

Hilaire Belloc

I let the Jehovah Witness carry on for a while before I tell her that this is not a Christian settlement and although the tribes that live here are friendly, they are incapable of being converted.

Robert Morley

I wonder if other dogs think poodles are members of some weird religious cult.

Rita Rudner

When my cat died my mother said, 'Don't cry, your cat's in heaven with God now,' and I thought, 'What does God want with a dead cat?'

Emo Philips

They say Hell is hot, but is it humid? Because I can take the heat; it's the humidity I can't stand.

Ronnie Shakes

We do not become more moral as we grow older; we just choose our sins more carefully.

Dean Inge

What God has created asunder, let not man put together.

Ralph Waldo Emerson

Three little boys were each asked to put a penny in the church collection and to quote a verse from the Scriptures as they did so. The first said, 'It is more blessed to give than to receive.' The second said, 'The Lord loves a cheerful giver.' The third said, 'The fool and his money are soon parted.'

Benny McHale

Men are the only animals who devote themselves assiduously to making one another unhappy. It is, I suppose, one of their godlike qualities.

H.L. Mencken

Charity is an amiable quality of the heart which moves us to condone in others the sins and vices to which we ourselves are addicted.

Ambrose Bierce

When they swore Clinton in, they used his family Bible. You know, the one with seven commandments.

David Letterman

There is no stigma attached to being a saint.

Padre Pio

Biography is now the only certain form of life after death.

David Cannadine

My favourite item from an Ulster newspaper went like this: 'Man and woman wanted to look after two cows, both Protestant.'

Frank Carson

Religion

My prayer to the Lord every day is this – I have been a great sinner. I do not deserve Heaven. Let me stay here.

Andres Segovia

Aunt Sadie so much disliked hearing about health that people often took her for a Christian Scientist, which, indeed, she might have become had she not disliked hearing about religion even more.

Nancy Mitford

Among the most famous bachelors are almost all of the Popes.

P.J. O'Rourke

I've made up my mind that for the next ten weeks, I'm going to keep one of the Ten Commandments each week until I've got through all ten of them.

H.L. Mencken

I was as unpopular as nipple piercing in a nunnery.

Douglas Adams

If everybody flew naked not only would you never have to worry about the passenger next to you having explosive shoes, but no religious fundamentalist would ever fly nude or in the presence of nude women.

Thomas Friedman

I think we should all treat each other like Christians. I will not, however, be responsible for the consequences.

George Carlin

The Church should send a satellite into space with a bishop in it. It would draw the attention of millions towards God.

Alastair Graham

God doesn't make mistakes. That's how He got to be God.

Archie Bunker

Nothing makes one so vain as being told that one is a sinner.

Oscar Wilde

If Abraham's only son had been a teenager, it wouldn't have been a sacrifice.

Scott Spendlove

Ambiguity is the Devil's volleyball.

Emo Philips

As a boy, I was expelled from a Catholic College for casting doubt on the Bible by asking how Noah was able, in the Palestine desert, to take a penguin on board the Ark.

Nikolaus Chrastry

'Oh no,' said God on the fourth day, 'I've gone and made a spider which can kill a man just by looking at them. I need somewhere to put it.' So on the fifth day he created Australia.

Jeremy Clarkson

Religion

Loving your neighbour as much as yourself is practically impossible. You might as well have a commandment that states, 'Thou shalt fly.'

John Cleese

My mother is a Muslim – she walks five steps behind my father. She doesn't have to. He just looks better from behind.

Shazia Mirza

As a child I experienced the rigours of the Scottish Sabbath, where the highlight was a visit to the cemetery.

T.C. Smout

It was Martin Luther's digestion that caused the Reformation. That diet of worms.

Patrick Murray

There is no memory with less satisfaction in it than the memory of some temptation we resisted.

James Cabell

You just have to work with what God sends, and if God doesn't seem to understand the concept of commercial success, then that's your bad luck.

Michael Frayn

I hear Joad has rediscovered God: I imagine he pronounces it with a soft G and a long O.

Lowes Dickinson

No man is free who has even one foot caught in a dingo trap.

John Law

At the holy season of Easter one is supposed to forgive all one's friends.

Oscar Wilde

Virtue is nothing more than vice tired out.

Josh Billings

I cannot stand Christians because they are never Catholics and I cannot stand Catholics because they are never Christians – otherwise I am at one with the Indivisible Church.

Oscar Wilde

There were times when Tolstoy thought of himself as God's brother, indeed God's elder brother.

Paul Johnson

I once replied to a street evangelist, 'You mean that Jesus is coming and you're dressed like that?'

Scott Caparro

I would be converted to any religion for a cigar and baptised in it for a box of them.

H.L. Mencken

My wife converted me to religion – I didn't believe in Hell until I met her.

Henny Youngman

Religion

I would like to go to Heaven. But if Jeffrey Archer is there, I want to go to Lewisham.

Spike Milligan

The Protestant Church looks after you from the womb to the tomb, but the Catholic Church looks after you from erection to resurrection.

Brendan Behan

It is unclear from historical documentation which war the Salvation Army fought, but it is apparent from their spoils that they won.

Dan Levin

Fortunately my parents were intelligent, enlightened people. They accepted me for exactly what I was: a punishment from God.

Dave Steinberg

The way of the transgressor is hard because it's so crowded.

Kin Hubbard

I was saved because witches always weigh less than a Bible.

Jane Wenham

I see my body as a temple or at least a relatively well-managed Presbyterian youth centre.

Emo Philips

Let the meek inherit the earth – they have it coming to them.

James Thurber

The early Christian gets the fattest lion.

H.H. Munro

If God wanted us to be brave, why did He give us legs?

Marvin Kitman

God punishes us mildly by ignoring our prayers and severely by answering them.

Richard Needham

I always like to associate with a lot of priests because it makes me understand anti-clerical things so well.

Hilaire Belloc

He had the morals of a Baptist Sunday School superintendent in Paris for the first time.

H.L. Mencken

A recent admission to hospital entailed mandatory form filling. 'Religion?' I was asked. 'None,' I replied. After a moment's hesitation, the auxiliary wrote: 'Nun.'

Julia Shipton

I have known clergymen, good men, kind-hearted, liberal, sincere, who did not know the meaning of a poker flush. It is enough to make one ashamed of the species.

Mark Twain

Just how many more witnesses do they need before Jehovah's trial starts?

Tom Shields

Religion

I'm Jewish. Jews don't exercise. We sell the equipment.

Joan Rivers

If God had not given us sticky tape, it would have been
necessary for us to invent it.

Emo Philips

Cardinal Goestheveezl became the shortest reigning prelate
in the history of the Church.

Joe Joseph

I generally avoid temptation, unless I can't resist it.

Mae West

And when God, who created the entire universe with all its
glories, decides to deliver a message to humanity, He will
not use as His personal messenger a person on cable TV
with a bad haircut.

Jerry Seinfeld

The younger men on *The Times* used to call Alexander
Woollcott 'God's big brother'.

Howard Teichman

Next time I'm in America, I may do a two-week intensive
priesthood course.

Robbie Williams

Richard Baerlein's father decided to calculate the chances of
life after death. He requested his family to give him a pile of
sandwiches and a Thermos flask of coffee and he then

retired to his room for the weekend. He emerged on
Monday morning announcing that the chances were 'little
better than five to two against'.

Jeffrey Bernard

Many clergymen grow beards to cover a multiple of chins.

Barry Hill

I'm a Muslim and I'm really looking forward to my
wedding day; I can't wait to meet my husband.

Shazia Mirza

God is good; but don't dance in a small boat.

Sean Desmond

Jesus loves you – well, someone has to.

John O'Connor

God! You've been keeping records on me. How many times
did I take the Lord's name in vain? One million and six?
Jesus Christ.

Steve Martin

Opportunity knocks only once; if you hear a second knock,
it's very probably a Jehovah's Witness.

John O'Connor

If God wanted people not to desire nuns, why did he dress
them in the most startling erotic clothes ever invented?

Simon Bell

Religion

If ever I utter an oath again may my soul be blasted to eternal damnation.

George Bernard Shaw

Like dear St Francis of Assisi, I am wedded to poverty; but in my case, the marriage is not a success.

Oscar Wilde

Abel started it.

Cain

A bishop is merely a clergyman with political interests.

John Hankin

Religion is when you kill each other to see who has the best imaginary friend.

Steven Wright

The reason there is so much smog in Los Angeles is so God can't see what they're doing down there.

Glen Campbell

I have always envisaged death and the Resurrection of the body as like finding your motorcar after a party.

Nancy Mitford

My mother is an orthodox paranoid, and while she doesn't believe in an afterlife, she doesn't believe in a present one either.

Woody Allen

There is no question that there is an unseen world. The problem is, how far is it from midtown and how late is it open?

Woody Allen

We will now sing hymn number forty-two – Holy, Holy, Holy; all the holies, forty-two.

Marty Feldman

Have a little fun. Soon enough you'll be dead and burning in hell with the rest of your family.

George Carlin

In every way, I wish to imitate my maker, and, like Him, I want nothing but praise.

Oscar Wilde

Surely Providence can resist temptation by this time.

Oscar Wilde

Remember the good Lord made your eyes, Pla-gi-ar-ize!

Tom Lehrer

We Bishops, in our proper dress, originated the mini-skirt. But we allowed Mary Quant to steal the thunder and make three million quid out of it last year.

Victor Pike

I see the Church of England as an elderly lady, who mutters away to herself in a corner, ignored most of the time.

George Carey

Religion

Never read the Bible or prayers as if it means something.
The liturgy is best treated and read as if it's someone
announcing the departure of trains.

Alan Bennett

The Lord giveth and the landlord taketh away.

John Raper

To die is to stop sinning suddenly.

Elbert Hubbard

Next to a circus there ain't nothing that packs up and
moves out of town quicker than the Christmas spirit.

Kin Hubbard

They were so old they were waiters at the Last Supper.

Tommy Lasorda

Science and Technology

Science and Technology

To protect yourself from nuclear radiation, all you have to do is to go down to the bottom of your swimming pool and hold your breath.

David Miller

I am an expert on electricity. My father occupied the chair of applied electricity at the State Prison.

W.C. Fields

Weather forecast for tonight: dark.

George Carlin

What is algebra exactly? Is it those three-cornered things?

J.M. Barrie

Quod Erat Demonstrandum is Latin for 'Don't argue with ME, you bastard.'

Russell Bell

The heart of the airport security system is the metal detector, a device that shoots invisible rays into your body. According to security personnel, these rays are perfectly harmless, although you notice that THEY never go through the metal detector. In fact, when nobody's around, they use it to cook their lunch.

Dave Barry

I saw Cher on TV promoting a sugar substitute. She said, 'You care more about what you put in your car than you do about what you put in your body.' Thanks, Cher. But I never put silicone breast implants in my car.

Denis Leary

The trouble with the Internet is that it is replacing masturbation as a leisure activity.

Patrick Murray

If the B-2 is invisible, why don't we just announce we've built a hundred of them and not build them?

John Kasich

The Irish Sea is naturally radioactive. The Sellafield discharges are less radioactive than the sea they are discharged into.

Cecil Parkinson

A tree is a tree. How many more do you need to look at?

Ronald Reagan

The most dreaded words in the English language are 'some assembly required'.

Bill Cosby

Electricity is of two kinds, positive and negative. The difference is, I presume, that one comes a little more expensive, but is more durable; the other is a cheaper thing, but the moths get into it.

Stephen Leacock

You ask me if I keep a notebook in which to record my great ideas. I've only ever had one.

Albert Einstein

Science and Technology

Beware of experts. The day humans blow up the world with The Bomb the last survivor will be an expert saying it can never happen.

Peter Ustinov

The best thing about the rain forests is that they never suffer from drought.

Dan Quayle

A Danish lady of one hundred and four was summoned to enrol in a nursery school because the computer only went up to ninety-nine and she appeared on the records as being five years old.

Peter Ustinov

You can stop almost anything from functioning by hitting it with a large rock.

Russell Bell

Well, if I called the wrong number, why did you answer the phone?

James Thurber

A stitch in time would have confused Einstein.

Steven Wright

Ghosts can walk through walls, how come they don't fall through the floor?

Steven Wright

Fish are so underrated these days, especially sand dabs – all of them really. I could go on and on about it. I do, actually.

People say to me, 'Don't go on about fish today, please, Jack'. And I say, 'Just tell me one thing – can you breathe under water?' And of course, I have them there.

John Cleese

A bishop wrote gravely to the *Times* inviting all nations to destroy 'the formula' of the atomic bomb. There is no simple remedy for ignorance so abysmal.

Peter Medaway

The wise individual doesn't get too attached to any of life's pleasures, knowing that wonderful science is hard at work proving it's bad for him.

Bill Vaughan

If builders built buildings the way computer programmers write programs, the first woodpecker that came along would destroy civilisation.

Reede Stockton

The only reason we had a son was to get someone to work the video. For ten years we used it as a night light.

Adrian Walsh

The ancient Greeks, aided by a warm climate, invented geometry and they used this advanced knowledge to conquer the surrounding cultures by piercing them with the ends of isosceles triangles.

Dave Barry

Everything that can be invented has been invented.

Charles Duell

Science and Technology

Sponges grow in the ocean. That kills me. I wonder how much deeper the ocean would be if that didn't happen?

Steven Wright

The greatest unsolved problem in science is this – how can you be sitting on a damp towel for half an hour and not realise it until you stand up?

Patrick Murray

Automatic simply means that you cannot repair it yourself.

Frank Capra

I am convinced UFOs exist because I have seen one.

Jimmy Carter

It is to be regretted that domestication has seriously deteriorated the moral character of the duck. In the wild state he is a faithful husband; but no sooner is he domesticated than he becomes polygamous, and makes nothing of owning ten or a dozen wives at a time.

Isabella Beaton

Mathematics was always my bad subject. I couldn't convince my teachers that many of my answers were meant ironically.

Calvin Trillin

Why is it that everything else can be written on paper, but mathematics and cave paintings have to be done in chalk?

A.A. Gill

Eighty-two point six per cent of statistics are made up on the spot.

Vic Reeves

Have you ever smelt a rain forest? They stink. They stink worse than a 13-year-old's bedroom.

A.A. Gill

An expert is a man who has stopped thinking. Why should he think? He is an expert!

Frank Lloyd Wright

The New York State Museum found my wife's shoe. On the basis of its measurements, they constructed a dinosaur.

Woody Allen

Life is anything that dies when you stamp on it.

Dave Barry

Beware of computer programmers who carry screwdrivers.

Leonard Brandwein

UNIX is basically a simple operating system, but you have to be a genius to understand the simplicity.

Dennis Ritchie

The factory of the future will have only two employees, a man and a dog. The man will be there to feed the dog. The dog will there to keep the man from touching the equipment.

Warren G. Bennis

Science and Technology

If rhino horn is such a powerful aphrodisiac, why are rhinos an endangered species?

Rory McGrath

The best defence against the atom bomb is not to be there when it goes off.

Winston Churchill

Printing broke out in the province of Kansu in AD 86. The early Chinese simply could not let well enough alone.

Bill Cuppy

The secret of creativity is knowing how to hide your sources.

Albert Einstein

The perfect computer has been developed. You just feed in your problems and they never come out again.

Al Goodman

The greatest invention in history is the safety pin. The second greatest is perforated toilet paper.

Tiny Tim

Death is a low chemical trick played on everybody except sequoia trees.

J.J. Furnas

He has an IQ of about room temperature.

Dan Hampton

The avocado is a lavatory-coloured fruit.

Mike Barfield

The Fourth Law of Thermodynamics states that if the probability of success is not almost one, then it is damn near zero.

David Ellis

Recent evidence suggests that normal body temperature is 89.4°F and that mankind is running a temperature.

Cully Abrell

Many snakes are actually quite short if you don't count the tail.

John Thompson

Monkeys and apes have the ability to speak but keep silent to avoid being put to work.

René Descartes

In France in the eighteenth century a combination lock was exhibited which required 3,674,385 turns of the dial to open and close it. It took one man 120 nights to lock and another man an additional 120 nights to unlock.

Bruce Felton

If everyone on earth stopped breathing for just an hour, the greenhouse effect would no longer be a problem.

Jerry Adler

Jocky Wilson is the minimum of mass into which a human being can be contracted.

Nancy Banks-Smith

Science and Technology

The ant sets an example to us all, but it is not a good one.

Max Beerbohm

An old lady of my acquaintance went into her greengrocer's and asked for a pound of potatoes. On being told that everything was kilos now, she said, 'All right, I'll have a pound of kilos then.'

Matthew Parris

Virtual reality is a cutting edge computer science project in which companies are investing millions of dollars in a frenzied attempt to reproduce an effect which can currently be achieved by simply looking out of the window.

Mike Barfield

My dog understands every word I say but ignores it.

Michael Green

The smallest hole will eventually empty the largest container, unless it is made intentionally for drainage, in which case it will clog.

Dave Grissom

The most overlooked advantage to owning a computer is that if they foul up there's no law against whacking them around a little.

Eric Porterfield

Chaos Theory is a new theory invented by scientists panicked by the thought that the public were beginning to understand the old ones.

Mike Barfield

Scientists have discovered a noise made just prior to the Big Bang which sounds something like 'oops'.

Cully Abrell

Sex is just the mathematics urge sublimated.

M.C. Reed

He was a multi-millionaire. He made all his money designing the little diagrams that tell which way to put batteries in.

Steven Wright

In Vegas I got into a long argument with the man at the roulette wheel over what I considered to be an odd number.

Steven Wright

If ants are such busy workers, how come they find time to go to all the picnics?

Marie Dressler

The best way to tell gold is to pass a nugget around in a crowded bar. If it comes back, it's not gold.

Lennie Lower

I don't understand electricity. All I know is that it soothes me.

Emo Philips

Don't buy fur. Do you realise that for every fur coat, twenty trees have to die to make the protest placards.

Emo Philips

Science and Technology

The mathematics of love: $1 + 1 = ?$; $2 - 1 = 0$

Mignon McLaughlin

The chopper has changed my life as conclusively as it did for Anne Boleyn.

Elizabeth Bowes-Lyon

For every action there is an equal and opposite government programme.

Bob Wells

When my screen froze, the manual suggested I reboot the computer. So I kicked it again.

Randy Budnikas

My wife is a sound driver. When parking the car she listens for the crunch and then stops.

Laurence Millington

A statistician is somebody that thinks that the average person has one breast and one testicle.

Aidan Moran

Why does not science, instead of troubling itself about sunspots, which nobody ever saw, or if they did, ought not to speak about, busy itself with drainage and sanitary engineering?

Oscar Wilde

Does that screwdriver really belong to Philip?

George Carlin

Science and Technology

If a computer cable has one end, then it has another.

Robert Lyall

It's not the heat; it's the humility.

Yogi Berra

I know where my new television set was manufactured. A label on the box said: 'Built-in Antennae.'

Steven Wright

Do not meddle in the affairs of cats, for they are subtle and will piss on your computer.

Bruce Graham

Two-thirds of the world's rainforest has been destroyed during the past ten years of my environmental campaigning. That shows how effective I've been.

Sting

Wow! They've got the Internet on computers now.

Homer Simpson

Nothing travels faster than light, with the possible exception of bad news.

Douglas Adams

The energy crisis is just a Californian problem.

George W. Bush

You can argue about foot and mouth disease until the cows come home.

Elliot Morley

Science and Technology

In 4 b.c., they had a YOK problem – they thought that civilisation would collapse in just four years because they would run out of numbers.

Derek Mitchell

Last year my friend upgraded his Girlfriend 3.1 to Girlfriend 1.0 (marketing name: Fiancée 1.0). Recently he upgraded Fiancée 1.0 to Wife 1.0 and it's a memory hogger, it has taken up all his space; and Wife 1.0 must be running before he can do anything. And Wife 1.0 came with unwanted plug-ins such as Mother-in-Law 1.0 and Brother-in-Law 1.0.

Roger Burton

Statistics are always true, unless you personally know who made them up.

Deepak Chopra

The Law of Probability Dispersal states that whatever hits the fan will not be evenly distributed.

Robert Murphy

Whatever happened to those pink-footed geese, the ones Peter Scott used to chase after on that tiny Arctic pony of his?

Robert Morley

Red squirrels – you don't see many of them since they became extinct.

Michael Aspel

A snake should not be in your yard unless it has your written permission.

Dave Barry

Science and Technology

The most overlooked advantage of owning a computer is that if they foul up, there's no law against whacking them around a little.

Joe Martins

Some people lose all respect for a lion unless he devours them instantly. There is no pleasing some people.

Will Cuppy

The current trend in television sets is to buy a screen so wide that it makes even Ally McBeal look as though she needs to shed a few pounds.

Barry Collins

How can we have any new ideas or fresh outlooks in science when ninety per cent of all the scientists who have ever lived have still not died?

Alan Mackay

Cats are smarter than dogs. You can't get eight cats to pull a sled through snow.

Jeff Valdez

Space is big, really big. You may think it's a long way down the road to the chemist's, but that's just peanuts.

Douglas Adams

In Canada it was thirty degrees below zero, and it would have been much colder if the thermometer had been longer.

Susanna Moodie

Science and Technology

I never met a robot I didn't like.

Isaac Asimov

Sylvia assisted her father in his experiments – one involved quite a serious fall, jumping off a fast-moving bus to prove that if you leaned forward you would land on your feet.

John Wells

When people run around and around in circles, we say they're crazy. When the planets do it we say they are orbiting.

Dave Barry

Most people are crazy about cars, but I'd rather have a goddamn horse. A horse is at least human, for Christ's sake.

J.D. Salinger

If it looks like a duck and quacks like a duck, we have at least to consider the possibility that we have a small aquatic bird of the family anatidae on our hands.

Douglas Adams

It is time for the human race to enter the Solar System.

Dan Quayle

There is a fierce smell of plutonium in many Dublin public toilets.

Joseph Duffy

A human being is a computer's way of making another computer. We are just a computer's sex organs.

Solomon Short

I thought that heavy water might have a practical use in something like neon signs.

Harold Urey

Science has taught us to pasteurise cheese – but what about the H-bomb? Have you ever thought what would happen if one of those fell off a desk accidentally?

Woody Allen

Flying isn't dangerous; crashing is what's dangerous.

Dave Barry

The propeller is just a big fan in front of the plane used to keep the pilot cool. When it stops you can see the pilot start sweating.

Rodney Dangerfield

If a man becomes a woman or a woman becomes a man, if they are priests they remain priests, willy-nilly.

Michael Scott-Joynt

Fifty-seven different types of alien life forms have been catalogued, some of which look just like humans. They could walk among us and you wouldn't know the difference. Certainly this would explain David Coulthard.

Jeremy Clarkson

Once a nuclear bomb has been dropped in your area it is unlikely that there will ever be another in the district. This is one reassuring point which should be put to the public to reduce panic during a nuclear war.

G.D. Kersley

Science and Technology

Disney World is just a people trap operated by a mouse.

Steven Wright

If the facts don't fit the theory, change the facts.

Albert Einstein

Scientists say there are over 3,000 spiders for every human being on earth. Does anybody want mine? I certainly don't.

Chuck Bonner

What's all this fuss about Plutonium? How can something named after a Disney character be dangerous? Anyway radiation cannot kill you because it contains absolutely no cholesterol.

Johnny Carson

Design flaws travel in groups.

Dave Barry

Our basketball offence is like the theorem of Pythagoras – there's no answer.

Shaquille O'Neal

How would you know if your goldfish was incontinent?

Ray Fitzgerald

Computers are like Old Testament gods: lots of rules and no mercy.

Joseph Campbell

Science and Technology

Entire new continents emerge from the ocean in the time it takes a Web page to show up on your screen.

Dave Barry

The Safari Park had a notice reading: 'Elephants Please Stay in Your Car.'

Spike Milligan

It is extremely difficult to tell the age of a snake unless you know exactly when it was born.

Will Cuppy

I like to melt dry ice so I can take a bath without getting wet.

Steven Wright

Where did the guy who messed up the invention of the drawing board go back to?

Steven Wright

People who count their chickens before they are hatched act very wisely: because once hatched, chickens run about so absurdly that it is impossible to count them accurately.

Oscar Wilde

Astrology proves at least one scientific fact – there's one born every minute.

Patrick Moore

A non-technical person is someone who cannot open a childproof bottle without an axe.

Dave Barry

Science and Technology

Britain is inching its way towards the metric system.

Harriet Harman

I'm so tired – I was up all night trying to round off infinity.

Steven Wright

I'm not so good a swimmer as I used to be, thanks to evolution.

Emo Philips

To bathe a cat takes brute force, perseverance, courage – and a cat. This last ingredient is usually the hardest to come by.

Stephen Baker

Can technology really be the answer when my toaster has never once worked properly in four years? I followed the instructions and pushed two slices of bread down in the slots, and seconds later they rifled upwards. Once they broke the nose of a woman I loved very dearly.

Woody Allen

Helicopters can't fly; they're just so ugly the earth repels them.

Dave Barry

I believe that mink are raised for being turned into fur coats and if we didn't wear fur coats, these little animals would never have been born. So is it better not to have been born or to have lived for a year or two and be turned into a fur coat?

Barbi Benton

Science and Technology

If you leave aside Three Mile Island and Chernobyl, the safety record of nuclear power is really very good.

Paul O'Neill

The statistics in this chapter are entirely my own invention.

Robert Morley

I don't kill flies but I like to torture them psychologically. I hold them above a globe. They freak out and think, 'Whoa, I'm way too high.'

Bruce Baum

Whose bicycle pump did Dunlop borrow to blow up the first pneumatic tyre?

Tom Shields

The attention span of a computer is as long only as its electrical cord.

Eugene Turnaucka

With every passing hour our solar system comes forty-three thousand miles closer to a globular cluster, M13 in the constellation Hercules, and still there are some misfits who continue to insist that there is no such thing as progress.

Ransom Ferm

I'm all for computer dating, but I wouldn't want my sister to marry one.

Emo Philips

Science and Technology

If you put garbage in a computer nothing comes out but garbage. But this garbage, having passed through a very expensive machine, is somehow ennobled and none dare criticise it.

Aaron Fuegi

A new computer printer can produce two hundred and fifty pages a minute. It certainly cuts down on the paperwork.

S.J. Wilcox

Dennis Priestly's darts are going into the sixty slot in angles that Hypotenuse never dreamed of.

Sid Waddell

Halley's Comet is a distinct blur.

Tom Shields

The difference between a battery and a woman is that the battery has a positive side.

Johnny Sharpe

I like dolphins. If dolphins were human, I'd like to be a dolphin.

Jason Donovan

The most powerful force in the Universe is gossip.

Mary Poole

Nothing is faster than light. To prove this to yourself, try opening the refrigerator door before the light comes on.

Aaron Fuegi

Pavlova's dog.

David Penhaligon

Some of these players can land darts on the nucleus of a proton.

Sid Waddell

Never trust a computer bigger than you can lift.

Dave Barry

The number of atoms in your body is one billion billion billion – even more than that if you're Robbie Coltrane.

Jeremy Clarkson

I avoid oysters, which are members of the phlegm family. I have never seen oysters reproduce, but I would not be surprised to learn that the process involves giant undersea nostrils.

Dave Barry

I believe in computer dating – but only if the computers really love each other.

Groucho Marx

Have you any idea how many little polyesters had to die to make that shirt of yours?

Steve Martin

British genius consists of an infinite capacity for making drains.

Lilian Knowles

Science and Technology

David Attenborough informs, entertains and educates, sometimes in the presence of unbelievable quantities of bat faeces.

Lynne Truss

Fifty per cent of the public doesn't know what 'fifty per cent' means.

Patricia Hewitt

There are ten types of people in the country: those who understand binary and those who don't.

Jeremy Paxman

A sundial – what will they think of next?

Samuel Goldwyn

I hate birds. They're not too bad in profile, but have you ever seen the sons of bitches head on?

Robert Benchley

Off-peak electricity is electricity which has been examined at the power station and found to be below standard. It is sold off cheaply in the evenings when people don't use so much.

Dave Barry

An elephant's computer has lots of memory but no mouse.

Russ Edwards

This guy called at my door taking a census. I asked him why and he said they wanted to find out how many people were living in the United States. I told him there was no point in asking me because I hadn't the faintest idea.

Gracie Allen

Social Behaviour and Manners

Social Behaviour and Manners

These are my principles. If you don't like them I have others.

Groucho Marx

I always take a nap before I go to bed.

W.C. Fields

I must particularly warn you against laughing; and I could heartily wish that you may be often seen to smile, but never heard to laugh. Frequent and loud laughter is the characteristic of folly and ill manners: it is the manner in which the mob express their silly joy at silly things. To my mind there is nothing so illiberal, and so ill-bred, as audible laughter.

Lord Chesterfield

It always rains on tents. Rainstorms will travel thousands of miles against the prevailing winds for the opportunity to rain on a tent.

Dave Barry

My only solution for the problem of habitual accidents is to stay in bed all day. Even then, there is always the chance that you will fall out.

Robert Benchley

We kept trying to set up a small anarchist community, but people wouldn't obey the rules.

Alan Bennett

Social Behaviour and Manners

I never accepted a knighthood because to be me is honour enough. Besides, they get one into disreputable company.

George Bernard Shaw

One should never put on one's best trousers to go out to battle for freedom and truth.

Henryk Ibsen

If you have anything of importance to tell me, for God's sake begin at the end.

Sara Duncan

Whether it is summer or winter, I always like to have the morning well aired before I get up.

Beau Brummell

In life it is difficult to say who does you the most mischief, enemies with the worst intentions or friends with the best.

Edward Bulwer-Lytton

In a civil war a general must know exactly when to move over to the other side.

Henry Reed

She had lost the art of conversation, but not, unfortunately, the power of speech.

George Bernard Shaw

If you can't laugh at yourself, make fun of other people.

Bobby Slayton

There are now groups of grown men going on self-discovery weekends, marching into the mountains, joining hands in moonlit forests, howling and beating drums. They pay money to do this. Personally, I like to do the same thing in my living room while I'm watching the Super Bowl. But I do it alone.

Denis Leary

Impotence and sodomy are socially OK but birth control is flagrantly middle class.

Evelyn Waugh

The nice thing about being a celebrity is that if you bore people they think it's their fault.

Henry Kissinger

Camping is nature's way of promoting the motel industry.

Dave Barry

To ask the Queen for a cigarette is rock bottom.

Jeffrey Bernard

Creep up behind a nightclub bouncer and hit him over the head with a wet fish. What follows is an example of 'response to stimuli' as well as a sojourn in the intensive care unit of your choice.

Russell Bell

The cocktail party is a device for paying off obligations to people you don't want to invite to dinner.

Charles Smith

Social Behaviour and Manners

Being a star has made it possible for me to get insulted in places where the average negro could never hope to go and get insulted.

Sammy Davis Jr

There is no stronger craving in the world than that of the rich for titles, except perhaps that of the titled for riches.

Hesketh Pearson

I was in a beauty contest once. I not only came in last, I was hit in the mouth by Miss Congeniality.

Phyllis Diller

I was driving down the highway, saw a sign that said 'Next Rest Area 25 miles'! I said, 'Wow, that's pretty big. People must get really tired around here.'

Steven Wright

He was the sort of fellow that would insist on being seated in the no-smoking compartment of the lifeboat.

John Pepper

Cockroaches and socialites are the only things that can stay up all night and eat anything.

Herb Caen

O wad some power the giftie gie us to see some people before they see us.

Ethel W. Mumford

Social Behaviour and Manners

I am firm; you are obstinate; he is a pig-headed fool.

Bertrand Russell

If you're going to do something tonight that you'll be sorry for tomorrow morning, sleep late.

Henny Youngman

To be positive is to be mistaken at the top of one's voice.

Ambrose Bierce

Never call a man a fool. Borrow from him.

W.C. Fields

I do not have to forgive my enemies, I have had them all shot.

Ramon Narvalez

One never trusts anyone that one has deceived.

Oscar Wilde

Clothes make the man. Naked people have little or no influence on society.

Mark Twain

Most of the time I don't have much fun. The rest of the time I don't have any fun at all.

Woody Allen

Nothing beats blackmail at securing absolute allegiance.

M.A. Sharp

Social Behaviour and Manners

Every day my grandfather made us stand in a little room together, side by side, looking straight ahead for three minutes without talking to each other. He told me it was elevator practice.

Steven Wright

Fashion is what one wears oneself.

Oscar Wilde

There's a name for you ladies, but it's not used in high society outside of kennels.

W.C. Fields

In Australia I had a long talk with the Governor's wife. We talked about the mating habits of the wallaby.

W.C. Fields

A man who is angry on the right grounds and with the right people, and in the right manner and at the right moment for the right length of time, is to be praised.

Aristotle

A friend that ain't in need is a friend indeed.

Kin Hubbard

The urge to gamble is so universal and its practice so pleasurable that I assume it must be evil.

Heywood Brown

Hermits have no peer pressure.

Steven Wright

Social Behaviour and Manners

A well tied tie is the first serious step in life.

Oscar Wilde

My favourite chair is a wicker chair. It's my favourite chair because I stole it. I was at a party, a very crowded party, and when no one was looking I went over to it and I unravelled it and stuck it through the keyhole in the door. The girl who was in it was almost killed.

Steven Wright

A friend in need is a pest – get rid of him.

Tommy Cooper

I was sitting in a restaurant the other day and there's a bloke sitting next to me with a really stupid haircut, so I hit him. Nobody takes the piss out of me.

Paul Merton

Speak softly and carry a big carrot.

Howard Laver

Very sorry I can't come. Lie follows by post.

Charles Beresford

The hardest thing in the world to stop is a temporary chairman.

Kin Hubbard

Dear Randolph Churchill – quite unspoiled by failure.

Noël Coward

Social Behaviour and Manners

Honesty is a good thing but it is not profitable to its possessor unless it is kept under control.

Don Marquis

Each of us as he receives his private trouncings at the hands of fate is kept in good heart by the moth in his brother's parachute, and the scorpion in his neighbour's underwear.

N.F. Simpson

If a woman likes another woman, she's cordial. If she doesn't like her, she's very cordial.

Irvin S. Cobb

I believe in the discipline of silence and could talk for hours about it.

George Bernard Shaw

The only way to atone for being a little over-dressed is by being always absolutely over-educated.

Oscar Wilde

Just when you're beginning to think pretty well of people, you run across somebody who puts sugar on sliced tomatoes.

Will Cuppy

We invite people like Betjeman to tea, but we don't marry them.

Lady Chetwode

I'm not superstitious. I'm afraid it would bring me bad luck.

Babe Ruth

Social Behaviour and Manners

Egotism is the anaesthetic that dulls the pain of stupidity.

Frank Leahy

And when they were up they were up,
And when they were down they were down,
And when they were only halfway up, I was arrested.

Spike Milligan

People are much more willing to lend you books than
bookcases.

Mark Twain

A depressed person is someone who, if he is in the bath,
will not get out to answer the telephone.

Quentin Crisp

His huff arrived, and he departed in it.

Alexander Woollcott

Love your enemies, just in case your friends turn out to be a
bunch of bastards.

R.A. Dickson

People who live in glass houses have to answer the bell.

Bruce Patterson

Of course I wouldn't say anything about her unless I could
say something good. And, oh boy, is this good.

Bill King

Why doesn't everybody leave everybody else the hell alone?

Jimmy Durante

Social Behaviour and Manners

My principal pastime is the daily avoidance of assorted professional beggars, alcoholics and deranged individuals.

George Salmond

There are no more liberals – they've all been mugged.

James Wilson

Philanthropy is the refuge of people who wish to annoy their fellow creatures.

Oscar Wilde

Nothing needs reforming so much as other people's habits.

Mark Twain

You probably wouldn't worry about what people think of you if you could know how seldom they do.

Olin Miller

Whenever people talk to me about the weather, I always feel certain that they mean something else.

Oscar Wilde

The secret of making oneself tiresome is not to know when to stop.

Voltaire

To be an ideal guest, stay at home.

E.W. Howe

If someone tells you he is going to make a 'realistic decision', you immediately understand that he has resolved to do something bad.

Mary McCarthy

Social Behaviour and Manners

We shall always keep a spare corner in our heads to give passing hospitality to our friends' opinions.

Joseph Joubert

When a fellow says, 'Well, to make a long story short,' it's too late.

Don Herold

Some people never use their initiative because nobody ever tells them to.

Mike Smith

My favourite way of wasting time is trying to say something in praise of paper towels.

Franklin P. Adams

There was laughter in the back of the theatre, leading to the belief that somebody was telling jokes back there.

George S. Kaufman

Other people are quite dreadful. The only possible society is oneself.

Oscar Wilde

The greatest happiness is to scatter your enemy, to drive him before you, to see his cities reduced to ashes, to see those who love him shrouded in tears, and to gather into your bosom his wives and daughters.

Genghis Khan

The little trouble in the world that is not due to love is due to friendship.

E. W. Howe

I have been complimented many times and they always embarrass me; I always feel that they have not said enough.

Mark Twain

A young lady is a female child who has just done something dreadful.

Judith Martin

You don't have to have an '-ology' to know that gardening is a symptom of mental instability.

A.A. Gill

The thing to remember about Cyril Connolly is that he is not as nice as he looks.

Maurice Bowra

Like everyone who talks of ethics all day long, one could not trust Koestler half an hour with one's wife, one's best friend, one's manuscript or one's wine merchant.

Cyril Connolly

The art of conversation is really within the reach of almost everyone except those who are morbidly truthful.

Oscar Wilde

I was in bed the other night and I phoned my neighbour and said: 'Would you mind turning the stereo down? The door's unlocked.'

Emo Philips

Social Behaviour and Manners

Nancy Spain is the only distinguished woman author and journalist to be dressed exclusively by the Army Surplus Store.

Roger Storey

I always make a point of arriving later than expected in order to transform the anxiety of the chairman into extravagant relief and enthusiasm when I do appear.

Robert Morley

Anyone throwing stones at this notice board will be prosecuted.

Lord Berners

Job endured everything – until his friends came to comfort him. Then he grew impatient.

Soren Kierkegaard

Nobody, not even in the provinces, should ever be allowed to ask an intelligent question about pure mathematics across a dinner table.

Oscar Wilde

Sit on hard chairs – soft ones spread the hips.

Joan Crawford

Men are the only animals that devote themselves, day in and day out, to making one another unhappy. It is an art like any other. Its virtuosi are called altruists.

H.L. Mencken

Don't be flattered if your guests ask for a doggie bag. They may just want to have the food analysed.

Phyllis Diller

Social Behaviour and Manners

If you are ever attacked in the street do not shout 'help!', shout 'fire!'. People adore fires and always come rushing. Nobody will come if you shout 'help'.

Jean Trumpington

Most human beings are likeable if you don't see much of them.

Robert Lynd

The only time he tells the truth is when he admits he's lying.

Gene Autry

If your hat blows off never run after it: others will be delighted to do it; why spoil their fun.

Mark Twain

When you leave the room, you feel as if someone fascinating had just come in.

Leo Rosten

Many a young man starts life with a natural gift for exaggeration which, if nurtured in congenial and sympathetic surroundings, or by imitation of the best models, might grow into something really great and wonderful. But as a rule, he comes to nothing. He either falls into careless habits of accuracy or takes to frequenting the society of the aged and the well informed, and in a short time he develops a morbid and unhealthy faculty of truth telling.

Oscar Wilde

Social Behaviour and Manners

Some folks can look so busy doing nothing that they seem indispensable.

Kin Hubbard

I am due at the club. It is the hour when we sleep there.

Oscar Wilde

What I really enjoy in life is farting in company, peeing on lavatory seats, preferably when women are about to use them, and blowing my nose into my fingers.

Bill Davis

A beggar is one who has relied on the assistance of his friends.

Ambrose Bierce

Being natural is such a difficult pose to keep up.

Oscar Wilde

With an evening coat and a white tie, anybody, even a stockbroker, can gain a reputation for being civilised.

Oscar Wilde

The difference between in-laws and outlaws is that outlaws are wanted.

Greville Janner

This is the earliest I've ever arrived late.

Yogi Berra

Before a man speaks it is always safe to assume that he is a fool. After he speaks it is seldom necessary to assume it.

H.L. Mencken

Social Behaviour and Manners

It is amazing what the human body can do when chased by a bigger human body.

Jack Thompson

If there was no other action around, my brother Chico would play solitaire – and bet against himself.

Groucho Marx

Even if they had the Mardi Gras in the streets, I still wouldn't go.

Samuel Goldwyn

Do unto others; then run.

Benny Hill

Whenever you see a man with a handkerchief, socks and tie to match, you may be sure he is wearing a present.

Frank Case

A friend is someone who will tell you she just saw your old boyfriend – and he's a priest.

Erma Bombeck

I have, all my life long, been lying till noon; yet I tell all young men and tell them with great sincerity, that nobody who does not rise early will ever do any good.

Samuel Johnson

I'm not going to stay in that hotel again. The towels were so thick there I could hardly close my suitcase.

Yogi Berra

Social Behaviour and Manners

I had to rescue David Frost from the water, otherwise
nobody would have believed I didn't push him in.

Peter Cook

Between the possibility of being hanged in all innocence,
and the certainty of a public and merited disgrace, no
gentleman of spirit could long hesitate.

Robert Louis Stevenson

Advice is like kissing: it costs nothing and it's a pleasant
thing to do.

George Bernard Shaw

Never transmit a sexual disease in public.

P.J. O'Rourke

Never wear a backwards baseball cap to an interview
unless applying for the job of umpire.

Dan Zevin

A good listener is usually thinking about something else.

Kin Hubbard

Nothing defines humans better than their willingness to do
irrational things in the pursuit of phenomenally unlikely pay-
offs. This is the principle behind lotteries, dating and religion.

Scott Adams

Once I lost ten blue chips to a player who bet that the pale
light we happened to notice filtering through the curtains
was dusk, not dawn.

Dick Miles

Why be difficult when with a little extra effort you can make yourself impossible?

Percy Grainger

The best etiquette for getting off a crowded train against a crowd of people forcing their way on is to shout, 'Excuse me, I think I'm going to be sick.'

Fran Collins

No matter how cynical you get, it is just impossible to keep up.

Lily Tomlin

He who lends a book is an idiot. He who returns a lent book is an even bigger idiot.

Joel Rosenberg

We have only one person to blame, and that's each other.

Yogi Berra

To be alone is to be in bad company.

Ambrose Bierce

A friend told me to shoot first and ask questions later. I was going to ask him why, but I had to shoot him.

John Wayne

Kenneth Tynan has the morals of a baboon and the guts of a butterfly.

Truman Capote

Social Behaviour and Manners

A clean desk is the sign of a cluttered desk drawer.

Gene Walker

There's nothing that I like better than sitting in front of a roaring fire with a copy of *War and Peace*. You know a big fat book like that will feed the fire for two hours.

Emo Philips

Cherie Blair's legs stiffen, but they do not curtsey.

Queen Elizabeth II

I've been travelling so much, I haven't had time to grow a beard.

Bob Horner

We shall never be content until each man makes his own weather and keeps it to himself.

Jerome K. Jerome

I couldn't warm to that fellow if we were cremated together.

Jimmy Durante

I never was mad really, but when you've been certified three times, you can't go around calling yourself 'Sane' Frankie Fraser, can you?

Frankie Fraser

His socks compelled attention without losing one's respect.

H.H. Munro

Social Behaviour and Manners

The working class has come a long way in recent years, all of it downhill. They look like one big Manson family.

Tony Parsons

Country manners. Even if somebody phones up to tell you your house is on fire, first they ask you how you are.

Alice Munro

Some of mankind's most esteemed inventions seem to have no purpose other than boredom. For example, there is the dinner party for more than two, the epic poem and the science of metaphysics.

H.L. Mencken

Lady Muriel was often in Eastern Europe, rescuing English governesses from revolution.

John Wells

Christmas cards are just junk mail from people you know.

Patricia Marx

I have very few superstitions before a game, but I always put my right boot on first, followed by my right sock.

Barry Venison

Nigel and I hit it off like a horse on fire.

Tony Britton

If an enemy is drowning and the water is up to his waist, pull him out; if up to his chin, push him in.

Baldassare Castiglione

Social Behaviour and Manners

Anything becomes a pleasure if one does it too often.

Oscar Wilde

You ponce in here expecting to be waited on hand and foot while I'm trying to run a hotel.

Basil Fawlty

They told me it was a birdbath but I didn't believe them. There isn't a bird alive who can tell the difference between Saturday night and any other night of the week.

Eamon Kelly

The only possible form of exercise is to talk, not to walk.

Oscar Wilde

A man's memory becomes the art of his continually varying and misrepresenting his past according to his interests in the present.

George Santayana

No one listens unless it is his turn next.

E. W. Howe

I always give one hundred per cent at work: twelve per cent on Monday, twenty per cent on Tuesday, thirty per cent on Wednesday ...

Josh Billings

Macbeth and Lady Macbeth stand out as the supreme type of all that a host and hostess should not be.

Max Beerbohm

Social Behaviour and Manners

Agreeing with a person cripples controversy and ought not to be allowed.

Mark Twain

Girls, you can learn to work the toilet seat: if it's up put it down. And yes, pissing standing up is more difficult than peeing from point blank range. We're bound to miss sometimes.

Denis Leary

I thought nothing of firing a revolver at a man or of thrusting a glass in his face, but as an Englishman I would never use a knife.

Arthur Harding

Even in civilised mankind faint traces of the monogamous instinct can sometimes be perceived.

Bertrand Russell

Hard work is simply the refuge of people who have nothing better to do.

Oscar Wilde

He hasn't been himself lately, so let's hope he stays that way.

Irvin Cobb

What keeps people apart is their inability to come together.

Richard J. Daley

I ran a respectable disorderly house – I let only gentlemen in. I never let in gunmen or convicts.

Mary Goode

Social Behaviour and Manners

War is undoubtedly hell, but there is no earthly reason why it has to start so early in the morning.

Fran Lebowitz

One can sympathise with everything, except suffering.

Oscar Wilde

If you haven't had a chocolate-covered dwarf in your shower, you haven't lived.

Kathy Self

Smile – it confuses people.

Scott Adams

Keep honking, I'm reloading.

W.C. Fields

It is difficult to say who do you the most mischief – enemies with the worst intentions or friends with the best.

Edward Bulmer-Lytton

You've got to get up early in the morning to catch me peeking through your bedroom window.

Emo Philips

Boodle's all-male club gave the old boys somewhere to binge, swear and fart in peace.

Robin Young

If you find yourself on the receiving end of an intemperate tirade on the telephone, wait for it to run its course, then say apologetically, 'I am so sorry, there seems to be a fault on the line and I didn't catch a word you said. Would you mind repeating it?'

Philip Hook

The difference between a diplomat and a lady is the following: when a diplomat says 'yes', he means 'perhaps'. When he says 'perhaps', he means 'no'. When he says 'no', he is not a diplomat. When a lady says 'no', she means 'perhaps'. When she says 'perhaps', she means 'yes'. But when she says 'yes', she is no lady!

Alfred Denning

There's nothing like looking at vacation pictures to put guests in a travelling mood.

Dan Bennett

It is said that Sir William Wilde, Oscar's father, was so patriotic that he carried a considerable portion of his country's soil about on his person.

Hesketh Pearson

I like the word 'indolence'. It makes my laziness seem classy.

Bern Williams

If you are off on a camping safari, take paper knickers. It saves washing and they are good for lighting the fire.

Lady Cobbold

Some people's idea of keeping a secret is lowering their voice when they tell it.

Franklin Adams

Social Behaviour and Manners

Gentlemen, you can't fight in here. This is the war room.

Stanley Kubrick

This door can be closed without slamming it. Try it and see how clever you are.

Spike Milligan

There was a time when a man wore a pink shirt only after a laundry disaster.

Doug Larson

Conversing with automatic cash dispensers is perfectly understandable and not as uncommon as you might think.

Lynne Truss

She is without one good quality, she lacks the tiniest spark of decency and is quite the wickedest woman in London. I haven't a word to say in her favour and she is one of my dearest friends.

Oscar Wilde

A dog is a yes-animal, very popular with people who cannot afford to keep a yes-man.

Robertson Davies

Not all coppers are bastards, but those that are make a very good job of it.

Charlie Kray

You could count our legal successes on the fingers of less than one hand.

Jack Elder

Social Behaviour and Manners

Women wearing Wonderbras and low-cut blouses lose their right to complain about having their boobs stared at.

P.J. O'Rourke

It was one of those parties where you cough twice before you speak and then decide not to say it after all.

P.G. Wodehouse

Getting caught is the mother of invention.

Robert Byrne

One should never listen. To listen is a sign of indifference to one's hearer.

Oscar Wilde

Goldwynisms! Don't talk to me about Goldwynisms. If you want to hear some real Goldwynisms, talk to Jesse Lasky.

Samuel Goldwyn

The nice thing about standards is that there are so many to choose from.

Ron Shepard

You can keep your dining room table clean by eating in the kitchen.

P.J. O'Rourke

Never squat with your spurs on.

Will Rogers

The truly wise man never plays leapfrog with a unicorn.

William Crosby

Social Behaviour and Manners

You know you're on a bad date when he gets really angry when you tell him you like his Siamese twin brother better.

David Letterman

Never floss a stranger.

Joan Rivers

Welcome thy neighbour to thy fallout shelter. He'll come in handy if thou runnest out of food.

Dean McLaughlin

Arguments with furniture are rarely productive.

Kehlog Albran

The important thing when you are going to do something brave is to have someone on hand to witness it.

Michael Howard

Michael Caine is an over-fat, flatulent sixty-two-year-old windbag, a master of inconsequence now masquerading as a guru, passing off his vast limitations as pious virtues.

Richard Harris

Trapped by the club bore, F.E. Smith once rang for a servant, to whom he said, 'Would you mind listening to the end of this gentleman's story?'

John Train

The correct way to punctuate a sentence that starts: 'Of course it is none of my business, but – ' is to place a period after the word 'but'. Don't use excessive force in supplying such a moron with a period. Cutting his throat

is only a momentary pleasure and is bound to get you
talked about.

Lazarus Long

A neighbour is somebody who has just run out of something.

Robert Benchley

I have decided to make occasional contact with the parallel
universe of young persons euphemistically described as
shop assistants.

Malcolm Southall

It has always been my aim to live a life so openly
scandalous that I would be immune from blackmail.

Lord Beaumont

If we had to identify, in one word, the reason why the
human race has not achieved, and never will achieve, its
full potential, that word would be 'meetings'.

P.J. O'Rourke

Maurice Chevalier was the fastest derrière pincher in the
West.

Jeannette McDonald

Electrocution is burning at the stake with all the modern
improvements.

P.J. O'Rourke

I always give beggars something – I give them a piece of my
mind.

David MacLean

Social Behaviour and Manners

I used to get postcards from Jack Ford from all over the world. One featured the rear end of a horse with the caption, 'Thinking of You.'

Ward Bond

When I am dead, Macaulay, you will be sorry you never heard me speak.

Sydney Smith

Get mad, then get even.

Jonathan Miller

The veil protects us from a lot of ugly women.

Jean-Marie Le Pen

Liza Minnelli's wedding reception was the night of a thousand facelifts.

Tina Brown

Knowledge is power – if you know it about the right person.

Ethel Mumford

George Kaufman had great integrity. You never had to watch him when he was dealing.

Harpo Marx

It is always necessary to aim at being interesting rather than exact, for the spectator forgives everything except boredom.

Voltaire

Social Behaviour and Manners

If nobody knows the trouble you've seen, you don't live in a small town.

Josh Billings

Lester Piggott is not pathologically mean. He's just tight.

Jeffrey Bernard

I am careful when I break with a woman, not to break with her husband. In this way, I have made my best friends.

Guy De Maupassant

If you can't stand the smell, get out of the shit-house.

Harry Truman

Never argue with idiots. They drag you down to their level, then beat you with experience.

Jess Brallier

I decided to stop drinking with creeps and to drink only with friends. I've lost 30 pounds.

Ernest Hemingway

I was so naïve as a kid, I used to sneak behind the barn and do nothing.

Johnny Carson

I want my epitaph to be what I once read on my dry cleaning receipt: 'It distresses us to return work that is not perfect.'

Peter O'Toole

Social Behaviour and Manners

The only way to get a drink out of a Vogon is to stick your fingers down his throat.

Douglas Adams

Some people have a wonderful way of looking at things. Like the ones who hire Negroes to baby-sit so they can go to a Ku Klux Klan meeting.

Dick Gregory

An accuser is one's former friend, particularly the person for whom one has performed some friendly service.

Ambrose Bierce

Those signs that say 'Baby on Board' just make you want to hit the car harder.

Sue Kolinsky

When Prince Charles speaks, everybody pretends to be fascinated, even though he has never said anything interesting except in that intercepted telephone conversation wherein he expressed the desire to be a feminine hygiene product.

Dave Barry

A rare book is a book that comes back to you when lent to a friend.

Alan King

He is in public relations, despite the fact that he looks like – and I say this as a friend – a street person who has failed to take his medication since 1972.

Dave Barry

You don't learn anything the second time you are kicked by a mule.

Josh Billings

When I go to the beach wearing a bikini, even the tide won't come in.

Phyllis Diller

I am a little surprised, not at Mrs Currie's indiscretion, but at a temporary lapse in Mr Major's taste.

Mary Archer

I met Romeo Benetti at a social function the other week and it's the first time I've been within ten yards of him and he hasn't kicked me. Even then I kept looking over my shoulder.

Kevin Keegan

Vince Lombardi is very fair. He treats us all like dogs.

Henry Jordan

Working with Woody Allen is like holding a puppy – it's warm and nice, but sooner or later he's going to piss all over you.

Sam Cohn

My chauffeur is a bit peculiar – he prefers to spend the weekend with his family rather than with me.

Michael Winner

Social Behaviour and Manners

I told Noël Coward that I was saddened because I'd arrived at the stage of life when all my friends were dying month by month. 'Personally,' said Coward, 'I'm delighted if mine last through luncheon.'

David Niven

The only law of hospitality she understood was that of speeding the parting guest.

E.F. Benson

I never take notice of letters marked 'Urgent'. It merely means urgent to the writer.

Napoleon Bonaparte

There are still some people who hitchhike, although not as many as before. A lot of folks gave up the practice after being buried in shallow graves near the side of the road.

George Carlin

What is called the vice of the upper classes is really the pastime of the working classes.

Oscar Wilde

I can't remember your name. But don't tell me.

Oscar Wilde

Statistically, there has not been anyone who stole more books of such obviously high quality from more libraries than Stephen Blumberg.

William Moffett

Let me put it this way: they were sort of on an interlibrary loan to me.

Stephen Blumberg

There's not a man in America who at one time or another hasn't had a secret desire to boot a child in the ass.

W.C. Fields

Never resign and never return to the office after a long lunch.

Cecil Wallace

He belongs to so many benevolent societies that he is destitute.

Edgar Howe

People say I'm indecisive, but I don't know about that.

George W. Bush

I am a man of regular habits. I am always in bed by four or five.

Oscar Wilde

Sport

Sport

Sure, luck means a lot in football. Not having a good quarterback is bad luck.

Don Schula

Any time Detroit scores more than 100 points and holds the other team below 100 points they almost always win.

Doug Collins

My wins are merely beginner's luck, gentlemen, although I have devoted some time to the game.

W.C. Fields

Someone threw a petrol bomb at Alex Higgins once and he drank it.

Frank Carson

There comes a time in every man's life and I've had plenty of them.

Casey Stengel

Nobody has ever bet enough on a winning horse.

Richard Sasuly

The news of the Pope's death puts a damper even on a Yankee win.

Phil Rizzuto

More lampshades were broken in Britain by golf clubs than by Hitler's bombers.

Val Doonican

In 1971 I was sent off the field for arguing with one of my own team-mates.

George Best

Sure there have been deaths and injuries in boxing, but none of them serious.

Alan Winter

I once got a ball out of a St Andrews bunker in two. I'm not saying God couldn't have got it out in one, but He would have had to throw it.

Arnold Palmer

Ninety-five per cent of putts which finish short don't go in.

Hubert Green

However unlucky you may be on the golf course it really is not fair to expect your adversary's grief for your undeserved misfortunes to be as poignant as your own.

Horace Hutchinson

Golf architects can't play golf themselves and make damn sure that no one else can.

Lee Trevino

These greens are so fast I have to hold my putter over the ball and hit it with the shadow.

Sam Snead

When golf first started, one under par was a birdie, two under par was an eagle and three under par was a partridge. They had to change that because you couldn't get a partridge on a par three.

John MacKay

Sport

It may have been the greatest four-wood anyone ever hit. It was so much on the flag that I had to lean sideways to follow the flight of the ball.

Gary Player

I was watching what I thought was sumo wrestling on the television for two hours before I realised it was darts.

Hattie Hayridge

I can never figure out what would make ten thousand people run twenty-six miles. Maybe there's a Hare Krishna behind them going, 'Excuse me, can I talk to you for just a second?'

Rita Rudner

Show me a man who is a good loser, and I'll show you a man who is playing golf with his boss.

Jim Murray

You can talk to a fade but a hook won't listen.

Lee Trevino

I owe everything to golf. Where else would a guy with an IQ like mine earn so much money?

Hubert Green

Pavarotti is very difficult to pass at the net in tennis with or without a racquet.

Peter Ustinov

Is my friend in the bunker or is the bastard on the green?

David Feherty

I was asked to be a linesman at the Wimbledon tennis championship. I excused myself by expressing myself flattered by the offer, but begged them to renew it when my eyesight had deteriorated sufficiently to be able to make wrong decisions with absolute conviction.

Peter Ustinov

A golfer needs a loving wife to whom he can describe the day's play through the long evening.

P.G. Wodehouse

In my singles match I saw Hope vanishing over the horizon with her arse on fire.

David Feherty

Never break your putter and your driver in the same round or you're dead.

Tommy Bolt

In the USA first-class golfers take as long to choose a wife as a club. Sometimes they make the wrong choice in each case.

Dai Rees

Proficiency at billiards is a sign of a misspent youth.

Samuel Johnson

If women were meant to play football, God would have put their tits somewhere else.

Gordon Sinclair

Sport

I have told the team that if we don't give away a goal, we don't lose.

Terry Venables

You can't lose an old golf ball.

John Willis

The other lads on the rugby team are calling me 'Lurpak' – the best butter in the world.

Steve Hampson

Golf and sex are about the only things you can enjoy without being good at it.

Jimmy Demaret

The fairway is a narrow strip of mown grass that separates two groups of golfers looking for lost balls in the rough.

Henry Beard

I've just had a hole-in-one at the sixteenth and I left the ball in the hole just to prove it.

Bob Hope

A goalkeeper is a goalkeeper because he can't play football.

Ruud Gullit

If your caddie says to you on the tee, 'Hit it down the left side with a little draw,' ignore him. All you do on the tee is try not to hit the caddie.

Jim Murray

Once rugby players have succeeded in getting their boots on the right feet, the mental challenge of the game is largely over.

Derek Robinson

It is now known that Darwin was a golfer – he set out in search of the missing links.

Sam Gross

Give me a millionaire with a bad back swing, and I can have a very pleasant afternoon.

George Law

If your adversary is badly bunkered, there is no rule against your standing over him and counting his strokes aloud, with increasing gusto as their number mounts up; but it will be a wise precaution to arm yourself with the niblick before doing so, so as to meet him on equal terms.

Horace Hutchinson

The word 'aerobics' came about when the gym instructors got together and said 'If we're going to charge ten dollars an hour, we can't call it "jumping up and down".

Rita Rudner

I can't cheat on my score – all you have to do is to look back down the fairway and count the wounded.

Bob Hope

If one synchronised swimmer drowns, do all the rest have to drown too?

Wright Stevens

Sport

Real golfers go to work to relax.

George Dillon

You don't have to be certifiably insane to be a jump jockey but it does give you the edge over the competition.

Graham Sharpe

Dear Lord, if there is cricket in heaven, let there also be rain.

Alec Douglas-Home

Hagen said that no one remembers who finished second. But they still ask me if I ever think about that putt I missed to win the 1970 Open at St Andrews. I tell them that sometimes it doesn't cross my mind for a full five minutes.

Doug Saunders

People will think I'm crackers taking over at Birmingham City. I'm voluntarily going back into the madhouse.

Trevor Francis

A professional will tell you the amount of flex you need in the shaft of your club. The more the flex, the more strength you will need to break the thing over your knees.

Stephen Baker

I am a jockey because I was too small to be a window cleaner and too big to be a garden gnome.

Adrian Maguire

A Coarse Golfer is one who has to shout 'Fore' when he putts.

Michael Green

No horse can go as fast as the money you put on it.

Earl Wilson

My favourite shots in golf are the practice swing and the conceded putt. The rest can never be mastered.

Lord Robertson

Most people play a fair game of golf – if you watch them.

Joey Adams

At Glasgow Rangers I was third choice left-back behind an amputee and a Catholic.

Craig Brown

A hole-in-one is an occurrence in which a ball is hit directly from the tee into the hole on a single shot by a golfer playing alone.

Roy McKie

I don't follow particular horses, although horses I back seem to.

Tommy Docherty

My trouble on the golf course is that I stand too close to my shots after I've hit them.

Bob Hope

If Ben Hogan means to win, you lose.

Henry Longhurst

Sport

Golf is a game in which you yell 'fore', shoot six and put down five.

Paul Harvey

An ante-post bet is simply a way of prolonging life. A man holding an ante-post voucher never dies before the race itself is over.

Jeffrey Bernard

Secretariat is everything I am not. He's young, he's beautiful, he has lots of hair, he's fast, he's durable, he has a large bank account, and his entire sex life is ahead of him.

Si Burick

If you're playing a poker game and you look round the table and you can't tell who the sucker is, it's you.

Paul Newman

I used to play golf with a guy who cheated so badly that he had a hole-in-one and wrote down zero on his scorecard.

Bob Bruce

Paul Kelleway would fancy his chances on a pregnant rhinoceros.

Nick Green

After shooting over 200 I asked my partner what I should give the caddie. He replied, 'Your golf clubs'.

Jackie Gleason

I was summoned to appear before the golf club committee for playing off the ladies' tee. I explained I was playing my third shot.

Bing Crosby

Golf is a game in which a sphere 1.68" in diameter is placed on a sphere 8,000 miles in diameter. The object is to hit the little sphere, not the big one.

Winston Churchill

If I had my way, any man guilty of golf would be ineligible for any office of trust in the United States.

H.L. Mencken

I'm hitting the woods just great, but I'm having a terrible time hitting out of them.

Harry Toscano

I've had more clubs than Nick Faldo.

Tommy Docherty

Any jockey can win on a great horse, but it takes a good jockey to lose on it.

Ernest Hemingway

Be funny on the golf course? Do I kid my best friend's mother about her heart condition?

Phil Silvers

Horse sense is something a horse has that prevents him betting on people.

Father Mathew

Sport

Any man who has to save up to go racing has no right to be on a racecourse.

Jeffrey Bernard

Local rules are a set of regulations that are ignored only by players on one specific course rather than by golfers as a whole.

Henry Beard

Playing golf with the President is handy. If you hit a ball into the rough and it drops near a tree, the tree becomes a Secret Service man and moves away.

Bob Hope

Give me a man with big hands, big feet and no brains and I will make a golfer out of him.

Walter Hagen

A man's gotta make at least one bet every day otherwise he could be walking around lucky and never know it.

Jimmy Jones

In the crowd I play with I find it more profitable to keep my eye on my partner than to keep my eye on the ball.

Jim Murray

The secret of missing a tree is to aim straight at it.

Michael Green

When I dislocated my shoulder the nurse said it was a lot less painful than having a baby. I said, 'Let's see what happens if you try to put it back again.'

Stuart Turner

Jack Nicklaus plays a kind of golf with which I am not familiar.

Bobby Jones

We can beat anyone on our day so long as we score.

Alex Toten

Daddy, why mustn't the ball go into the little hole?

Herbert V. Prochnow

Paul Gascoigne was waddling around the pitch like a recently impregnated hippopotamus.

Marcus Berkmann

The least thing upset him on the links. He missed short putts because of the uproar of the butterflies in the adjoining meadows.

P.G. Wodehouse

If you want to take long walks, take long walks. If you want to hit things with a stick, hit things with a stick. But there's no excuse for combining the two and putting the results on TV. Golf is not so much a sport as an insult to lawns.

Dave Barry

I once 'skied' a ball so high I had to shout, 'Don't touch it, Lord, there's a two-stroke penalty if you do'.

Lee Trevino

Some male athletes have breasts I've only dreamed about.

Ruby Wax

Sport

There's a fine line between fishing and just standing on the shore like an idiot.

Steven Wright

The secret of football is to equalise before the opposition scores.

Danny Blanchflower

The invention of the ball was one of the worst tragedies ever to befall mankind and to force small boys on to soggy playing fields every afternoon to kick or throw or hurl these objects at each other for a couple of hours before returning the ball to precisely where they had first found it is a near criminal waste of time, energy and childhood.

Robert Morley

In baseball I see no reason why the infield should not try to put the batter off his stride at the critical moment, by neatly timed disparagements of his wife's fidelity and his mother's respectability.

George Bernard Shaw

They call it golf because all the other four-letter words were taken.

Walter Hagen

In Russia, if a male athlete loses he becomes a female athlete.

Yakov Smirnoff

Tony Cascarino is the biggest waste of money since Madonna's father bought her pyjamas.

Frank Lauder

Anybody who finds it easy to make money on the horses is probably in the dog food business.

Franklin P. Jones

Michael Chang has all the fire and passion of a public service announcement, so much so that he makes Pete Sampras appear fascinating.

Alex Ramsay

If you want to know what you'll look like in ten years, look in the mirror after you've run a marathon.

Jeff Scaff

I was swinging like a toilet door on a prawn trawler.

David Feherty

I'm not saying my game is bad at the moment, but if I grew tomatoes, they'd come up sliced.

Lee Trevino

If you hit a pony over the nose at the outset of your acquaintance, he may not love you but he will take a deep interest in your movements ever afterwards.

Rudyard Kipling

Jack Nicklaus isn't really a great golfer. He's just been on a thirty-year lucky streak.

Henry Beard

Sport

I'm not happy with our tackling. We're hurting them, but they keep getting up.

Jimmy Murphy

The cocktail party – as the name itself indicates – was originally invented by dogs. They are simply bottom sniffings raised to the rank of formal ceremonies.

Lawrence Durrell

Burrough Hill Lad has had more operations than Joan Collins – and maybe more men working on him.

Jenny Pitman

When the force is with Devon Malcolm and he puts his contact lenses in the correct eyes, he can be devastating.

Mike Selvey

One way to stop a runaway horse is to bet on him.

Jeffrey Bernard

It is extremely cold here. The English fielders are keeping their hands in their pockets between balls.

Christopher Martin-Jenkins

A loving wife is better than making 50 at cricket or even 99; beyond that I will not go.

James Barrie

He hit an opponent around the head with his stick during a polo match. In a sport rooted in protocol both on and off the pitch, there is only one more serious crime – abuse of a pony.

Lin Jenkins

Cricket is the only game that you can actually put on weight when playing.

Tommy Docherty

Golf balls are attracted to water as unerringly as the eye of a middle-aged man to a female bosom.

Michael Green

I take my new football recruits into the woods and start them running. Those that run around the trees are chosen as guards; those that run into the trees are chosen as tackles.

Vince Lombardi

Mickey Mantle can hit them with the left and the right. He's completely amphibious.

Yogi Berra

When you are putting well, you are a good putter; when your opponent is putting well, he has a good putter.

John D. Sheridan

Ted Dexter was a master of placing both feet in his mouth at the same time.

Ian Botham

If in the paddock the owner is surrounded by a herd of young children, don't back his horse. But if the owner is accompanied by a beautiful lady, plunge to the hilt.

Robert Morley

Sport

A coarse golfer is one who normally goes from tee to green without touching the fairway.

Michael Green

The secret of playing cricket is to put bat to ball.

W.G. Grace

The real beauty about having Lester Piggott ride for you in the Derby is that it gets him off the other fellow's horse.

Vincent O'Brien

When Charlie Cooke sold you a dummy, you had to pay to get back into the ground.

Jim Baxter

There are certain things you don't believe in. The Easter Bunny. Campaign promises. The Abominable Snowman. A husband with lipstick on his collar. And a guy who tells you he shot a 59 on his own ball. Out of town of course.

Jim Murray

Ally MacLeod thinks that tactics are a new kind of peppermint.

Billy Connolly

Someone once said that nobody murders Troon. The way I played the Open there they couldn't even arrest me for second degree manslaughter.

Lee Trevino

I don't know who designed the Road Hole at St Andrews, but I hear he's escaped.

Mark James

I don't want to be a millionaire, I only want to live like one.

Walter Hagen

They say, 'Trevino is wondering whether to play a five or a six iron to the green, when all the time I'm gazing at some broad in the third row of the gallery, wondering where my wife is.'

Lee Trevino

My swing is so bad I look like a caveman killing his lunch.

Lee Trevino

I saw Sir Edmund Hillary out there in Saurgrass and he had to walk around the greens.

Tom Weiskopf

I have a tip that can take five strokes off anyone's golf game. It's called an eraser.

Arnold Palmer

I once played a round with Jack Nicklaus and I asked him what impressed him most about my golf. 'Your score keeping', he replied.

Bob Hope

The biggest mistake I ever made at the Monte Carlo Rally was to let my wife go shopping by herself.

Mario Andretti

Sport

Tainton boasted that his mother had given birth to him on the hunting-field after which minor intrusion into a day's sport she went on to be up with the kill at Torne Wood.

John Mortimer

That miss on the red will go straight out of my head as soon as I collect my pension book.

John Parrott

When Peter Beardsley appears on television, Daleks hide behind the sofa.

Nick Hancock

You can take a man's wife, you can even take his wallet. But never on any account take a man's putter.

Archie Compston

Secretariat and Rivia Ridge are the most famous pair of stablemates since Joseph and Mary.

Dick Schaap

I only have to read Joe Louis' name and my nose starts to bleed again.

Tommy Farr

For most amateurs the best wood in the bag is the pencil.

Chi Chi Rodriguez

I was three over: one over a house, one over a patio, and one over a swimming pool.

George Brett

We were so fired up, when the referee ran on to the pitch, three of us tackled him.

Graham Dawe

Gerald Ford made golf a contact sport.

Bob Hope

Snooker is just chess with balls.

Clive James

Arnold Palmer is the biggest crowd pleaser since the invention of the portable sanitary facility.

Bob Hope

When male golfers wiggle their feet to get their stance right they look exactly like cats preparing to pee.

Jilly Cooper

Every team needs a mad bomber with the conscience of a rattlesnake.

Johnny Bach

Putts should be conceded only in the following circumstances:
(i)   When your opponent is two inches from the pin and three down.
(ii) Your opponent is nine feet from the hole and is your boss
(iii) Immediately after you have holed out in one.

Tom Scott

Bobby Robson's natural expression is that of a man who fears he may have left the gas on.

David Lacey

Sport

The PGA tour has a simple test to see if a player is on drugs – if Isao Aoki speaks and the player understands him, the player is on something.

Bob Hope

I never exaggerate. I just remember big.

Chi Chi Rodriguez

It's not whether you win or lose – but whether I win or lose.

Sandy Lyle

The ideal board of football directors should be made up of three men – two dead and one dying.

Tommy Docherty

I can close any boxing cut in the world in fifty seconds, so long as it ain't a total beheading.

Adolph Ritacco

It's a marriage. If I had to choose between my wife and my putter – I'd miss her.

Gary Player

The long ball down the middle is like pouring beer down the toilet – it cuts out the middle man.

Jack Charlton

In one year I travelled 450,000 miles by air. That's eighteen and a half times around the world, or once around Howard Cosell's head.

Jackie Stewart

Golf is a game in which the ball lies poorly and the players well.

Art Rosenbaum

I went down to the dugout to pass on some technical information to the team like the fact that the game had started.

Ron Atkinson

Fellows become bookmakers because they are too scared to steal and too heavy to become a jockey.

Noel Whitcome

I've heard it said that sprinters should be allowed to use any drug or other means to improve their performances. Right then, I'll have a motor bike.

Paul Merton

In the language of football, 'resign' is a code word meaning 'he was given the choice of quitting, being fired, or having the fans blow up his house'.

Gene Klein

The first ninety minutes of a football match are the most important.

Bobby Robson

Being paired with Arnold Palmer is like a two-shot penalty.

John Schlee

Sport

You can hit a 200 acre fairway 10 per cent of the time and a two-inch branch 90 per cent of the time.

Henry Beard

Arnold Palmer has won about as much money playing golf as I've paid on lessons.

Bob Hope

If Jesus Christ rode his flaming donkey like Jim Old rode that horse, then he deserved to be crucified.

Rod Simpson

Being left-handed is a big advantage. No one knows enough about your swing to mess you up with advice.

Bob Charles

I'm using a new putter because the old one didn't float too well.

Craig Stadler

Sonny Liston is so ugly that when he cries, the tears run down the back of his head.

Muhammad Ali

When I tee the ball where I can see it, I can't hit it. And when I put it where I can hit it, I can't see it.

Jackie Gleason

Songwriter Hoagy Carmichael, an avid golfer, once teed up on a par three hole, picked up a club and hit the ball. It bounced once on the green, hit the pin and dropped in for a hole in one. Hoagy didn't say a word, but took another ball from his pocket, teed up, then observed, 'I think I've got the idea now.'

Buddy Hackett

Arnold Palmer turned golf into a game of 'Hit it hard, go find it and hit it hard again!'

John Schulian

No one who ever had lessons would have a swing like mine.

Lee Trevino

When losing heavily at a game of doubles in tennis, a good ploy is to whisper to one of your opponents when changing ends, 'Your partner is playing very well.'

Michael O'Connell

A caddy is someone who accompanies the golfer and didn't see the ball either.

Joe Francis

Jack Dempsey hits like an epileptic piledriver.

Harry C. Witwert

These are my suggested rules for golf:
Shallow, porcelain-lined open drains sloping in the direction of the green should be introduced at all difficult parts of the course. Every other green should be bowl-shaped with the hole dead in the middle. High rubber walls should be erected around ponds, woods, railway embankments and other hazards. In bunker play any shot which does not propel the ball onto the green or fairway

Sport

shall not count against the player. Any player who is two or more down may ask his caddie to take every other shot for him. In desperate cases like dormie five, the player may carry the bag and the caddie take all the shots.

John D. Sheridan

He took a swing like a man with a wasp under his shirt and his pants on fire, trying to impale a butterfly on the end of a scythe.

Paul Gallico

The principal difference between Babe Zahanas and myself is that I hit the ball like a girl and she hits the ball like a man.

Bob Hope

If the golfer's object was merely to sink the ball in the hole, he could walk around the course with a bag of golf balls and drop each one in.

Arnold Lunn

The difference between a sand bunker and water is the difference between a car crash and an airplane crash. You have a chance of recovering from a car crash.

Bobby Jones

They asked me if the train passing near the final green hadn't disturbed my putting. I said 'What train?'

Gary Player

Ballesteros spends so much time in the woods that he carries an axe as one of his clubs.

David Feherty

Pessimists see a cup that is half-empty. Optimists see a cup that is half-full. Queens Park Rangers haven't even seen the cup.

Frank Lauder

The most common mistake at St Andrews is just turning up.

Mark James

Driving Mark McCormack's getaway car is the best job in golf.

George Low

The bowling of Cunis, like his name, is neither one thing nor another.

John Arlott

It is hard to tell whether Americans have become such liars because of golf or income tax.

Will Rogers

A real Irish football fan is one who knows the true nationality of every player on the Republic of Ireland team.

Jack Charlton

Arnold Palmer would go for the flag from the middle of an alligator's back.

Lee Trevino

I've never had a coach in my life. When I find one who can beat me, then I'll listen.

Lee Trevino

Never bet with anyone you meet on the first tee who has a deep suntan, a 1 iron in his bag, and squinty eyes.

Dave Marr

The English rugby team – I've seen better centres in a box of Black Magic.

Max Boyce

If it wasn't for golf, I'd be a caddie today.

George Carcher

It hit a spectator, but my ball is OK.

Jerry Pate

To win the US Open, all you have to do is to shoot the lowest score.

Ben Hogan

I cannot understand why people say Ben Hogan is so untalkative. He speaks to me on every green and says, 'You're away.'

Jimmy Demaret

I have finally discovered the secret of the Old Course at St Andrews. Take fewer putts.

Jack Nicklaus

They say I cannot punch, but you should see me putting the cat out at night.

Chris Finnegan

A struggling golfer should take two weeks off and then quit the game.

Jimmy Demaret

What would I have to shoot to win the tournament? The rest of the field.

Roger Maltie

The three ugliest words in golf are – still your shot.

Dave Marr

The reason the pro tells you to keep your head down is so you can't see him laughing.

Phyllis Diller

My car absolutely will not run unless my golf clubs are in the trunk.

Bruce Berlet

A tap-in is a putt that is short enough to be missed one-handed.

Henry Beard

I believe in letting the other guy lose.

Pete Rose

I've hit two balls into the water. I've a good mind to jump in and make it four.

Simon Hobday

Sleep came to Bruce Woodcock, as it must come to all British heavyweights, midway in the fifth round.

Red Smith

My back swing off the first tee put the pro in mind of an elderly woman of dubious morals trying to struggle out of a dress too tight around the shoulders.

Patrick Campbell

I get upset over a bad shot just like anyone else, but it's silly to let the game get to you. When I miss a shot I just think what a beautiful day it is, and what fresh pure air I'm breathing. Then I take a deep breath. I have to do that. That's what gives me the strength to break the club.

Bob Hope

If it wasn't for golf, I don't know what I'd be doing. If my IQ had been two points lower, I'd have been a tree somewhere.

Lee Trevino

Gerald Ford doesn't realise he can't hit a ball through a tree trunk.

Jack Nicklaus

'Stance' is defined by the Rules of Golf as 'that which you have taken up when you place your feet on the ground in position for and preparatory to striking at the ball. The location of the feet before they are placed on the ground is left to the discretion of the individual player.'

John D. Sheridan

We've lost seven of our last eight matches. The only team that we have beaten is Western Samoa. It's a good job we didn't play the whole of Samoa.

Gareth Davies

Don't talk about Michael Johnson's style. Look, if that guy ran with his fingers up his bum he could still run 42 seconds for 400 metres.

Roger Black

There is only one man allowed to say 'There's nothing wrong with defeat', and that's Nelson Mandela's chiropodist.

Jack Powell

Saint Paul was the first golfer – he fought the good fight and finished the course.

Billy Graham

Always remember your bones cannot break in a bobsleigh – they shatter.

John Candy

Paul Ince with a big white bandage on his head was running around the field looking like a pint of Guinness.

Paul Gascoigne

Bob Hope has a beautiful short game. Unfortunately it's off the tee.

Jimmy Demaret

Sport

Colin Montgomerie is a few fries short of a happy meal. His mind goes on vacation and leaves his mouth in charge.

David Feherty

Jack Lemmon has been in more bunkers than Eva Braun.

Phil Harris

We lost the test through fifteen-man rugby. It was just that we didn't have the ball.

Ian McGeechan

I had a rather bizarre telephone call with Kenny Dalglish and I understood only part of it. I assume it was a bad line.

Victor Green

Few pleasures on earth match the feeling that comes from making a loud bodily function noise just as the other guy is about to putt.

Dave Barry

One of the O'Flanagan twins who played rugby for Ireland was punched by a French forward but the other twin persuaded the referee not to send him off. However, the twins did ensure that the French forward eventually left the field – on a stretcher.

Richard Harris

My only feeling about superstition is that it's unlucky to be behind at the end of the game.

Duffy Dougherty

No matter how I try I just can't seem to break 64.

Jack Nicklaus

The best thing you can do with a horse that hangs left is to put a bit of lead in his right ear to act as a counterbalance – with a shotgun.

Lester Piggott

Manchester City are the only team in the world to get the crowd to autograph the ball after the game.

Bernard Manning

Hubert Green swings like a drunk trying to find a keyhole in the dark.

Jim Murray

If you can keep your head when all about you are losing theirs, you're at the wrong end of the football pitch.

Bill Munro

Basketball is a simple game to understand. Players race up and down a fairly small area indoors and stuff the ball into a ring with Madonna's dress hanging on it.

Dan Jenkins

Any money I put on a horse is a sort of insurance policy to prevent it from winning.

Frank Richardson

England's coach Jack Rowell, an immensely successful businessman, has the acerbic wit of Dorothy Parker and, according to most New Zealanders, a similar knowledge of rugby.

Mark Reason

I sometimes got birthday cards from fans. But it's always the same message – they hope it's my last.

Al Norman

What do I think of William Shakespeare? I'll moider da bum!

Tony Galento

Seve Ballesteros drives into territory Daniel Boone couldn't find.

Fuzzy Zoeller

The key to an ice hockey match is the first punch. If you're left-handed and they're expecting a right, it helps a lot.

Wayne Cashman

It's easy to beat Brazil. You just stop them getting twenty yards from your goal.

Bobby Charlton

A puck is a hard rubber disc that ice hockey players strike when they can't hit each other.

Jimmy Cannon

In football it is widely accepted that if both sides agree to cheat then cheating is fair.

Charles B. Fry

It ain't getting it that hurts my players, it's staying up all night looking for it. They got to learn that if you don't get it by midnight, you ain't gonna get it, and if you do, it ain't worth it.

Casey Stengel

Mountain climbers rope themselves together to prevent the sensible ones from going home.

Earl Wilson

Ice hockey is a form of disorderly conduct in which a score is kept.

Doug Larson

I watched the Indy 500, and I was thinking that if they left earlier they wouldn't have to go so fast.

Steven Wright

We are in such a slump that even the ones that aren't drinkin' aren't hittin'.

Casey Stengel

The only time I feel superstitious is when somebody hits me hard on the chin.

Jack Dempsey

The sole Dutch Guiana entrant in the 1956 Olympics was runner Wim Esajas. He slept all morning to relax for the event and arrived at the stadium at 2 p.m. only to learn that the race had been run in the morning. He returned home where he was beheaded.

Peter Sherwood

Sport

I would not advise any golf professional to marry until after the age of thirty. Marriage demands a division of interests and golf, particularly tournament golf, demands every minute of a man's attention.

Henry Cotton

The present state of English rugby is serious but not hopeless; the present state of Irish rugby is hopeless but not serious.

Noel Henderson

Lanny Wadkins doesn't have to worry about offending his friends out here on the tour, because he doesn't have any.

Hal Sutton

If I catch one of my amateur friends playing with a one-iron, he had better be putting with it.

Tommy Bolt

The two mistakes I see most often from amateurs are lifting up and hitting the equator of the ball, sending it into the next country, or taking a divot of sand large enough to bury a cat.

Sam Snead

I knew it was okay to die after the Wimbledon final, but not during it. It would have put Goran off.

Srdjan Ivanisevic

Tiger Woods' idea of an up and down is a birdie on a par three.

Des MacHale

I detest games – I never like to kick or be kicked.

Oscar Wilde

One way to solve the problem of golfers' slow play is to knock the ball into them. There will be a short delay while you have a hell of a fight, but from then on they'll move faster.

Horace Hutchinson

Good Goran was frustrated, but he didn't want to break a racket. But bad Goran pushed my arm down that extra two inches for the break.

Goran Ivanisevic

The main difference between Tony Cascarino and Boris Becker is that Becker hits the net sometimes.

Tom Shields

Only a fool would attempt to predict the score of a Rangers – Celtic match. I think it will be a score draw.

Hughie Taylor

I don't know why that putt hung on the edge. I'm a clean liver. It must be my caddy.

Joanne Carner

She kept up with the lads for fourteen pints, but then they started talking about football.

Martin Kemp

Sport

When your shot has to carry over a water hazard, you can either hit one more club or two more balls.

Henry Beard

Hit the ball up to the hole. You meet a better class of person there.

Ben Hogan

A good wife is someone who lets you keep your fishing maggots in the fridge during warm weather.

Paul Carman

I've had fourteen bookings this season – eight of which were my fault, but seven of which were disputable.

Paul Gascoigne

Driving a race car is like dancing with a chain saw.

Cale Yarborough

When Neil Armstrong set foot on the moon, he found a baseball that Jimmy Fox hit off me in 1937.

Lefty Gomez

Pool has been offered as a recreation in asylums for about 150 years. Alas, more people have been driven crazy by pool during that time than have been cured by it.

Mike Shamos

I have never got over the shock of seeing my first cricket ball. I simply couldn't believe that there was anything so dangerous loose in what up to then had seemed a safe sort of world.

Robert Morley

I would not be bothered if we lost every game, as long as we won the league.

Mark Viduka

Wolverhampton Wanderers' strikers couldn't score in a brothel.

Tommy Docherty

Birmingham City are a club with plenty of luck. Unfortunately it's all bad luck.

Jasper Carrott

I don't retire and go fishing because fish don't applaud.

Bob Hope

He can run any time he wants. I'm giving him the red light.

Yogi Berra

The name 'February' comes from the Latin word 'Februarius', which means 'fairly boring stretch of time during which one expects the professional ice-hockey season to come to an end but it does not'.

Dave Barry

The only polite thing to do when engaged in sky diving, hang gliding, ice climbing or any other dangerous sport is to die. That's what everyone is waiting around for.

P.J. O'Rourke

Sport

Ice hockey fans love the fighting. The players don't mind. The coaches like the fights. What's the big deal?

Don Cherry

I have seen jockeys do things to horses I bet on that they will have to answer for on Judgement Day if there is any justice at such a time.

Damon Runyon

I believe every human has a finite number of heartbeats. I don't intend to waste any of mine running around exercising.

Neil Armstrong

Footballers are going on strike? When can they start?

Anne Burton

Ardiles strokes the ball like it is part of his anatomy.

Kevin Keegan

Good pitching will always stop good hitting and vice versa.

Casey Stengel

If Shakespeare had been in pro basketball he would never have had time to write his soliloquies. He would always have been in a plane between Phoenix and Kansas City.

Paul Westhead

Ice hockey combines the best features of figure skating and World War II.

Alfred Hitchcock

Alex Ferguson is the best manager I've ever had at this level. Well, he's the only manager I've actually had at this level.

David Beckham

He's a man who likes to keep his feet on the ground – he sails a lot.

Alan Titchmarsh

He dribbles a lot and the opposition don't like it – you can see it all over their faces.

Ron Atkinson

Don't cut off your nose yourself.

Casey Stengel

I don't have to tell you people about scuba diving. So that will save some time.

Emo Philips

Argentina are the second best team in the world, and there's no higher praise than that.

Kevin Keegan

Leeds is a great club and it's been my home for years, even though I live in Middlesbrough.

Jonathon Woodgate

Match results of the Under Eleven league will not be published so that teams will not be embarrassed when they lose. Reports can highlight which boys have scored goals,

Sport

whether it was a great game, who was man of the match but winning or losing is not an aspect we like to go into at junior levels.

Trevor Saunders

Ted Simmons didn't sound like a baseball player. He said things like 'Nevertheless' and 'If, in fact'.

Dan Quisenberry

There will be very few siestas in Madrid tonight.

Kevin Keegan

We murdered them nil-all.

Bill Shankly

This season I want to gain 1,500 or 2,000 yards, whichever comes first.

George Rogers

Although I was the referee, I scored a goal for the losing side because I wanted to cheer them up after the terrorist attacks on New York.

Brian Savill

I don't think jogging is healthy, especially morning jogging. If morning joggers knew how tempting they looked to motorists, they would stay at home and do sit-ups.

Rita Rudner

I was 6'1" when I started boxing, but with all those uppercuts I'm now up to 6'5".

Chuck Nepner

Small wonder that Manchester United is in such a pickle when the star player talks in a squeak so high-pitched only dogs can hear him and the manager speaks goat.

Jeremy Clarkson

Suffice it to say this will be remembered as a season best forgotten.

Terry Badoo

I'm a volatile player – I can play in the centre, on the right and occasionally on the left side.

David Beckham

Sometimes in football you have to score goals.

Thierry Henry

The midfield picks itself – Beckham, Scholes, Gerrard and A.N. Other.

Phil Neal

A perfect game has never happened in a World Series, and it still hasn't.

Yogi Berra

The putt was a little heavy, but nearly perfect – a bit like Kate Winslet.

Peter Alliss

If you're 0–0 down, there's no better person to get you back on terms than Ian Wright.

Robbie Earle

Sport

I can set up John Prescott with a trainer and I will guarantee he will become British champion within five fights.

Frank Malone

Everyone knows that for Manchester United to get a penalty we need a certificate from the Pope and a personal letter from the Queen.

Alex Ferguson

That would have been a goal if the goalkeeper hadn't saved it.

Kevin Keegan

Kicking is very important in football. In fact some of the more enthusiastic players even kick the football occasionally.

Alfred Hitchcock

Over a season, you'll get goals disallowed that are good and you'll get goals that are good disallowed.

Kevin Keegan

Temp – now there's a big word.

Barry Venison

I would rather watch a man at his toilet than on a cricket field.

Robert Morley

Isn't that nice? The wife of the Cambridge president is kissing the cox of the Oxford crew.

Harry Carpenter

I have a lifetime contract. That means I can't be fired during the third quarter if we're ahead and moving the ball.

Lou Holtz

Men carrying brooms represent the second best chance of a British medal at the Winter Olympics in Salt Lake City next month.

David Powell

Winning doesn't really matter as long as you win.

Vinny Jones

Most chess games have all the raw-nerved excitement of the home-shopping channel with the sound turned down.

Richard Morrison

You've got to believe you're going to win, and I believe we will win the World Cup until the final whistle blows and we're knocked out.

Peter Shilton

The great thing about golf – and this is the reason why a lot of health experts like me recommend it – you can drink beer and ride in a cart while you play.

Dave Barry

I believe that professional wrestling is clean and everything else in the world is fixed.

Frank Deford

Sport

Football is football; if that weren't the case, it wouldn't be the game it is.

Garth Crooks

Colin Montgomerie couldn't count his balls and get the same answer twice.

David Feherty

In my prime I could have handled Michael Jordan. Of course, he would only have been twelve years old then.

Jerry Sloan

Me and George and Billy are two of a kind.

Micky Rivers

Once he'd got past the point of no return, there was no coming back.

Murray Walker

I see Kate Hoey, our Sports Minister, has come eleventh in the most beautiful women in sport. I'd really hate to meet the girl who came twelfth on a dark night.

Ken Bates

Fiona May lost out on the gold medal only because the Spanish athlete jumped further than she did.

David Coleman

I would give up golf if I didn't have so many sweaters.

Bob Hope

There are no handles to a horse but the 1910 model has a string to each side of its face for turning its head when there is anything you want it to see.

Stephen Leacock

This is an interesting circuit because it has inclines. And not just up but down as well.

Murray Walker

The drivers have one foot on the brake, one on the clutch and one on the throttle.

Bob Varsha

He was dead before he hit the floor and he never regained consciousness.

David Coleman

When I say that Alex Ferguson needs to stand up and be counted, I mean that he needs to sit down and take a good look at himself in the mirror.

Gary Mabbutt

One accusation you cannot throw at me is that I've always done my best.

Alan Shearer

A winner never quits and a quitter never wins. But those who never win and never quit are called idiots.

Jarjar Stinks

Last time I saw a mouth like yours, pal, Lester Piggott was sitting behind it.

Billy Connolly

These American horses know the fences like the back of their hands.

Harvey Smith

I don't even understand offside, so how can I be expected to understand a Manchester United contract?

Victoria Beckham

Last week I missed a spectacular hole-in-one by only five strokes.

Bob Hope

She is so cross-eyed, she can watch a tennis match without ever moving her head.

Phyllis Diller

My wish is to end all the killing in the world. My hobbies are hunting and fishing.

Bryan Harvey

Scotland are the nymphomaniacs of world rugby.

George Hook

I love boxing. Where else do two grown men prance about in satin underwear, fighting over a belt? The one who wins gets a purse. They do it in gloves. It's the accessory connections I love.

John McGivern

I don't know why the Yankees' record is so bad this season. I wish I knew because I'm getting tired of answering that question.

Yogi Berra

The garryowen in rugby is basically a Hail Mary kick – send it up in the air and hope for the best.

Tony Ward

Sex is better than scoring ninety-nine not out at Lord's. Further than that I will not go.

Geoffrey Boycott

Greg Goossen is only twenty and with a good chance in ten years, he'll be thirty.

Casey Stengel

I'm too old to compete ever again in the NBA Slam Dunk contest. Maybe down the road.

Kobe Bryant

The tide is very much in our court now.

Kevin Keegan

Curling is crown green bowling redesigned by Salvador Dali.

Ronald White

There are too many drugs in sport, but not enough in angling.

Phil Kay

Sport

All that remains is for a few dots and commas to be crossed.

Mitchell Thomas

I was surprised, but like I always say, nothing surprises me in football.

Les Ferdinand

Never play golf for money against a man nicknamed 'One-Iron'.

Tom Sharpe

Curling was invented in the sixteenth century by bored Scottish farm labourers who passed the time by pushing a frozen cow pat up and down icy rivers.

Gillian Harris

I am not learning Japanese for the World Cup. I'm still trying English.

David Beckham

There's no in between – you're either good or bad. We were in between today.

Gary Lineker

If that had gone in it would have been a goal.

David Coleman

I'd love to be a mole on the wall in the Liverpool dressing room at half time.

Kevin Keegan

Par is anything I want it to be. For instance, the hole right here is a par 47, and yesterday I birdied the sucker.

Willie Nelson

Curling is the only sport where they have to speed up the action replays.

A.A. Gill

At the Winter Olympics, why on earth don't they do those sliding things all together instead of one at a time? Then it would be a proper race and take a couple of minutes instead of a few days and it would be exciting.

A.A. Gill

My gold handicap is my honesty.

Bob Hope

If the Red Sox ever tested me for attention deficit disorder, I don't remember it.

Manny Ramirez

It takes skill and courage to ski down a hill at 80 mph dressed in nothing but lycra.

Ronald White

Moses Kiptanui – the nineteen-year-old Kenyan, who turned twenty a few weeks ago.

David Coleman

There are going to be six laps left at the end of this race.

Murray Walker

Sport

Why does there have to be a style judge for the ski jump, which is, to the unpractised eye, simply controlled falling from a tenth-storey window?

A.A. Gill

Dutch goalkeepers are protected to a ridiculous extent. The only time they are in danger of physical contact is when they go into a red-light district.

Brian Clough

Some of the goals were good; some of the goals were sceptical.

Bobby Robson

The atmosphere is so tense you could cut it with a cricket stump.

Murray Walker

If they don't put a stop to the fighting at ice hockey matches, we'll have to start printing more tickets.

Conn Smythe

It's like learning to play golf. Just when you think you've mastered it, they move the goalposts.

Adrian Love

I have to exercise very early in the morning before my brain figures out what I'm doing.

Ruby Wax

I listened to a football coach who spoke straight from the shoulder. At least I couldn't detect a higher origin in anything he said.

Dixon Fox

Female streakers should not be allowed on a cricket pitch because you're allowed only one bouncer per over.

Bill Frindall

I'd like to play for an Italian club like Barcelona.

Mark Draper

If you don't believe you can win, there is no point in getting out of bed at the end of the day.

Neville Southall

I couldn't have won the World Series without my players.

Casey Stengel

Without being too harsh on David Beckham, he cost us the match.

Ian Wright

I went into a pawnshop to buy a chess set, but they didn't have a full one.

George Carlin

Watching women playing cricket is a bit like watching men knitting.

Len Hutton

Golf is no closer to being a sport than being hanged out-of-doors is a reliable way of getting a tan.

Jim Bishop

Sport

The hardest part of my famous Twickenham try was not resisting the English pack, but dragging the entire Irish pack over with me.

Ginger McLoughlin

The motto of Irish rugby has always been kick ahead – any head.

Fergus Slattery

Men are amused by almost any idiot thing – that is why professional ice hockey is so popular.

Dave Barry

The true coarse golfer takes a divot when he putts.

Milton Berle

What does it profit a man if he gains the whole world and three-putts the eighteenth green?

Fred Corcoran

Rally points scoring is twenty points for the fastest, eighteen points for the second fastest, right down to six points for the slowest fastest.

Murray Walker

What makes a sane and rational person subject himself to such humiliation? Why on earth does anyone want to become a football referee?

Roy Hattersley

This would have been Senna's third win in a row if he had won the two before.

Murray Walker

I don't wear a helmet. I have nothing to protect. No brain, no pain.

Randy Carlyle

If Alain Prost wants to catch Ayrton Senna, he'll have to get on his bike.

James Hunt

A golf ball can stop in the fairway, rough, woods, bunker or lake. With five equally likely options, very few balls choose the fairway.

Jim Bishop

Acne seems to be an occupational hazard for football strikers, as in 'Duncan Ferguson picked his spot before tucking the ball away'.

Tom Shields

Jimmy Connors was such an out-and-out 'personality' that he managed to get into a legal dispute with the president of his own fan club.

Martin Amis

Watching the Aussies at cricket is like watching a porn movie. You always know what's going to happen in the end.

Mick Jagger

I played snooker like a pig with a shotgun.

Mark Williams

Sport

A fishing line has a worm at one end and a fool at the other.

Samuel Johnson

Have you ever seen a jogger smile?

Jo Brand

When a professional golfer hits the ball to the right it's called a fade. When an amateur hits it to the right, it's called a slice.

Peter Jacobson

There are only two things in this world I just can't grow accustomed to – a man and a woman living together without being married, and taking a Mulligan at golf.

Harvey Penick

How did I make a twelve on a par five hole? It's simple – I missed a four-foot putt for an eleven.

Arnold Palmer

My biggest thrill came the night Elgin Baylor and I combined for 73 points in Madison Square Garden. Elgin had 71 of them.

Rod Hundley

If there wasn't such a thing as football we'd all be frustrated footballers.

Mick Lyons

One of the advantages of bowling over golf is that you very seldom lose a bowling ball.

Don Carter

We didn't underestimate them – they were just better than we thought.

Bobby Robson

Who is this Babe Ruth and what does she do?

George Bernard Shaw

When you are 4–0 up you should never lose 7–1.

Lawrie McMenemy

Sport is a universal language. Yes. If you learn to speak it, you can communicate at a superficial level with idiots all over the world.

Andy Millar

If we played like this every week we wouldn't be so inconsistent.

Bobby Robson

The trouble with jogging is that by the time you realise you're not in shape for it, it's too far to walk back.

Franklin Jones

It's terrible how they treat umpires in the US. When they first go out on the field the band starts to play 'Oh Say Can You See?'

Goodman Ace

We actually got the winner three minutes from time but then they equalised.

Ian McNail

Sport

In the rough at Muirfield not only could you lose your golf ball, but if you left your golf bag down you could lose that, too. You could even lose a short caddy.

Jack Nicklaus

It would have been a birdie if the ball hadn't stopped before it reached the hole.

David Coleman

Don King's head looks like my crotch.

Roseanne Barr

Time was if you had forty white men with sticks chasing a black man, it was the Ku Klux Klan. Nowadays it's the US Open.

Martin Blake

England played out the last half hour of the game against Brazil apparently under the impression that they were leading.

Tom Humphries

The closest Michael Parkinson ever came to a hole-in-one was ten.

Jimmy Tarbuck

There would have been serious trouble between David and Jonathan if either had persisted in dropping catches off the other's bowling.

P.G. Wodehouse

I felt a lump in my mouth as the ball went in.

Terry Venables

Most of the people who can remember when Notts County were a great club are now dead.

David Coleman

Somewhat surprisingly, Cambridge have won the toss in the Boat Race.

Harry Carpenter

Runners-up at Wembley, Leicester, never the bride, always the bridegroom.

Peter Jones

He had an eternity to play that ball, but he took too long over it.

Martin Tyler

We could be putting the hammer in Luton's coffin.

Ray Wilkins

David Leadbetter wanted me to change my takeaway, my backswing, my downswing and my follow-through. He said I could still play right-handed.

Brad Bryant

My wife was in the bathroom and I put my *Spitting Image* puppet into bed and put a sheet over it and hid. She did say that it was actually more active than I was.

Steve Davis

Sport

Nothing can compare to becoming a father, not even winning the men's singles at Wimbledon.

Tim Henman

Can I take a punch? Now that's a question that is never likely to be answered.

Muhammad Ali

Those people who row single-handedly across the Atlantic – wouldn't it be easier if they used both hands.

Steven Wright

I'd have played Tom Finney in his overcoat.

Bill Shankly

I asked the manager for a ball to train with. He couldn't have looked more horrified if I'd asked for a transfer. He told me they never used a ball at Barnsley. The theory was we'd be hungry for it on Saturday if we didn't see it for the rest of the week. I told him that, come Saturday, I probably wouldn't recognise a ball.

Danny Blanchflower

Birmingham City – you lose some, you draw some.

Jasper Carrott

Pat Jennings does actually have faults – he might be a bit vulnerable to a hard low shot from the edge of the six-yard box.

Don Howe

Leighton James is very deceptive – he's even slower than he looks.

Tommy Docherty

Mark Waugh is thirty-seven, the same age as his twin brother Steve.

Ian Healy

You'd think if anybody would be able to form a decent wall it would be the Chinese.

Ron Atkinson

Curling is half sport, half housework.

Clive James

Good news: ten golfers a year are hit by lightning.

George Carlin

Polo will become the new sport and will wipe snooker and darts off the small screen.

Ronald Ferguson

It was like the referee had a brand new yellow card and wanted to see if it worked.

Richard Rufus

I hear Elvis is living now in Michigan or Minnesota. Well, we'd like him to come and be on our bench. We don't care how much he weighs.

Jerry Glanville

Sport

My best score ever is 103. But I've been playing golf for only fifteen years.

Alex Karras

There is nothing wrong with that car except for the fact that it is on fire.

Murray Walker

If I were you, I would give your driver to your worst enemy.

John Jacobs

The secret in the rough is to take a few dozen practice swings with a 2-iron. (A scythe is good too.)

Tom Callahan

A policeman told me he'd caught a dozen courting couples in the stand at Hartlepool and asked me what to do about it. I told them to fix the bloody fence and board them in. Best gate of the season it would have been.

Fred Westgarth

Theatre and Criticism

Theatre and Criticism

Don't pay any attention to the critics. Don't even ignore them.

Sam Goldwyn

The unique thing about Margaret Rutherford is that she can act with her chin alone.

Kenneth Tynan

The crowd were behind me all the way, but I shook them off at the railway station.

Tom O'Connor

My dear delightful company, I have just watched your performance of *The Importance of Being Earnest*. It reminds me of a play I once wrote.

Oscar Wilde

The trouble with nude dancing is that not everything stops when the music stops.

Robert Helpmann

A politically correct American revival of *Guys and Dolls* is to be called *Loathsome Oppressors and Women of Vision and Strength*!

Nigel Rees

Danny La Rue denies that he is a wealthy man, but I happen to know for a fact that he has a little bit tucked away.

Jimmy Tarbuck

I want my Hamlet to be so male that when I come out on the stage, they can hear my balls clank.

John Barrymore

W.H. Auden's face looks like a wedding cake left out in the rain.

Stephen Spender

The trouble with Freud is that he never had to play the old Glasgow Empire on a Saturday night after Rangers and Celtic had both lost.

Ken Dodd

We would see Charles Laughton floating in his own pool and it was just the reverse of an iceberg – 90 per cent of him was visible.

Peter Ustinov

This must be an extremely wealthy town – I see that each of you bought two or three seats.

Victor Borge

Edith Evans took her curtain calls as though she had just been un-nailed from the cross.

Noël Coward

Eddie Izzard is a comedian so politically correct that he wears a skirt.

Paul Vallely

To people who say to me that the Abbey Theatre is not what it used to be, I reply 'It never was'.

Lennox Robinson

Theatre and Criticism

Kylie Minogue looks like one of those nine-year-olds from Dagenham done up in her mother's lipstick, to appear on a talent show.

Jonathan Margolis

If you were a shape-changing movie creature, needing a supply of virgins to survive, would you choose to live in America?

Simon Rose

Dear Ingrid Bergman – speaks five languages and can't act in any of them.

John Gielgud

I can't say it was the worst ever *Richard II*, because I imagine that in Upper Volta there may have been school productions for English-as-a-second-language classes, but it must have been a close-run thing.

A.A. Gill

Trying to direct Robert Morley was about as useful as trying to alter the sequence on a set of traffic lights.

John Gielgud

I've always thought I would be particularly good in Romeo and Juliet – as the nurse.

Noël Coward

The script of *Murder One* is as tight as an egg-fed nun's bum.

A.A. Gill

I once stayed in a theatrical boarding house that had two toilets, one upstairs and one downstairs. There was one rule that you broke at your peril – no solids downstairs.

Les Dawson

Very few people go to the doctor when they have a cold. They go to the theatre instead.

W. Boyd Gatewood

In the ballet suddenly Sigmund hears the flutter of wings, and a group of wild swans flies across the moon. Sigmund is astounded to see that their leader is part-swan and part-woman – unfortunately, divided lengthwise. She enchants Sigmund, who is careful not to make any poultry jokes.

Woody Allen

Even Donald Sinden managed to put aside his habitual act of Queen Victoria playing Widow Twankey to turn in a heavyweight country-class lord.

A.A. Gill

Milton Berle knows the secret of making people laugh and he sure knows how to keep a secret.

Arnold Strang

At my most recent performance the audience were so tightly packed they could not applaud horizontally; they had to applaud vertically.

W.C. Fields

Theatre and Criticism

A drama critic has the same effect on one as a bicycle without a saddle.

Brendan Behan

Very good actors never talk about their art. Very bad ones never stop.

John Whiting

With the collapse of vaudeville new talent has no place to stink.

George Burns

My favourite comedian is Frank Carson. Over the years I have enjoyed his joke very much.

Ken Dodd

Critics – the very word suggests an insect.

Dylan Moran

I once had a nightmare in which I heard the judge say, 'The prisoner is sentenced to face a mixed audience of St Louisians, Washingtonians and Kansas Citizens every night for the remainder of his life. Bailiff, lead him to the theatre and let the punishment begin'.

W.C. Fields

The question actors most often get asked is how they can bear saying the same things over and over again night after night, but God knows the answer to that is, don't we all anyway; might as well get paid for it.

Elaine Dundy

If there is one pleasure on earth which surpasses all others, it is leaving a play before the end. I might perhaps except the joy of taking tickets for a play, dining well, sitting on after dinner, and finally not going at all. That, of course, is very heaven.

Angela Thirkell

Shaw has the emotional range of a Pat Boone record with a scratch.

A. A. Gill

To me Edith Evans looks like something that would eat its young.

Dorothy Parker

I am a Camera – Me no Leica.

Walter Kerr

I spent four years studying mime under Marcel Marceau – unfortunately he was teaching welding at the time.

Paul Merton

I won't play Hamlet unless he gives me a stroke a hole.

Groucho Marx

Jackie Collins is to writing what her sister Joan is to acting.

Campbell Grison

The first thing a comedian does on getting an unscheduled laugh is to verify the state of his buttons.

Alva Johnston

Theatre and Criticism

Better an eternity in Hell with Little and Large, Max Bygraves and Dick Emery than a single Christmas with the Osmonds.

Clive James

Dustin Hoffman is the luckiest Jewish midget that ever lived.

Martin Rackin

Samantha Fox in a leather suit looks like a badly wrapped black pudding.

Janet Street-Porter

Mrs Siddons was so dramatic she stabbed the potatoes at dinner.

Sydney Smith

The consistent thing about all American courtroom drama is that invariably the only vaguely human being on the credits is the psycho multiple murderer.

A.A. Gill

It was without doubt the most cringe-making, knuckle-chewing livivacious bit of screamingly ghastly dramatic television ever – and I haven't forgotten Brian Blessed going up Everest.

A.A. Gill

Groucho Marx was a major comedian, which is to say that he had the compassion of an icicle, the effrontery of a carnival shill and the generosity of a pawnbroker.

S.J. Perelman

The first time I saw Barbra Streisand perform she was so good, I wanted to run up to the stage, put my arms around her – and wring her neck.

Judy Garland

The best heckle I ever had was one night when I went on stage and said I was going to do the weatherman sketch. 'Here is the weather,' I began – 'Meteorologist,' shouted a bloke from the audience.

Malcolm Hardee

All my shows are great. Some of them are bad. But they're all great.

Lew Grade

Some critics are emotionally desiccated, personally about as attractive as a year-old peach in a single girl's refrigerator.

Mel Brooks

Heywood Broun once described Geoffrey Steyne as the worst actor on the American stage. Steyne sued but lost the case. The next time Broun reviewed a play in which Steyne appeared he said simply 'Mr Steyne's performance was not up to its usual standard.'

Robert E. Drennan

Avoid crowds during the influenza epidemic – see *Someone in the House.*

George S. Kaufman

Theatre and Criticism

In a 1956 production of *King Lear* in New York, Orson Welles, who had fractured his ankle in a fall, played the title role from a wheelchair.

Mark Fowler

I have more talent in my smallest fart than Barbra Streisand has in her entire body.

Walter Matthau

Bo Derek turned down the role of Helen Keller because she couldn't remember the lines.

Joan Rivers

Critics – unless the bastards have the courage to give you unqualified praise, I say ignore them.

John Steinbeck

After my act there was a lot of booing but also a lot of clapping. But the clapping was for the booing.

Milton Berle

Hermione Baddeley is touring in the *Diary of a Nobody* as if she wrote it herself.

Hermione Gingold

The voice was marvellously clear and we all went into the wings to see the cause of the improvement. There was Frank Benson, hanging upside down in a tree as Caliban, and for the first time on the whole tour the false teeth fitted him properly.

Robert Morley

When I worked with Bette Davis I was never so scared in my life. And I was in the war.

John Mills

I am happy with every part of my costume except the wig. I feel as if I am looking out of a yak's asshole.

Coral Browne

Possibly because of my shape, the role of Portia always eluded me.

Robert Morley

During the performance of the play, I leaned forward and politely asked the lady in front if she would mind putting on her hat.

George S. Kaufman

I have never been able to see how the duties of a critic, which consist largely in making painful remarks in public about the most sensitive of his fellow-creatures, can be reconciled with the manners of a gentleman.

George Bernard Shaw

I gather that the Head of Plays at the BBC has turned it down. Well, that seems a pretty good recommendation to me.

Innes Floyd

The chief pleasure in going to the theatre in Brighton is in leaving it, and leaving it as noisily as possible.

Alan Bennett

Theatre and Criticism

When I die, I want to be cremated and ten per cent of my ashes thrown in my agent's face.

W.C. Fields

As Lavinia, Miss Leigh receives the news that she is about to be ravished on her husband's corpse with little more than the mild annoyance of one who would have preferred foam rubber.

Kenneth Tynan

Cher has just one expression. She makes Roger Moore look like the world gurning champion.

Jo Brand

The opening night audience is mostly friends of the cast and backers of the show, and they come to applaud their money.

Al Hirschfeld

Give me a couple of years and I'll turn that actress into an overnight success.

Samuel Goldwyn

Tommy Cooper had a great rapport with himself.

Russ Abbot

If a circus is half as good as it smells, it's a great show.

Fred Allen

Just point me in the direction of the stage and tell me the name of the play.

Junuis Booth

Gaxton, I am watching your performance from the rear of the house. Wish you were here.

George Kaufman

I think the Animal Rights people should boycott *The Mousetrap*.

Patrick Murray

Army generals say the biggest threat to the entertainer Wayne Newton when he arrives in Afghanistan is friendly fire.

Jimmy Fallon

William Inge handles symbolism rather like an Olympic weightlifter, raising it with agonising care, brandishing it with a tiny grunt of triumph, then dropping it with a terrible clang.

Benedict Nightingale

Actually I am a golfer. That is my real occupation. I was never an actor; ask anybody, particularly the critics.

Victor Mature

At a London Theatre during the interval of a production of Shakespeare's *Antony and Cleopatra*, two anxious patrons approached the theatre manager and asked, 'Tell us, is this, or is this not, *Bunty Pulls the String*?'

Tom Stoppard

I played a sheep in a nativity play aged six. I was the stupid kid trying to upstage Jesus.

Nicole Kidman

Theatre and Criticism

Hook and Ladder is the sort of play that gives failures a
bad name.

Walter Kerr

Critics search for ages for the wrong word, which, to give
them credit, they usually find.

Peter Ustinov

I've told my mother that it's called *The Geneva Monologue*
and that's it about women in banking.

Maureen Lipman

I recently attended a matinee of *Waiting for Godot*. I
thought the orchestra rail was quite beautiful.

Jessie Bull

A coarse actor is one who can remember his lines but not
the order in which they come.

Michael Green

'Tis ever thus with simple folk, an accepted wit has but to
say, 'Pass the mustard,' and they roar their ribs out.

W.S. Gilbert

I never sleep through a performance. I always make sure I
am awake for the intermission.

Max Benchley

Margaret Rutherford is filled with a monstrous vitality: the
soul of Cleopatra has somehow got trapped in the
corporate shape of an entire Lacrosse team.

Kenneth Tynan

Steve Coogan's stand-up comedy is about as funny as a hole in a parachute.

Bernard Manning

I have never had to try to get my act across to a non-English-speaking audience, except at the Glasgow Empire.

Arthur Askey

The editor asked me to cut fifteen minutes from my play, *Ah, Wilderness!*, so I decided to cut the third intermission and play it in three acts rather than four.

Eugene O'Neill

A play is basically a means of spending two hours in the dark without being bored.

Kenneth Tynan

We had a topless lady ventriloquist in Liverpool once. Nobody ever saw her lips move.

Ken Dodd

Ken Dodd's act is like watching an old man having constipation against the clock.

A.A. Gill

Arthur Pinero's play is the best I have ever slept through.

Oscar Wilde

Perhaps it is true that dramatic critics can be bought, but judging from their appearances, most of them cannot be at all expensive.

Oscar Wilde

Theatre and Criticism

I used to start my act with, 'Hello, I'm Jim Tavare and I'm schizophrenic.' One night a voice rang out from the darkness, 'Well, why don't you both **** off then?'

Jim Tavare

One critic deemed *Fergus's Wedding* about as funny as an outbreak of venereal rash.

Declan Lynch

If you attend this drama and if you don't knit, bring a book.

Dorothy Parker

I would ask members of the audience not to laugh individually but to laugh together please. If everybody laughs individually, we'll never get out of here.

Victor Borge

The cast was terrific. They could play the Albanian telephone directory.

Noël Coward

I came from a long line of performers and actors. It's called the dole queue.

Jack Dee

One night in *King Lear* they coughed so much I stopped and started coughing as a sort of hint. But they didn't get it.

Tom Courtenay

I frequently come to the play without knowing what it is. One merely comes to meet one's friends and show that one's alive.

Fanny Burney

Henry Irving's left leg is a poem.

Oscar Wilde

Modern dancing is old-fashioned.

Samuel Goldwyn

You don't expect me to know what to say about a play when I don't know who the author is, do you? If it's by a good author, it's a good play, naturally. That stands to reason.

George Bernard Shaw

I don't know his [Ralph Richardson's] name, but he's got a face like half a teapot.

King George VI

Chaplin is the best goddamned ballet dancer in the business.

W.C. Fields

I once did twelve successive comedy shows in Wolverhampton without a single laugh.

Barry Took

One of the good things about being an actor is that you can continue to make money from repeat fees after you are dead.

Richard Briers

Theatre and Criticism

Meryl Streep will do whatever a part demands even if it demands speaking in a foreign accent whose origins only Streep and her dialogue coach know.

Joe Joseph

I have no intention of uttering my last words on the stage, darling. Room service and a couple of depraved young women will do me quite nicely for an exit.

Peter O'Toole

I can't stand Shakespeare's plays, but Chekhov's are even worse.

Leo Tolstoy

Playwriting and safe cracking are similar occupations – lonely work, tedious and tense and not especially rewarding considering the time, effort and risk involved. And unless each job comes off to perfection the newspapers treat both the playwright and the safecracker as common criminals.

George Kaufman

If you want to see what Cher will look like when she's dead, all you've got to do is to look at her now.

Joan Rivers

The theory is if you're fat, wear silly trousers and you've got a big red nose, you're gonna be funny. Well, it didn't work for Mussolini, did it?

Alexei Sayle

I'd like to work with Streisand again in something appropriate; perhaps *Macbeth*.

Walter Matthau

Oliver Hardy was two-thirds of the comedy duo, Laurel and Hardy.

Barry Phelps

I studied dramatics under Douglas MacArthur for twelve years.

Dwight D. Eisenhower

Every actor yearns to have a voice as resonant and penetrating as those in the audience who whisper.

Cullen Hightower

Speak low, speak slow, and don't say much.

John Wayne

At the end of my first week as theatre manager, I sent a telegram to my father which read: 'Last Supper and Original Cast Wouldn't Draw in this House.'

George S. Kaufman

Milton Berle was the Thief of Badgags.

Walter Winchell

Stephen Fry once came on set in a TV comedy and spoke his lines. They turned on the canned laughter machine and it refused to work.

Bernard Manning

Theatre and Criticism

The play got mixed notices – terrible and rotten.

George S. Kaufman

Riverdance is dancing for amputees.

Richard Littlejohn

They all laughed at me when I said I wanted to be a stand-up comedian, but they're not laughing at me now.

Joe Manning

I got kicked out of *Riverdance* for using my arms.

Steven Wright

It is called the opening night because it is the night before the play is ready to open.

George J. Nathan

Given a good play, a good team and a decent set, you could have a blue-arsed baboon as director and still get a good production.

Peter O'Toole

I'm a comic because I haven't enough brain to be anything duller.

Fred Emney

He's an actress.

John Sullivan

It is said that no actor can survive playing opposite a child or a dog. It is just as lethal playing opposite the Irish Abbey

Players. Apart from being able to act you off the stage, they can also drink you under the table.

Sidney Gilliat

The aim of the music hall is, in fact, to cheer the lower classes up by showing them a life uglier and more sordid than their own.

Max Beerbohm

In the 1930s there was a revue called *Not to Worry* that was so bad that on the first night the management did not raise the curtain after the interval. They showed no such leniency on the second night.

Milton Shulman

The first qualification of a drama critic is the capacity to sleep while sitting bold upright.

William Archer

There is something about seeing real people on the stage that makes a bad play more intimately, more personally offensive than any other art form.

Anatole Broyard

How do I intend to play Nero? Straight.

Charles Laughton

Japanese kabuki theatre is only just preferable to root-canal work.

A.A. Gill

Theatre and Criticism

I am a sacred cow.

Cilla Black

Michael Caine started acting relatively late in life.

Hugh Leonard

The great thing for an actor is to be homosexual. Then nobody can say anything about you – it virtually guarantees discreet press coverage. However, it is too late for me to change my sexual proclivities. Far too late.

Rex Harrison

Bedtime Story was shot by Ralph Levy, unfortunately not fatally.

Penelope Gilliat

My father once took me to the floor of the set when he was shooting *Casino Royale* with a lot of nude girls in a bath, because he wanted me to understand how arduous an actor's life could be.

David Niven Jr

It is my ambition to see actors at the Abbey Theatre paid as much as the lavatory attendants. The number of actors trying to get into the Abbey is equal only to the number trying to get out.

Bryan O'Higgins

Diane Keaton is a vacuum cleaner on heat.

John Simon

We have now acted in theatres, on radio, in films and on live television – they can't think of anything else, can they? My God! I hope not.

Orson Welles

The only good thing about the theatre is that you can leave at the interval.

Philip Larkin

I loved the way all the actresses smelt. I didn't realise until years afterwards that it was gin.

Rhys Ifans

There are many advantages of puppets. They never argue. They have no crude views about art. They have no private lives. They recognise the presiding intellect of the dramatist and have no personalities at all.

Oscar Wilde

My play was reduced from four acts to three, necessitating cutting a scene which cost me terrible exhausting labour and heart-rending nervous strain – it must have taken me fully five minutes to write.

Oscar Wilde

I am not an actor and I have sixty films to prove it.

Victor Mature

At matinee audiences in Bridlington you could see the dampness rising from the wet raincoats like mist on the marshes.

Les Dawson

Theatre and Criticism

I think it so kind of the mimic to tell us who he is imitating.
It avoids discussion, doesn't it?

Oscar Wilde

Academic critics treated Cyril Connolly as if he were a
hunting parson who had blundered into the Oriel Common
Room when Newman and Keble were discussing the illapse
of the Holy Ghost.

Noel Annan

Few women care to be laughed at and men not at all,
except for large sums of money.

Alan Ayckbourn

Joan Crawford is a movie star. I am an actress.

Bette Davis

Miscellaneous

Miscellaneous

We don't necessarily discriminate. We simply exclude certain types of people.

Gerald Wellman

Show me a man who is content, and I'll show you a lobotomy scar.

Sean Connery

It happened as quick as a flashlight.

Sam Goldwyn

How come the dove gets to be the peace symbol? How about the pillow? It has more feathers than the dove, and it doesn't have that dangerous beak.

Jack Handey

'Aviatrix' means deceased person.

Dave Barry

Rolf Harris is the only performer that dogs can ask for by name – Rolf, Rolf.

A.A. Gill

There are many strange jobs on offer in the country. I once met a chap whose job it was to stick the chicken crap and feathers onto free range eggs so you knew they were the real thing.

Craig Charles

'You haven't got the guts to pull that trigger' is almost always a bad thing to say.

Russell Bell

Miscellaneous

This *Travel Guide* is dedicated to Wilbur and Orville Wright without whom airsickness would still be just a dream.

Dave Barry

Ariana Stassinopoulos is so boring that you fall asleep halfway through her name.

Alan Bennett

When in doubt, go shopping.

Sarah Ferguson

Marshal Foch was just a frantic pair of moustaches.

T.E. Lawrence

His neck was the width of a fat man's thigh. He looked like Lou Feringo's idiot cousin.

Zoë Heller

Not enough farmers give their sheep pocket money.

Charlie Chuck

When I was told that curiosity killed the cat, I asked what exactly the cat was so curious about.

Wright Stevens

A liberal is a man who is too broadminded to take his own side in an argument.

Robert Frost

We do try to anticipate your questions so that I can respond 'no comment' with some degree of knowledge.

William Baker

Miscellaneous

I propose getting rid of conventional armaments and replacing them with reasonably priced hydrogen bombs that would be distributed equally throughout the world.

Idi Amin

When Fortune empties her chamberpot on your head, smile and say, 'We are going to have a summer shower'.

John A. MacDonald

Generals detest generals on their own side far more than they dislike the enemy.

Peter Ustinov

Look wise, say nothing, and grunt. Speech was given to conceal thought.

William Osler

How many whales do we really need? I figure five. One for each ocean. We save their semen in a huge mayonnaise jar, we procreate them when we need to.

Denis Leary

This is Bollocks the butler speaking. What splendid news about mad-cow disease. That explains the last twenty years and I thought I was the one who was barmy. Please leave a spring-like message after the Moooooooo.

Willie Rushton

How do the men who drive the snow plough get to work in the morning?

Steven Wright

Miscellaneous

There are four things that will never come back: the spoken word; the speeding arrow; the past and hot pants.

Russell Bell

F.E. Smith is very clever, but sometimes his brains go to his head.

Margot Asquith

I have often wished to cultivate modesty, but I am too busy thinking about myself.

Edith Sitwell

Tragedy is when I cut my finger. Comedy is when you fall into an open sewer and die.

Mel Brooks

Like most of those who study history, Napoleon III learned from the mistakes of the past how to make new ones.

A.J.P. Taylor

Let the scintillations of your wit be like the coruscations of summer lightning, lambent but innocuous.

Edward Goulbum

I don't believe in fairies, even if they exist.

Brendan Behan

Turbulence is what pilots announce that you have encountered when your plane strikes an object in midair.

Dave Barry

Miscellaneous

Brevity is the.

Kevin Gildea

It rolled off my back like a duck.

Sam Goldwyn

It's like carrying something or other, somewhere or other, as the case may be.

W.C. Fields

I played a lot of tough clubs in my time. Once a guy in one of those clubs wanted to bet me $10 that I was dead. I was afraid to bet.

Henny Youngman

Monogamy is OK in the office but at home I prefer white pine.

Samuel Goldwyn

Woke up this morning, I was folding my bed back into a couch. I almost broke both my arms because it's not one of those kinds of beds.

Steven Wright

I once heard two ladies going on and on about the pains of childbirth and how men don't seem to know what real pain is. I asked them if either of them ever got themselves caught in a zipper.

Emo Philips

The other day on the underground I stood up and enjoyed the pleasure of offering my seat to three ladies.

G.K. Chesterton

I wonder what language truck drivers are using now that everyone else is using theirs.

Beryl Pfizer

Generals are fascinating cases of arrested development – after all, at five we all of us wanted to be generals.

Peter Ustinov

It is nice to make heroic decisions and to be prevented by 'circumstances beyond your control' from ever trying to execute them.

William James

And it is written, a wise man never plays leapfrog with a unicorn.

Emo Philips

The Army is a place where you get up early in the morning to be yelled at by people with short haircuts and tiny brains.

Dave Barry

How do pebbles know how to get into a shoe, but never know how to get out?

Casper Dante

I've just signed a contract to do commercials for a mattress company and fulfilled my life's ambition. I'll get paid for lying down.

Lee Trevino

Miscellaneous

[Anything in parenthesis can be ignored].

Bill Seeger

I may not agree with what you say but if you say it I'll punch you in the mouth.

Laurence J. Peter

If the phone doesn't ring, it's me.

Jimmy Durante

How would I like to be remembered? In somebody's will.

Robert Redford

Everywhere is within walking distance if you have the time.

Steven Wright

In any organisation there will always be one person who knows what is going on. That man must be fired.

John Conway

I cannot stand this proliferation of paperwork. It's useless to fight the forms. You've got to kill the people producing them.

Vladimir Kabaidze

Predicting the future is easy. It's trying to figure out what's going on now that's hard.

Fritz Dressler

Why do kamikaze pilots wear helmets? Smacks of indecision to me.

Sean Meo

You've no idea what a poor opinion I have of myself – and how little I deserve it.

W.S. Gilbert

Nero renamed the month of April after himself, calling it Neroreus, but the idea never caught on because April is not Neroreus and there is no use pretending that it is.

Will Cuppy

If Dracula cannot see his reflection in the mirror, how come his hair is always so neatly combed?

Steven Wright

Whenever I pick up someone hitchhiking I always like to wait for a few minutes before I say anything to them. Then I say, 'Put your seatbelt on – I wanna try something. I saw it in a cartoon but I'm pretty sure I can do it.'

Steven Wright

I may have faults but being wrong ain't one of them.

Jimmy Hoffa

Those press-on towels are a real rip-off, aren't they? I used six of them and I couldn't even get my arms dry.

Jack Dee

If Dorothy Parker isn't more careful with her suicide attempts, one of these days she's going to hurt herself.

Alexander Woollcott

Miscellaneous

The private papers left by Herbert Morrison were so dull and banal that they would have to be burned to provide any illumination at all.

John Zametica

Once at the airport I leaped onto the conveyor belt just as the luggage was coming through. When the airport police arrived I said to them, 'Just one more round and I promise to get off. I've always wanted to do this, all my life.'

Spike Milligan

The main thing about being a hero is to know when to die. Prolonged life has ruined a great number of heroes.

Will Rogers

Mutiny is such an unpleasant word – think of it more as a management reshuffle.

Alistair Swinerton

Cheops built the Great Pyramid of Gizeh about 3050 BC. Then he felt better.

Will Cuppy

There is nothing so pathetic as a forgetful liar.

F.M. Knowles

Third class mail – what's that? They strap the letter to a crazy person and he wanders at random.

Richard Lewis

I'm so unlucky that if I was to fall into a barrel of nipples
I'd come out sucking my thumb.

Freddie Starr

Work is the refuge of people who have nothing better to do.

Oscar Wilde

I got a new dog. He's a paranoid retriever. He brings back
everything because he's not sure what I threw him.

Steven Wright

But enough of me, let's talk about you. What do you think
of me?

Ed Koch

There are two classes of pedestrian – the quick and the dead.

George Robey

How long was I in the army? Five foot eleven.

Spike Milligan

He flung himself upon his horse and rode madly off in all
directions.

Stephen Leacock

A coward dies a hundred deaths, a brave man only once.
But then once is enough, isn't it?

Harry Stone

Nothing I do can't be done by a ten-year-old with twenty-
five years of practice.

Harry Blackstone

Miscellaneous

I've just solved the parking problem. I bought a parked car.

Henny Youngman

One can survive everything nowadays, except death.

Oscar Wilde

My idea of exercise is a good brisk sit.

Phyllis Diller

A Jiffy Bag is an envelope used to alert Post Office employees to damage opportunities.

Mike Barfield

If only I had a little humility, I'd be perfect.

Ted Turner

The general idea in any first class laundry is to see that no shirt or collar ever comes back twice.

Stephen Leacock

He was a self-made man who owed his lack of success to nobody.

Joseph Heller

I regard you with an indifference closely bordering on aversion.

Robert Louis Stevenson

A lady came up to me on the street and pointed to my suede jacket. 'You know a cow was murdered for that jacket?' she sneered. I replied in a psychotic tone, 'I didn't know there were any witnesses. Now I'll have to kill you too.'

Jake Johanson

If there are two or more ways to do something, and one of those ways can result in a catastrophe, then someone will do it.

Edward Murphy

Yesterday I told a chicken to cross the road. It said 'Why?'

Steven Wright

In theory there is no difference between theory and practice, but in practice there is.

J.L. Van De Snapscheut

Anyone who starts a sentence, 'Of course I can take a joke along with the best of them,' is lying and about to prove it.

A.A. Gill

If you think you're too small to be effective you've obviously never been to bed with a mosquito.

Josh Billings

They're playing the Mayonnaise – the French army must be dressing.

Groucho Marx

Don't bother to agree with me – I've already changed my mind.

Samuel Goldwyn

I am a big fan of Superman or anyone who can make his living in his underwear.

David Mamet

Miscellaneous

Dese are de conditions dat prevail.

Jimmy Durante

Consensus means a lot of people saying collectively what nobody believes individually.

Abba Eban

John Tyler has been called a mediocre man; but this is unwarranted flattery.

Theodore Roosevelt

All is fair in love, war and tax evasion.

Tom Sharpe

With further ado.

Jimmy Durante

A collision at sea can ruin your entire day.

Thucydides

I wouldn't trust him with a ten-foot pole.

Joseph Hammond

By a sudden and adroit movement I managed to hit his fist with my left eye.

Artemus Ward

Answer me this: why doesn't Tarzan have a beard?

George Carlin

Viewed as a drama, World War One was somewhat disappointing.

D.W. Griffith

I have a bumper sticker that says, 'Don't honk if you can't read this.' Everywhere I drive, I leave confused people in my wake.

Craig Tanis

I was nearly drafted. It's not that I mind fighting for my country, but they called me up at a ridiculous time: in the middle of a war.

Jackie Mason

A man who is not afraid of the sea will soon be drowned for he will be going out on a day he shouldn't. But we do be afraid of the sea, and we do be drowned only now and again.

J.M. Synge

We'll jump off that bridge when we come to it.

Lester Pearson

My shoes are size two and a half, the same size as my feet.

Elaine Paige

The first cuckoo I ever heard outside of a cuckoo clock, I was surprised how closely it imitated the clock and yet, of course, it could never have heard a clock.

Mark Twain

When Christopher Columbus set sail, he didn't know where he was going. When he got there, he didn't know where he was, and when he got back he didn't know where he had been. And he did it all on borrowed money.

Mac Cole

Miscellaneous

For every set of horseshoes people use for luck, somewhere out there there's a barefoot horse.

Allan Sherman

We do feature a smoking section on this flight; if you must smoke, contact a member of the flight crew and we will escort you to the wing of the airplane.

Victoria Wood

The future always starts today.

Henry McLeish

I made up my mind but I made it up both ways.

Casey Stengel

Checking in at Luton Airport recently, I was asked, 'Has anyone put anything in your luggage without you knowing?'

Pauline Pearson

A bird in the hand makes blowing your nose difficult.

Solomon Short

The past is history.

Dave Bennett

I can see the carrot at the end of the tunnel.

Stuart Pearse

I'm generally as busy as Germaine Greer's hairdresser, and he'd have to be busy.

Barry Humphries

My car doesn't have a manual because it's an automatic.

Steven Wright

History is filled with events that did not happen.

Carolyn Quinn

I wonder if Superboy wore his nappies over his romper suit?

Joe Joseph

Mr William Huskisson MP attended the opening of the Manchester–Liverpool Railway and was unfortunately run over by the train.

John Julius Norwich

A horse show is a lot of horses showing their asses to a lot of horses' asses showing their horses.

Denis Leary

I want to hire a telepath. A really good one will know where to find me.

Steve Wright

Lots of guys like to drive a BMW because it's the only car name they can spell.

Jeremy Clarkson

The journey of a thousand miles begins with a broken fan belt.

Steven Wright

Miscellaneous

At least Lord Birt's role as transport advisor keeps him occupied.

Stephen Byers

There was a point to this story, but it has temporarily escaped the chronicler's mind.

Douglas Adams

If at first you don't succeed, reload and try again.

Scott Adams

They met on the Circle Line and they've been going around together ever since.

Leslie Thomas

I cannot disguise my proboscuity.

Jimmy Durante

I'm a psychic amnesiac. I know in advance what I'm going to forget.

Mike McShane

I joined the army, and succeeded in killing about as many of the enemy as they of me.

Bill Arp

A good way to threaten somebody is to light a stick of dynamite. Then you call the guy and hold the burning fuse up to the phone. 'Hear that?' you say. 'That's dynamite, baby.'

Jack Handey

The last words of Tarzan were, 'Who greased that vine?'

Sandy Ransford

He played five aces – now he's playing a harp.

Paul Lyons

Air travel efficiency would improve if more travellers started going to less popular places.

Dan Quayle

My car mechanic is pretty good. Otherwise, why would I go back to him every week?

Tom Collins

Then came the war – North Africa, promoted in the field (they wouldn't let me indoors). Mentioned in dispatches: nothing positive. Just mentioned.

Spike Milligan

Every decent man carries a pencil behind his ear to write down the price of fish.

J.B. Morton

Life is like a kick in the groin. It's a kick. In the groin.

Woody Allen

The train has been punctual for once in its life. How shocked the directors would be if they knew it, but, of course, it will be kept from them.

Oscar Wilde

Miscellaneous

I was trying to daydream, but my mind kept wandering.

Steven Wright

I really believe that is was Kate Winslet's weight that really sank the *Titanic*.

Jeremy Clarkson

The kilt, being a practical outdoor garment, failed him only once, and that occurred during a short-lived interest in beekeeping.

J.M. Bannerman

Broken promises don't upset me. I just think, Why did they believe me?

Jack Handey

I have all the answers, it's just that none of them are right.

Rich Hall

The Gulf War was like teenage sex. We got in too soon and we got out too soon.

Thomas Harkin

During my army training the instructor said to me, 'It's been three weeks since I've seen you in camouflage class.' I said, 'I'm getting pretty good at it.'

Emo Philips

Maintain thy airspeed lest the ground rise up and smite thee.

William Crosby

I had to quit the ballet after I injured a groin muscle. It wasn't mine.

Rita Rudner

If Freud had worn a kilt in the prescribed Highland manner, he might have had a very different attitude to genitals.

Anthony Burgess

I have a bumper sticker that says, 'So many pedestrians, so little time.'

Emo Philips

It's utterly impossible, but it's got possibility.

Samuel Goldwyn

I filled in the application form and where it said, 'Sign here,' I wrote, 'Capricorn.'

Gracie Allen

Why do airline pilots have to tell us everything they are doing – I'm taking it up, I'm bringing it down? Do I knock on the cockpit door – I'm having peanuts now, I just thought you'd like to know.

Jerry Seinfeld

Some people have peculiar mirrors in their bathrooms. They go to wash in the morning and the person they see in the mirror is Catherine Zeta-Jones. Possibly these men haven't put in their contact lenses.

Joe Joseph

Miscellaneous

I have a great memory; it just happens to be short.

Yogi Berra

The future has changed a lot in the last three years.

Yogi Berra

The starting pay of an American pilot is $16,800. Never let somebody fly you up in the air who makes less than the kid at Taco Bell.

Michael Moore

Floating in his own pool, Charles Laughton was just the reverse of an iceberg – ninety per cent of him was visible.

Peter Ustinov

The new coal mine has still to get off the ground.

Arthur Scargill

John Dillinger, the bank robber, once wrote Henry Ford an unsolicited testimonial on the merits of the Ford as a getaway car.

Barry Phelps

Truth is so precious it must be surrounded by a bodyguard of lies.

Winston Churchill

Of all the '-isms' of the twentieth century, tourism may yet turn out to have been the worst.

Aga Khan III

'If' is a very big proposition.

John Major

I'll just say what's in my heart: ba-bump, ba-bump, ba-bump.

Mel Brooks

Does it go without saying that nothing goes without saying?

Des MacHale

In the days of King Henry the Eighth, the authorities knew that if they made any mistakes during the funeral of the King's wife they would always have the consolation of trying again next year.

John Smith

I called a psychic hotline and we spoke for six hours. How come she didn't know I wasn't going to pay the bill?

Michael Aronin

His uncle and two cousins were killed in an automobile by a train which refused to change its course.

Kin Hubbard

A compromise is an agreement between two men to do what both agree is wrong.

Edward Cecil

I may be gullible, but at least I've got this magic fish.

Jack Handey

Miscellaneous

There are pros and cons on both sides of the argument.

Samuel Goldwyn

I don't wear makeup. I use knives.

Phyllis Diller

He told me what I was looking for was right under my nose. I asked him if he could be more specific.

Jimmy Durante

The manufacturers of Levi's once begged me not to wear their jeans.

Jeremy Clarkson

If the British Army landed on the coast of Germany, I would call out the police to arrest them.

Otto von Bismarck

Setting off to a costume party dressed as a ghost, I was given a lift by a car full of men in white sheets. When those Klansmen discovered I was a New York Jew, they wanted to lynch me on the spot, but I calmed them down with an eloquent discourse on brotherhood. Not only did they cut me down and let me go, but that night I sold them two thousand dollars' worth of Israel bonds.

Woody Allen

The trouble with many British Rail passengers is that they think the railways are being run for their benefit.

Jeremy Clarkson

Some see the glass as half-empty; some see the glass as half-full. I see the glass as too big.

George Carlin

I would sooner lose a train by the A.B.C. than catch it by Bradshaw.

Oscar Wilde

The pilot performed a perfect landing through the fog by sight alone, but a hundred or so items of underwear were never the same again.

Hugh Leonard

March is a month that helps to use up some of the bad weather that February just couldn't fit in.

Doug Larson

Index

Index

Index

Index

Index

Index

Index

Index

Index

Index

Index

Index

Index

Index

Index

Index

Index